Contemporary

New Testament Interpretation

Contemporary

New Testament Interpretation

WILLIAM G. DOTY
Douglass College
Rutgers University

PRENTICE-HALL, INC.
Englewood Cliffs, New Jersey

Library of Congress Cataloging in Publication Data

Doty, William G.
  Contemporary New Testament interpretation.

  Bibliography: p.
    1. Bible. N.T.—Criticism, interpretation, etc.
—History—20th century.   I.   Title.
BS2350.D67   225.6   71-38839
ISBN 0-13-170142-8
ISBN 0-13-170134-7 (pbk.)

Printed in the United States of America

10   9   8   7   6   5   4   3   2   1

Prentice-Hall International, Inc., London
Prentice-Hall of Australia, Pty. Ltd., Sydney
Prentice-Hall of Canada, Ltd., Toronto
Prentice-Hall of India Private Limited, New Delhi
Prentice-Hall of Japan, Inc., Tokyo

Contents

v

3

The Search for Proper Methods, 52

4

Contemporary Perspectives on Authentic Translation, 87

5

Primitive Christianity and Interpretation Today, 132

Appendices, 157

Index, 171

Preface

That this book has been written is more a matter of prodigious tutorship and parentage and companionship than of personal accomplishment. My teachers in New Testament Studies—Karlfried Froehlich, Robert W. Funk, Neill Q. Hamilton, and Howard C. Kee—taught me to be impatient with their conclusions and my conclusions; my parents saw to it that I learned my own formulations were not exceptionally important; and my students with my wife have demanded critical analysis rather than facile evasiveness. To all of them this book may partially express my appreciation.

Portions of the book took shape for professional meetings or as lectures. I am grateful not only for the stimulus but also for the criticisms of my students at the Garrett Theological Seminary, at Vassar College, and at Rutgers and Douglass Colleges of Rutgers University. Professor Christine Downing made substantial criticisms toward revision, and other colleagues have read and commented on the manuscript—I am grateful to all of them.

The book by James M. Robinson and Helmut Koester, *Trajectories Through Early Christianity*, has been published (Philadelphia: Fortress Press, 1971) since production of this text began. It was not possible to change page references in Chapter 4 to correspond to the Robinson/Koester volume.

New Brunswick, New Jersey

vii

Contemporary

New Testament Interpretation

Introduction

The best way of accomplishing literary analysis of the New Testament (NT) is by using an all-inclusive approach that listens to early Christian language with a full range of literary, historical, theological, and hermeneutical sensitivities. Since the late nineteenth century, developments in NT scholarship stemming from literary criticism* and from hermeneutics* (the principles and theory of interpretation) have been of growing importance for a modern biblical criticism that is richly contoured and neither arid nor pietistic.

To be sure, literary criticism has traditionally been restricted to matters of literary style and form, carefully differentiated from "interpretation" by being placed among questions of an "introductory" nature in biblical study. But form and content are now understood to have such a vitally close interrelation that theological and interpretive analysis cannot be strictly separated from formal analysis.

The study of the NT and other primitive Christian literature enfolds a great variety of approaches. The beginning college or seminary student usually faces only one aspect (technically called New Testament Introduction) with a few problems of a theological nature thrown in for good measure. The student's time is as severely limited as the instructor's —there is just so much that can be included in a one-term or one-year course. The main purpose of this book is to give such a student an opportunity to gain perspective into some of the various disciplines and

* See Glossary.

methodologies used by the scholars he is likely to read. No single volume can satisfy all the needs, but at least the reader will be able to gain a sense of the ways questions are posed, and why certain issues now dominate NT studies. In reviewing the field I have come to rather personal conclusions, and I feel that at these points it is more important to share my conclusions than to pretend objectivity. There are value judgments, therefore, and the reader is urged to engage in dialogue with the author at these junctures.

The book proceeds on several levels. In Chapters 1 and 2 the course of theological interpretation is reviewed, with no attempt to be all-inclusive or purely objective. A term such as "the new hermeneutical approach," to designate an approach that seeks dialogue and encounter with biblical texts rather than using them to prove or illustrate theological doctrines, may be appropriate for the current scene. However I do not always share the values and methods of the specific theological school centered around Ernst Fuchs and others, usually called "the new hermeneutic," and discussed in Chapter 2. I think this school is too preoccupied with the technical data of theological language theory, and that it has moved too quickly into its own linguistic jargon.

"The Search for Proper Methods," Chapter 3, both reviews and engages the problem of methodology as crucial to interpretation. There we see the strands that intertwine—or should intertwine—in the whole process of biblical interpretation, especially in exegesis* (technical exposition) of a particular text.

Chapters 4 and 5 move away from the historical orientation of Chapters 1–3 to demonstrate how our heritage now influences our thinking. Chapter 4, "Contemporary Perspectives on Authentic Translation," illustrates two areas in which the new hermeneutical approach is being developed: first with respect to historical analysis of primitive Christianity, and then with respect to the orders of language expression in the NT.

The role of eschatology* as permeating primitive Christianity is discussed in Chapter 4 and in Chapter 5, in which a tradition history* of early Christian literature is followed by discussion of contemporary problems of interpretation and theology.

It is true that the materials of primitive Christianity are primarily religious in orientation; hence their religious aspects must be fully respected. I think it is important, however, to develop analyses that do not necessarily issue in faith claims or theology. Although trained as a theologian, I am more appreciative of my historical and analytical roles

* See Glossary.

within a secular state university. Perhaps the distinctions are not entirely valid, since my understanding of the content of Jesus' parables or of Paul's letters comes out of my analysis of how the parable or the letter functions, and the reader will find that I have often fused historical analysis, literary criticism, and theological interpretation.

Much of what is at issue has to do with locating NT studies—deciding how the various moments of historical and literary study, non-religious interpretive study, and theological study fit together. I have not so much attempted to impress my own new interpretations upon materials and methods as to bring together widely dispersed lines of re-search. It is the task of interpretation-as-a-whole that confronts us, and part of this task consists today in overcoming an increasing tendency toward atomistic studies that are done with great care, but that often leave the total dimensions of the issues out of sight. The project is not new, for indeed the search for adequate modes of interpretation is what characterizes the history of biblical sciences. In each generation scholars have felt that their own unique pattern of exegesis would be satisfactory in an ultimate way—although a review of the history of exegetical pride soon puts the lie to this assumption. In advocating a holistic approach, I am indirectly arguing for a necessary replacing of methodological attention in such a way that theological ghettos can be broken down.[1]

Perhaps our interpretive tasks take on meaning precisely as we come to respect the extent to which all life is interpretation—hermeneutics. Twentieth-century man has come more and more to the realization that what is "out there" becomes real, has power, only as it is released into contemporary contexts. We are increasingly sensitive to the power of the interpreter over literary and historical texts.

Hermeneutics is the classical identification of the careful attempt to delineate what happens in the interpretive act; it places questions such as How is understanding possible? What points of contact exist between contemporary men and texts of the past? How can we safe-guard the independence of the text so that we do not merely hear our own projected meanings but rather hear the author's own meanings?

Hermeneutics, then, is part of the training of any technician who

[1] Two books by the former British barrister, Owen Barfield, contain rich and penetrating reflections on the necessity to face up to and rethink the terminological and conceptual distances of today's academic disciplines: *Worlds Apart (A Dialogue of the 1960's)*, and Chapter 4 of the *Speaker's Meaning* (both Middletown, Conn.: Wesleyan University Press, 1963 and 1967, respectively). The more holistic approach is now possible because of the understanding of hermeneutics that has taken shape during the period since about 1950. If the features of my work fail to coincide with the terms and features of recent theological interpreters (such as Ernst Fuchs, associated with the "new hermeneutic"), it is because I emphasize the literary end of the spectrum and do not consider such interpretation as being necessarily tied to specialized theological reflection.

deals with contemporary interfaces with the past: it is crucial to the literary critic (theory of criticism), to the philosopher and sociologist (theories of knowledge and communication), and to the historian (theories of historical method—historiography). Studies in religion show increasing awareness of the necessity to approach religious phenomena with a multi-faceted methodology and with critically honed methods. Because hermeneutics, understood as theory of interpretation and as methodological precision, tended to disappear from the formal structure of theological training in the late nineteenth century, a great deal of interpretive work that has appeared since that time remains undigested. The twentieth-century emphasis upon hermeneutics, as in this book, represents the conscious attempts to renew self-conscious historical criticism* in disciplined rapprochement with the contemporary disciplines of human enquiry.

Harvard Professor Emeritus Amos N. Wilder, in a succession of articles and in his two most recent books, *Early Christian Rhetoric: The Language of the Gospel,* and *The New Voice: Religion, Literature, and Hermeneutics,*[2] argues for an enrichment of interpretation while recognizing the failure of much contemporary theologizing. Wilder's earlier interests in the relationship of the NT and ethics are present in his recent writings,[3] but not in such a way as to lead him to propose that an adequate modern hermeneutic must include concern for politics and ethics. He sees that ethics and aesthetics, for example, are not far apart.[4]

It is with Wilder's emphasis upon the NT writings as essentially *new* utterance, however, that I find the greatest affinity here. He stresses the "new dynamics in human speech" (*Early Christian Rhetoric,* p. 9), the "speech event" of early Christian language. Jesus, who "spoke as the birds sang" (p. 13), brought God's willing into man's *present* time with such clarity that man's *future* could (in primitive Christianity) be approached through modes of newness. The NT writings, both formally and with respect to their religious expression, were new in utterance. No one familiar with the great importance placed on the understanding of a hallowed covenant between God and the Israelite community will miss the radical nature of the early Christian claim to represent the *new* covenant community (in Greek, *kaine diatheke,* either "new covenant"

---

* See Glossary.

[2] Cambridge: Harvard University Press, 1971, 1st ed. 1964; New York: Herder and Herder, 1969.

[3] "The Teaching of Jesus: II. The Sermon on the Mount," *The Interpreter's Bible* (New York and Nashville: Abingdon Press, 1951), Vol. VII, 155–164; and especially in his *Eschatology and Ethics in the Teaching of Jesus* (New York: Harper & Row, Publishers, 1950).

[4] *Early Christian Rhetoric,* p. 68.

or the traditional "new testament.") It is with hopes of recovering—re-exposing—some of the dynamism of these cultural beginnings that interpretive work on the NT is concerned.

The reader will note a large number of references to German authors and terms, reflecting the great influence of German biblical scholarship. Foreign language words are given in English, with the foreign language word or phrase in parentheses when important.

Since there are a number of references to the writings of Rudolf Bultmann, brief titles are used in the notes and text, with full bibliographic references given in Appendix 2. Periodicals are abbreviated according to the system used in *New Testament Abstracts* (published since 1956 at Weston College, George W. MacRae, S.J., and Simon E. Smith, S.J., eds.). The three volumes of the series, *New Frontiers in Theology: Discussions among German and American Theologians*, edited by James M. Robinson and John B. Cobb, Jr., are abbreviated as follows:

NF I   = Volume I, *The Later Heidegger and Theology* (New York, Evanston, and London: Harper & Row, Publishers, 1963).

NF II = Volume II, *The New Hermeneutic* (New York, Evanston, and London: Harper & Row, Publishers, 1964).

NF III = Volume III, *Theology as History* (New York, Evanston, and London: Harper & Row, Publishers, 1967).

Robert W. Funk's *Language, Hermeneutic, and Word of God* (New York, Evanston, and London: Harper & Row, Publishers, 1966) is abbreviated: Funk, *Language*.

Full bibliographical information is given only in the first reference to a book or article; afterwards only abbreviated titles are used. ET means English Translation; NT stands for New Testament. A reference glossary is provided in the Appendix.

1

Linguistic and Theological Sensitivities: The Context and Features of Contemporary Interpretation

FROM THE NEW TESTAMENT TO THE TWENTIETH CENTURY

The question, How is the NT to be interpreted? does not make for a very lively discussion in the English-speaking tradition. We have not developed great schools of interpretation and often have to justify strenuously any critical or historical interpretation that seems to conflict with more popular religious approaches. Until this decade, little attention was paid to hermeneutics as a formal pattern of scholarship, and so the contemporary scene is marked by a recurrent phenomenon: we find the categories of discourse set in Europe, where hermeneutics has continued to be extensively debated. It is due primarily to the Marburg Professor Emeritus Rudolf Bultmann and his students that we speak in terms of "hermeneutics," "the hermeneutical circle,"* "pre-understanding,"* and all the various "-geschichtes"* (Heilsgeschichte,* Formgeschichte,* Redaktionsgeschichte*).[1]

There is nothing lamentable about this European flavor, but we must often struggle to comprehend such terms, and when we press them through the filters of our own language, their original diversity may be-

---

* See Glossary.

[1] As a component, Geschichte can be translated into "history" (and so Heilsgeschichte, "the history of salvation," or "saving history"), or by convention, "criticism" (so Formgeschichte and Redaktionsgeschichte, "form criticism" and "redaction criticism"). These terms are discussed in context later.

come unnaturally specified. We also have the problem that certain phrases carry negative connotations in English that are not present in German, French, or Dutch. One thinks of the difficulty of translating *Auslegung* as "exegesis," or of translating *Heilsgeschichte* as "history of salvation," or of the connotations of "-criticism," when used as the component translation word in "form-criticism" or "redaction-criticism." Being alert to this difficulty of translation when we are operating within an English-speaking context helps us to be alert when the issue of interpretation itself is raised. To interpret, to translate, does not mean only to find equivalent words. To interpret correctly means to move fully from one context into another without loss of the original statement's power. "Translation" itself literally refers to "carrying over" (*L. translatio*, pp. of *transferre*).

Our own situation is marked by problems of interpretation, but such problems are not uniquely modern: wrestling with problems of transferral of meaning marked the period of the early church itself. In fact we may say that our hermeneutical heritage began in the early church. Presentations referring to a "pure" primitive Christianity that became successively removed from its origins are no longer acceptable. We now recognize that Christianity itself was fundamentally preoccupied with translation, insofar as the primitive Christian phenomenon was not restricted to only one cultural matrix, but soon took on many forms within the whole Graeco-Roman arena. So the problem of interpretation is rooted in the writings of the NT itself, and it is not improper to refer to the NT as a collection of writings *that are themselves interpretations.*

We have, for instance, no single sentence that anyone can absolutely guarantee with the words "Jesus said this." What we have is the record of the story told by this man's followers, for whom the guiding principle was: either he said it (as the historical Jesus,* Jesus of Nazareth), or he says it (now!) as the Christ of faith.* [2] And the situation is similar with respect to the early interpretations of Paul. The Pastoral Letters (Timothy

---

* See Glossary.

[2] See the development of criteria for authenticity of Jesus' words by Norman Perrin, *Rediscovering the Teaching of Jesus* (New York and Evanston: Harper & Row, Publishers, 1967). Bultmann's classical formulation (*History,* p. 205) is more tersely stated by Gerhard Ebeling, *The Nature of Faith,* trans. R. G. Smith (Philadelphia: Fortress Press, 1961), p. 52: "Whenever provenance from the Jewish world or from early Christian ideas is out of the question, we are in all probability dealing with an historically faithful tradition about Jesus." The criteria are useful when one attempts to reduce the gospels' traditions to a probably authentic core. It should be realized, of course, that such an approach must then be supplemented by evaluation of material that in all likelihood Jesus did emphasize in common with the Palestinian Judaism of his day. Otherwise Jesus is treated as significant only when he breaks with Judaism, an idea I consider to be a subtle but misleading theological (Christian) influence upon historical scholarship.

and Titus), for example, represent what their authors believed Paul *would have said* if he had been able to address their own later situations.

The writing ascribed to James is also an interpretation: it attempts to translate Paul "rightly," to regain Paul's teaching for the church by showing that if we read him correctly, he is not a dangerous heretic, but says what the orthodox James wants him to say. James M. Robinson notes that the "letter" of Ephesians:

> seems to have rendered a similar service for Colossians at an intermediary stage in the development of the Pauline school, before the gnosticizing* and the Catholicizing* wings of the Pauline school had completely split.[3]

The issue in all these cases is the recovery of the original—that is to say, these later writings claim that if the earlier writings are read correctly (and that means according to the later theologies), then their use in the church is safeguarded from erroneous application by heretics.

Further examples of this interpretive process can be given: Jude and II Peter contain approximately 40 percent of the same material. The second author was trying to interpret the earlier author in a way that was compatible with his own theology. And whoever wrote II Thessalonians "interpreted" the eschatology of I Thessalonians in such a way as to bring it into accord with post-Pauline apocalyptic* expectation; in this case it is especially evident that "interpretation" meant re-interpretation —a conforming of an original text to what a later (or differently oriented) author thought. Paul's sense of the End-time being immediately near his own day is "corrected" more explicitly by II Peter 8–9, where we learn that though it seems the Lord is slow in coming, "with the Lord one day is as a thousand years," and so the immediacy of primitive Christian eschatology gives way to the possibility of some millennia passing before the End. The author of II Thessalonians is not as explicit, but has the same intentions.

There are many instances of this process in the synoptic* gospels: in "The Strange Exorcist" (Mk 9:38–41/Lk 9:49–50), for example, Luke shortens the earlier Markan form to make it more compatible with his own church's method of dealing with non-Christian exorcists (healers); Matthew, on the other hand, omits the incident completely, since for his church non-Christian healers were so troublesome as to be an "unmentionable" problem.

---

* See Glossary.

[3] "A Critical Inquiry into the Scriptural Bases of Confessional Hermeneutics," *JournEcumenStud* 3(1966); repr. in *Encounter* 28(1967), 17–34; the quotation is from p. 29. It may be that the Johannine letters saved the reputation of the somewhat unorthodox author of the fourth gospel.

The passage concerning a woman with a hemorrhage (Mk 5:25–34/ Mt 9:20–22 and Lk 8:43–48) betrays a similar modification of an earlier account. Matthew makes the healing of the woman turn upon Jesus' word to her, whereas in Mark the healing comes as she touches Jesus' garment. Evidently Matthew is shocked by Mark's crude magical understanding, since he alters the story to fit his own more refined concept of Jesus.

Finally, a single example showing how interpretation could take place by the expansion of an earlier account is seen in Mk 8:14–15/ Mt 16:5 and Lk 12:1. Luke seems to have felt that the sense in which Jesus referred to the "leaven of the Pharisees" would be obscure to his readers, so he added the phrase, ". . . which is hypocrisy." Whether or not Jesus had "hypocrisy" in mind is questionable.[4]

The same interpretive process is evident in deciding which of the many early Christian writings were to be officially approved or "canonized" (included in the canon,* the official list of scriptural books). The process of weeding out the Christian writings and canonizing some of them was itself a hermeneutical method of securing the tradition and giving it a selective interpretation. This is seen especially when the church authorities who published the NT canon stamped "approved" on later writings of the NT by identifying them with the names of apostolic leaders (John, Paul, Peter, James). Earlier, with even greater consequences, was the official decision as to how one of the major sources of Jesus-traditions, called "Q,"* was to be utilized in the church. Instead of leaving Q free to be used by anyone, the church decided that only those Q-materials worked into their editions of the gospel by Matthew and Luke were valid. So Q was secured from idiosyncratic use by the canonization of the gospels of Matthew and Luke.

By their interpretive, selective work, Mark and his followers determined how gospel sources were to be used, and hence determined the nature of the "gospel" form. We ask now whether or not this was done correctly. If the bounds and the use of the source materials were determined by their inclusion in the canonical gospels, we ask how we might perform the same task for our own contexts. After all, the literary standards of today are quite different from those prevailing in antiquity. We do not so much call the early writers to account as to take full cognizance of the fact that anyone who sets out to interpret the NT walks a path

---

[4] Luke does not seem overly arbitrary in this case, since "leaven" had a negative connotation in Judaism. Nevertheless the change is important, since it fits into the pattern of anti-Pharisaism of the NT, a bias against Judaism that has influenced Jewish-Christian relations for centuries and that we have only begun to correct in this century. Some of the Pharisees themselves were even more critical of a false application of the Pharisaic interpretation of Judaism than was Jesus.

* See Glossary.

already laid by the NT writers themselves. The NT is like a photo-montage of statement/restatement/tradition/new statement.

Of course one responds to the NT in various ways: one eventually makes value judgments and decisions of faith (faith determines how one responds more to certain traditions than to others). Most of the work in this book concerns the way one approaches the NT before deciding whether it is worth staking one's life on its teachings; but there have always been faith colorations upon methodology, and part of recalling the history of NT methodology has to do with recognizing presuppositions at work in supposedly "objective" critics.[5]

Faithful response to the NT may also be understood as a matter of translation; that is, decisions of faith come about as the appropriation of portions of the past for the purpose of meeting contemporary situations. Similar projects are easily seen in the NT: John's gospel, to give only one example, may be understood as an attempt to translate the story of Jesus Christ by a creative adaptation of Jesus-traditions that were most meaningful in John's own sociological setting and philosophical-religious milieu. Christian or non-Christian faith claims rest largely upon the materials in the NT, part of the canon of Christianity. These claims can be made only after first choosing the portions of the NT thought to be relevant to contemporary sensitivities, and then deciding whether such portions are to be transformed into contemporary language or left anchored to their initial linguistic formulations in Greek-speaking primitive Christianity.

There is always the sense that what one takes to be the center of the NT has pride of place over the specific language of the earlier NT traditions, although Catholics and Protestants have always been divided over the extent to which this holds true. The critical interpreter, at any rate, cannot but feel that the primacy of "the gospel" (what one takes to be the irreducible core of the NT) has been used to justify forced interpretations throughout the church's history. Elaborate sets of rules for interpretation, especially the four-fold pattern prominent in the Middle Ages, were devised to organize and regulate scriptural interpretation.[6]

---

[5] The context of a critic's thought influences the types of issues he discusses, as I have demonstrated in the work of Gustav Adolf Deissmann; see "The Classification of Epistolary Literature," *CathBibQuart* 31(1969), 183–199, esp. pp. 185–189.

[6] See William F. Lynch, S.J., *Christ and Apollo: The Dimensions of the Literary Imagination* (New York: Sheed and Ward, Inc., 1960), especially Supp. IV, "On Medieval Exegesis." The old saw that tied the levels of meaning together was by Nicholas of Lyra (14th century): *Littera gesta docet, quid credas allegoria./ Moralis quid agas, quo tendas anagogia.* A traditional paraphrase reads: The letter (the literal sense) shows us what God and our fathers did; allegory shows us where our faith is hid; the moral meaning gives us rules for daily life; and anagogy (the spiritual meaning) shows us where we end our strife (that is, discloses the hope of future life).

See also Raymond E. Brown, *The SENSUS PLENIOR of Sacred Scriptures*

We cannot begin to treat in detail the history of interpretation that is so important in gaining a sense of the freedom Christians have or have not had in appropriating the NT. It will be helpful to mention only the comparatively modern developments—but then we are not suggesting that the contemporary approach to the interpretation of the NT is different from what went on between the first century and today. Rather we want to be quite clear that contemporary reappropriation and reinterpretation stand in a rich heritage; the history of a religion is in many ways the history of the ways its sacred writings have been interpreted.

The Renaissance reorientation of exegesis was directed to misuses of the four-fold method, taking into account the results of research then being done on the ancient languages. Critical scientific exegesis as we now know it was beginning. The role of scripture interpretation within the church has always been a decisive one, and when in the sixteenth century certain church leaders began to implement the late-Renaissance criticism, the reorientation and reinterpretation was so extensive that a virtual re-forming of religion was necessary.

One way of describing the Protestant Reformation is to call it a *word-event*. The use of this phrase, which has become almost a slogan among contemporary Protestant theologians, reflects a rich and complex way of viewing history. *Word-event* refers to more than merely the socio-economic-political forces operative in a historical period; it views the Reformation as a manifestation of the power of words. We are so accustomed to saying that something is "just a matter of words" that we fail to put the crucial question to this statement, namely, What else is there? To speak of the Reformation as an event of language is to suggest that what took place within the myriad historical events of the Reformation period was a basic reorientation of the way the world was presented to men. We speak of the "linguisticality of existence," since a man's language is his fate (*L. fatum*, that which is spoken), and our experiencing of the world cannot be separated from our means of articulating it.

The Reformation was a word-event insofar as its adherents claim that through the reshaping of established religious authority and interpretation the Reformers gave new presence to God's actions in behalf of man. Of course we may not ignore the cultural, social, and economic factors, but speaking of the Reformation in this way helps us to comprehend how language itself may be expressive of deep forces—in this case, forces of renewal. It also allows proper focus on the revitalization of

---

(Diss., St. Marys' University, 1955). chaps. 1 & 2. Brown refers to Cassian's treatment of Jerusalem according to the four-fold sense: "historically, it is a Jewish city; allegorically, it is the Church of Christ; tropologically, it is the soul of man; anagogically, it is the heavenly city" (p. 56, n. 106.)

scriptural interpretation, since a central focus of Reformation thought involved new interpretations of the biblical writings.

Luther's own experiences of man's ability to perceive God directly (or at any rate through a "reformed" and revitalized church) came from his assigned homework as a teaching biblical scholar in the church. His thought as well as Calvin's was deeply influenced by exegetical study, and their hope was that the "Word" that was perceived in Scripture could become a vital word once again. Through the formal process of *explication, meditation,* and *application,* Reformation interpreters sought to hear again that living voice (*viva voce*) of the scriptures. *Explication* was emphasized as Reformation and post-Reformation scholars sought to base their theologies on what they considered the *original* voices of scripture rather than on what they felt were only subsequent layers of ecclesiastical interpretation.[7]

In the period following the formal organization of Reformation churches, the most significant development for Protestant biblical research was the growth of the historical-critical method. The method cannot be defined by any one aspect. "Historical-critical" is one of those terms (like "Renaissance" or "scientific") that takes on significance as one works through its history. In fact historical criticism is perhaps best understood by describing what it is not. The historical-critical method is not pietistic, it tries not to be misled by what seems obvious in the text, and it seeks to analyze texts with as little influence as possible being exercised by the interpreter.

Gerhard Ebeling thinks that the real fruition of the method came about only after the first World War, and this is appropriate as long as we are considering its impact on contemporary scholarship. The term and the first working-out of the historical-critical method, however, go back to Ferdinand Christian Baur (1792–1860), whose exposition had a great influence upon subsequent nineteenth-century and early twentieth-century scholarship.[8] Baur's historical criticism attempted to overcome the failings of positivist or empiricist historiography; he sought to take historical analysis beyond statistical reconstruction to the imperative philosophical impulses that create historical movements. He urged historians to heed the implicit *tendencies* underlying explicitly stated mo-

---

[7] It should be noted that in the late Reformation period, and especially in Lutheranism and Calvinism, interpretation often became just as arbitrary as the traditional interpretation the early Reformers had criticized.

[8] Gerhard Ebeling, "The Significance of the Critical Historical Method for Church and Theology in Protestantism," in *Word and Faith,* trans. J. W. Leitch (Philadelphia: Fortress Press, 1963), pp. 17–61. See also Heinz Liebing, "Historical-Critical Theology," *JournTheolChurch* 3(1967), 55–69; James M. Robinson, "For Theology and the Church," *JournTheolChurch* 1(1965), 1–19; and Robert W. Funk, "The Hermeneutical Problem and Historical Criticism," *NF* II, 164–197.

tives and events, and his subsequent analyses of the dialectics and dynamics of the primitive Christian movement have evoked many new comprehensions of that movement.

Historical criticism has come to designate the approach to the writing and study of history that demonstrates, collects, edits, and tries to interpret history in self-critical consciousness. Such analytic self-criticism is necessary as the historian pursues accuracy of reconstruction. And such accuracy depends not upon a positivist detailing of what took place at 9:21 A.M. on 14 September 1753, but upon a fully comprehensive analysis of all operative influences in a given context—political, sociological, philosophical, or whatever else.

Although use of the historical critical method has important consequences for biblical criticism, it has as many consequences for the whole theological task. There is a sense in which no theology may be anything but historical-critical theology in the modern world if it is not to be regarded as pre-scientific, and hence uselessly archaic. Careful judgmental criticism (the word derives from the Greek *krinein*, "to judge") is prerequisite to any formulation of modern thought. "Criticism" implies criticism of all tradition, including one's own, and theological criticism has little alternative except retreat behind a vague ahistorical spiritualism.

Theological historical criticism as well as historical criticism in any field deals not just with "facts," but also with impulses, reasons, and "content." Baur emphasized the content factor and so paved the way for those who followed to place even more emphasis upon the ways contents are evaluated and interpreted—upon *hermeneutics*, the theory and scientific criticism of interpretation.

The issue of hermeneutics was raised to the forefront of modern studies by the influential works of Friedrich D. E. Schleiermacher (1768–1834) and Wilhelm Dilthey (1833–1911). Schleiermacher's *Hermeneutik* was compiled posthumously from his lecture notes and student class notes; it was in this book especially that there was a major reorientation of the process of interpretation, both in philosophy and in theology. In fact what happened was a reconceiving of the whole hermeneutical enterprise.

Before Schleiermacher's work, hermeneutics was thought of as supporting and clarifying an interpretation that had already been sketched out. A theological hermeneutics was to function in such a way as to confirm the dogmatic teachings of the church. Schleiermacher broadened this narrow concept of hermeneutics to include understanding as such, and as found in all disciplines. According to one historian:

> In the thinking of Schleiermacher, hermeneutics achieves the qualitatively different function of first of all making understanding possible, and de-

liberately initiating understanding in each individual case. Hermeneutics becomes universally applicable.[9]

Schleiermacher's concern was to formulate universal rules for the process of interpretation; he reasoned that an instance of hermeneutical understanding was a case of the universal being represented in the individual (the infinite in the finite). In his later writings Schleiermacher moved toward what we would today call an existential theory of interpretation: the interpreter must develop his own sensitivities until he can "identify with" the original writer.[10]

Such "existential identification" was also an aim of Wilhelm Dilthey, but he emphasized the full powerful potential of the original context. Hence Dilthey broadened hermeneutics even further, to include not only written and oral discourse, but also human conduct. For him the hermeneutical task included not only the interpretation of what texts say, but also the whole situational nexus in which authors write. Hermeneutics developed into the "stature of a methodology for the humanities which secures scientific understanding."[11] Hermeneutics in the humanities differs from scientific investigations, however, in that the interpreter shares a common dimension (the meaning of being a human being) with the texts. As Dilthey put it: "All ultimate questions about the value of history find their answer in this—that, in it, man comes to know himself." The interpreter's own involvement is emphasized, since "we cannot go behind life but can only try to understand it from within."[12]

Both Schleiermacher and Dilthey were consistent in trying to get inside the interpretive act. They sought to grasp how understanding can be shared by a contemporary reader and a writer of the past. Their

---

[9] Heinz Kimmerle, "Hermeneutical Theory or Ontological Hermeneutics," *JournTheolChurch* 4(1967), 107; see also Gerhard Ebeling, *Word and Faith*, 316ff. Richard Palmer's *Hermeneutics: Interpretation Theory in Schleiermacher, Dilthey, Heidegger, and Gadamer* (Evanston: Northwestern University Pess, 1969) is a thorough and insightful study of the hermeneutics of those listed in its title.

[10] References in Kimmerle, pp. 107–109; see also W. Pannenberg, "Hermeneutics and Universal History," *JournTheolChurch* 4(1967), 127–129, who quotes Schleiermacher: "That which is to be understood is now no longer a specific *content* expressed in the text, but rather 'the process of emerging from the inwardness of thought into speech.'" In most studies of Schleiermacher, the term "psychological analysis" is used rather than "existential analysis"; the former term is less useful because of the connotations it often carries that the analysis will portray the author's psychological needs and personality traits.

[11] Kimmerle, 109; Dilthey is discussed on pp. 109–110, and by Pannenberg in the article just mentioned, pp. 129–130.

[12] Wilhelm Dilthey, *Pattern and Meaning in History: Thoughts on History and Society,* trans. H. P. Rickman (New York: Harper and Brothers, 1961), pp. 92 and 160, see 116 ff., esp. 119. Rickman characterizes Dilthey's concept of hermeneutics as "interpreting the products of human activity which reveal the qualities of human life . . . ," p. 43.

principle of psychological or existential identification left much to be desired, however, since such a principle leads to the belief that no communication is possible *unless* coidentity is present, and that is clearly not always possible.

The various directions subsequent hermeneutical theory took are already present in Schleiermacher and Dilthey (the theme of understanding, the importance of involvement with the text, the "self"), but it was not until well into this century that a more satisfactory hermeneutics was to be found—a hermeneutics that spoke of the tension between interpreter and text while adequately conceiving their necessary relationships. The theological liberalism that developed toward the end of the last century tried to deal with this tension, but failed. Liberal interpreters reduced the tension between text and interpreter so much that biblical writings were only assimilated to liberal theological convictions. The distance between the contemporary situation and the ancient text was reduced rather than appreciated, and the portrait of Jesus and his followers was painted in the colors of nineteenth-century liberalism. Contemporary research is still in the debt of Albert Schweitzer for portraying the ways in which liberal scholars writing biographical accounts of Jesus projected liberal values (the fatherhood of God and the genial brotherhood of all men; progress as the greatest good; the religious leader as ahistorical guru) onto their portraits of Jesus. In wider perspective, we now see how extensively liberal "culture protestantism" identified its own status quo, nationalistic and chauvinistic though it was, with what God really wanted for society. It must still be asked today, whenever a religious leader invokes a deity at a political meeting, whether or not the participants implicitly identify the political status quo with God's will.

THE CONTRIBUTIONS OF BARTH AND BULTMANN

The first World War came at a time when theology was very much in the hands of the theological liberals, but also at the point where such liberalism was becoming unsatisfactory. Karl Barth (1886–1968), in his exegetical study of Romans (the *Römerbrief* of 1918; 2nd ed. 1921), articulated the disenchantment with liberal theology felt by those who recognized the tragic lessons of the early twentieth century. These lessons indicated that men, contrary to the ideals of liberal theology, are not getting progressively better and better. Men, even given adequate training and education, will not relinquish their self-seeking desires; the War seemed to indicate that rational means of resolving conflicts were not attainable.

For Barth, the religious optimism of liberal theology was ill-founded. In his opinion man's life is completely impoverished when he thinks of

God as a projection of manhood, or when he thinks he has a secure grasp of God's rational plan for the world. Against the liberal's religious optimism and sense of the close fellowship of man and God, Barth proclaimed the "totally other" God. He spoke of revelation as that process by which a supreme God deigns to disclose himself to man. God is not man, not even perfect man, and man's place is to await God's disclosing of himself. This process of awaiting God's Word is not something to be done quiescently, however, nor something over which man has control. It is not something that can be guaranteed by the most arduous scientific research, but demands an additional spiritual element—here Barth's place in contemporary hermeneutical theory begins to be evident. Barth thought that nineteenth-century historical criticism, for all its academic excellence with regard to matters of the original text and historical situation, had become too arid and lifeless. It lacked the sensitivity to seek the real *meaning* of what the biblical writers were saying. Instead, said Barth, we must ask what the real spiritual content is, and we must seek God's revealing of himself *through*, not *in*, our scientific-exegetical preparation. We must attempt to reach the central impact of the scriptural passage:

> I, as the one who seeks to understand, must press on to the point where I am located close to the riddle of the *subject*, not just facing the riddle of the *ancient document* itself; at that point, therefore, where I almost forget that I am not the author, where I have understood him nearly so well that I can make him speak in my name, and can myself speak in his name.[13]

Barth's exegesis has often been termed a "pneumatic" (spiritual) exegesis, and the term is fitting as long as it does not suggest a sort of spiritualist procedure that ignores historical-critical preparation.[14] His primary contribution was his emphasis upon the otherness of God and upon the necessity of moving beyond technical analysis of scripture to the underlying meaning in the text. The new hermeneutical approach goes beyond such a view in denying that hermeneutic can be separated into "theory of interpretation" and "exegesis," but the impact of Barth's

[13] Barth, *Der Römerbrief*, 2nd ed., p. XII (Zürich: Theologischer Verlag); see Georg Eichholz, *Tradition und Interpretation* (Munich: Chr. Kaiser Verlag, 1965), p. 194.

[14] Barth refers to the term pneumatic exegesis as "an unpleasant catch-word . . . not of my coining," *The Epistle to the Philippians,* trans. J. W. Leitch from 6th ed., 1947 (Richmond: John Knox Press, 1962), p. 7. Barth stood in a long succession of those who deplored over-concentration upon the details of scholarly analysis: appeals to the "deeper sense of scripture" were frequent not only in Pietistic exegesis, but in the seventeenth-century reaction to the new sciences of biblical research. See also H. S. Nash, "Exegesis or Hermeneutics," *The New Schaff-Herzog Encyclopedia of Religious Knowledge* IV(1909), 242.

work was that the "meaning" questions attained an important place alongside the technical questions.

In studying Rudolf Karl Bultmann (b. 1884), we come to the scholar whose lasting influence is felt in all phases of biblical interpretation (scientific exegesis, historical reconstruction, literary analysis, and biblical theology), not to mention his influence upon hermeneutical theory and within systematic theology (especially "dialectical" or "kerygmatic" theology). Barth came to be known as a dogmatic theologian, Bultmann more as a biblical theologian; but Bultmann's sustained interests in problems such as interpretation theory and the nature of theological language make it difficult to speak of him exclusively as a biblical theologian. In the following section, only one of the many aspects of Bultmann's theological writings is stressed, namely his understanding of hermeneutics. Of course this is still not to narrow the subject very much, for in many ways Bultmann's whole enterprise *is* hermeneutics.[15]

Meaning of God-Language and Myth, Demythologizing   Following the broad hermeneutical perspective of the German philosopher Martin Heidegger,† Bultmann understands interpretation to be the central issue in all theological work. Interpretation is necessary because in the Bible we are confronted with texts in which (our Christian forebears tell us) God speaks, yet his language is no longer our language. First of all, God does not speak in the language to which contemporary man is accustomed; God does not speak in such a way as to become an object, or something to which language *refers*. For Bultmann, then, most God-language is indirect language. It is not language that we can lay hold of or that we can write down and classify according to the models of the sciences.[16]

---

[15] Bultmann's basic perspective is easily grasped in his *Jesus Christ and Mythology;* his analysis of hermeneutics is found especially in "The Problem of Hermeneutics." Edwin M. Good's "The Meaning of Demythologization," in *The Theology of Rudolf Bultmann,* ed. C. W. Kegley (New York: Harper & Row, Publishers, 1966), pp. 21–40, is a cogent secondary study; Norman Perrin, *The Promise of Bultmann* (Philadelphia and New York: J. P. Lippincott Company, 1969) will be helpful for those not familiar with Bultmann. Footnotes in this section contain only brief references to Bultmann's writings; full bibliographic references are given at the end of the book.

† Martin Heidegger (b. 1889) is one of this century's most outstanding German philosophers. Concerned with the meaning of Being (*das Sein*), Heidegger's works have pursued the ontology of thought and the ways Being is manifested through language. His major works translated into English include *An Introduction to Metaphysics* (1953, ET 1959), *Being and Time* (1927, ET 1962), and *Discourse on Thinking* (1959, ET 1966). A brief popular introduction by John Macquarrie, a theologian who has concentrated on Heidegger's relation to theology, is found in his *Martin Heidegger* (Richmond: John Knox Press, 1968).

[16] Bultmann, "A Chapter in the Problem of Demythologizing," pp. 3 f.; "How Does God Speak?", p. 169; "General Truths," pp. 155 ff.

Few men, however, realize that God-language cannot be objective. Men have plenty to say about God, his acts, and so forth—that is just the problem. By assuming that God can be grasped in everyday language, man believes he is really—actually—talking about God. Such talk (for example about God's "descent" from or Christ's "ascension" to "heaven") is what Bultmann calls mythological language.[17] Myth makes things or objects out of the nonobjectifiable. If mythological language is to be truly understood, therefore, we must grasp its intentionality—its meaning. In short, we ought to demythologize* (the prefix "ent-" of the German *entmythologizieren* is not as strong as the English "de-"); we ought to interpret the myth.

Bultmann specifically states that he advocates interpreting the myths, not getting rid of them; "A Chapter in the Problem of Demythologizing" begins:

> It is not the intention of Demythologizing to eliminate some elements contained in the New Testament (or in the Bible) and to retain others. In my first article about the New Testament and Mythology (1941) I stressed that I did not wish to eliminate but to interpret the mythological elements in the New Testament.

The interpreter attempts to attain to the interior meaning of mythological formulations, and indeed this is one of the main applications of hermeneutical work: ". . . *de-mythologizing* [*sic*] *is an hermeneutic method, that is, a method of interpretation, of exegesis.*"[18]

Because of the fact that Bultmann's use of "myth" is not always consistent, and because of obvious problems in deciding which myths need extensive interpretation, Bultmann's program of demythologizing has been attacked from many sides. Perhaps the main point of his program comes through more clearly today if we substitute the term "deliteralizing" for his "demythologizing"; the advantage lies in the fact that we can more readily understand the necessity of recognizing the restrictiveness of taking image-language "literally." "Myth" can have very positive connotations for us, and emphasis upon *de*mythologizing has led to many needless attacks from modern literary and biblical critics. This critique will be expanded in Chapter 4.

Existentialist Interpretation   Bultmann criticizes two earlier ways of dealing with the meaning of mythological texts: first, he deals with "Liberal Theology [which] eliminated the mythological elements because

---

[17] "Die christliche Hoffnung . . . ," pp. 84 ff.; "New Testament and Mythology."

* See Glossary.

[18] *Jesus Christ and Mythology*, p. 45.

they were no longer credible for men of modern times."[19] The value of liberal theology was that it reassured Christians that they did not need to sacrifice their intellects in order to assent to conceptions that are simply silly in our century. Its danger, however, was that many distinctively Christian elements were eliminated; the residue, after the myth was deleted, was a pond of "general religious ideas." Such a procedure also falsely elevated subjectivity (only that is true which I accept as true) at the expense once again of basic Christian tenets.[20]

Second, historicism, in its various rationalistic forms, was also criticized. Bultmann felt that it became lost in the search for sources of the mythology, as it sought (falsely, according to him[21]) to create a purely objective reconstruction of facts. This approach was unsatisfactory, according to Bultmann, because history itself, in the sense of chronicle, has little to tell one about one's own situation in life.

Bultmann found an alternative way of interpretation in a modified form of existentialism. According to this way of understanding, such texts as those of the NT are treated as concrete expressions of the meaning of existence. Bultmann's "existentialist interpretation" provides a means of dealing with materials whose imagery and world are not our own. The interpreter looks in texts for that which he can understand; he asks in what ways the texts speak of the meaning of the world—of the meaning and worth of being human. ("We must ask for the existential meaning of the mythological concepts . . . for what can be heard in these concepts about human existence . . ."—"A Chapter . . . ," p. 2.)

Pre-understanding   Because we share certain existential concerns with the authors of texts, it can be said that we do not approach texts with blank minds. We have a pre-judgment (*Vorurteil*) and a pre-understanding (*Vorverständnis*[22]) with us as we begin the hermeneutical encounter with the text.

Pre-judgment is out of the question if we wish to interpret appropriately; to enter the hermeneutical circle or situation with pre-judgments is to foreclose the encounter with the text before it is begun—we would be judging what the text had to say (or that it had anything to say) before we

---

19 "A Chapter . . . ," p. 1.

20 "New Testament and Mythology," p. 13; see also "Liberal Theology."

21 "On the Problem of Demythologizing," pp. 36 ff.

22 The term appears frequently; see esp. "Is Exegesis without Presuppositions Possible?" and Chapter 4 of *Jesus Christ and Mythology*. Gerhard Ebeling, *The Problem of Historicity in the Church and its Proclamation*, trans. Grover Foley (Philadelphia: Fortress Press, 1967), p. 18, rightly suggests the term "point of contact" for *Vorverständnis*. Carl Michalson's comment is a classic: "*Vorverständnis* is Bultmann's alternative to hermeneutical voyeurism," from *Worldly Theology: The Hermeneutical Focus of an Historical Faith* (New York: Charles Scribner's Sons, 1967), p. 84.

began. Pre-judging the miracle stories of the NT as "impossible," or "absurd," for example, precludes the possibility that they may have something to say, even to citizens of an atomic age.

An example of pre-judgment at work with a vengeance is found in the translating of the King James Version of the Bible. Since King James instructed his translators to maintain the transliteration "baptism" (from the Greek *baptidzo*) so as not to give support to either dunkers or sprinklers, and to keep the translation "church" (for *ekklesia*) so as not to support either Romanists or radical separatists, his translators began their task with set concepts of what these two words meant in early Christianity. The consequence was that the narrow meanings of baptism and church were established in the English tradition; the translator's final product was determined from the start. It is only in this century that we have regained the impact of *ekklesia* as a separatist, sect-type phenomenon in the Hellenistic world, and that we have come to appreciate the wide range of ways of performing and understanding baptism in the NT.

The interpreter should rigidly exclude pre-judgments in the interests of faithfully listening to the text; but excluding pre-understandings is a more difficult task, since they are more subtle and more implicit in the approach to reality as a whole. One's pre-understandings reflect one's philosophy of life, one's systems of values, and the ways these are expressed. For Bultmann it is vitally important to be aware of how pre-understandings operate, since they determine the questions we place to the text, and since it is primarily only answers to these questions that we seek. The interpreter's work and training must include careful consideration of how pre-understandings have become dominant in his own worldview.

The question of pre-understanding is not just a matter of attempting to interpret as efficiently as possible. It is not just a factor that can be replaced by something better in the training of the interpreter; nor is it something that can be used as a shibboleth in accusing another interpreter of having a sloppy (false, precocious) pre-understanding. One's pre-understanding is as present in the final outcome of his interpretation as it is in the way he sets up his questions and tools and begins to work. We neither begin nor complete interpretation in a sterile sphere devoid of all outside considerations.[23]

Pre-understanding has to do with basic matters of understanding, since it informs one's life-stance and world-view—what one expects and

---

[23] One of my students compared Bultmann's *Vorverständnis* concept to Heisenberg's Uncertainty Principle in physics: "A scientist making a measurement of some quantity which is part of the physical system cannot stand independent of the system or make his measurement independently of the system. Indeed his very presence presumes to change the characteristics of the system and hence the system itself."

how open one is to the text. Bultmann correctly senses that pre-understanding is not unrelated to learning. Pre-understandings can change—and it is with changing and modifying perspectives that much of primitive Christianity was concerned. In the parables of Jesus, for instance, Jesus called not for more learned discussions about how the Law might be kept, not for better upkeep of the Temple, and not for currency reforms, but for a dramatic reorientation of personal actions. According to contemporary interpreters, Jesus takes his listeners along with him in the parables to the point at which they recognize that they have become actors in the parable's drama. But unlike a theatre play observed from comfortably plush seats, this drama has moved in such a way as to include its listeners, who then have to decide on the merits of this parabolic viewing of the world. The listener has only the choices of turning back to the tried-and-true ways of life or of entering upon the path shown through the parable's small and somewhat opaque window. The parable asks the hearer to give up his pre-understandings about the nature of things in exchange for the values of the parabolic world.[24]

Content-Exegesis   Since it is impossible to operate with absolutely no pre-understandings, it follows that there is no "neutral" exegesis. Of course the scholar tries to be as objective as possible, but Bultmann feels that the idea of a completely objective exegesis ought to be relinquished. "There is no bare interpretation of 'what is there,' but in some way . . . the interpretation of the text always goes hand in hand with the exegete's interpretation of himself."[25]

Legitimate interpretation must therefore reject three traditional approaches: the idealist approach, which seeks the presence of rationalistic ideals; the psychological approach, which limits what occurs to interpenetration of psychic circumstances; and the historicist approach, which explains all phenomena in terms of interactions between supposedly "objective" historical factors. Each of these approaches projects its categories upon the materials and hence endangers the independence of the text.

In their place, Bultmann favors a substance-exegesis (or material-exegesis, or content-exegesis, *Sachexegese* or *Sachkritik*) "which grows from the text itself."[26] Such interpretation does not occur apart from

---

[24] This point is made by Dan Otto Via, Jr., *The Parables: Their Literary and Existential Dimension* (Philadelphia: Fortress Press, 1967), p. 54, with reference to Fuchs and Linnemann. See also A. C. Thiselton, "The parables as language-event: some comments on Fuchs's hermeneutics in the light of linguistic philosophy," *Scot JournTheol* 23(1970), 437–468.

[25] "The Problem of a Theological Exegesis," p. 242.

[26] "Karl Barth, *The Resurrection of the Dead*," p. 72; see also Bultmann's review of the second edition of Barth's *Römerbrief* in *ChristWelt* 36(1922), 320 ff. (ET

historical-critical analysis (precisely "what is said"), but complements it and asks in each case whether "what is said" is really "what is meant."[27] It is the subject matter of the text itself—the content with which the text is concerned—that should determine the interpretation of that text, and not pre-conceived ideas belonging to one or another pattern of interpretation.

Historie/Geschichte   The distinction between what is said and what is meant finds a parallel in Bultmann's distinction between history-as-chronicle (our everyday concept of history—as when we think of *The New York Times* or *Life* magazine as "recording history") and history-as-meaningful-history. The distinction in German, which has only been pressed in our century, is between *Historie** and *Geschichte*.

Bultmann, as an exceptionally well-trained student of classical antiquity and primitive Christianity, has spent most of his life working with historical data (*Historie*), so he is not proposing a distinction that would permit a carefree speculation about what texts mean as a sort of high-stakes theological parlor game. When it comes to analysis of the historian's working papers, however, he emphatically suggests that analysis of "what happened when and where" has only limited value in the attempt to get inside texts and listen to what they are saying.

Geschichte is interpreted history; it is history as meaningful-history, and that means as meaningful-for-me. The fact that a man named Jesus ambled about the Israeli homeland for some thirty years at one point in history was probably of some importance for those who knew him. But a straight record of what this Jesus said and did, a life of Jesus in the *historische* sense alone, would have little impact upon most modern men. Many men have had ascribed to them miracles, healings, resurrections, forecasting of events, and so forth. It is only as the relating of such events proceeds, not for the sake of chronicle but for the sake of sharing an insight into life's meaning, that this Jesus' history touches my own. It is only the "inner history" that ultimately matters. The late Carl Michalson

---

in James M. Robinson, ed., *The Beginnings of Dialectic Theology,* Vol I [Richmond: John Knox Press, 1968], 100–120); and see Walter Schmithals, *Die Theologie Rudolf Bultmanns: Eine Einführung* (Tübingen: J.C.B. Mohr (Paul Siebeck), 1967, 2nd ed.), p. 251; *An Introduction to the Theology of Rudolf Bultmann,* trans. J. Bowden (Minneapolis: Augsburg Press, 1968). James Robinson translates *Sachkritik* as "criticism in terms of the subject matter," *NF* II, 31.

[27] "The Problem of a Theological Exegesis," pp. 241–242. It is sometimes said that Bultmann conceives of this process as one of determining how words mechanically refer to objects, but such an understanding would be inconsistent with Bultmann's other statements on demythologizing where he is cognizant of the fact that words can also refer to feeling-states, theological complexes of ideas, or "world."

* See Glossary.

caught up the dynamics of this sort of *geschichtliche* history in a few terse statements:

> . . . history is not a mere fact of the past. History is what has happened with such meaning that it can continue to support our lives with meaning. In history one does not "go back." History is what is brought forward as the basis for one's meaningful life.[28]

According to Bultmann, the NT is primarily meaning-history, and one does not respond to it merely because of enjoyment of ancient facts. Rather, one finds the NT expressions of the meaning of life (as in stories about Jesus) to be concerned with ultimate reality, that is to say, with questions about life that we also ask. Bultmann was faithful to the distinction between *Geschichte* and *Historie* when he formulated his famous dictum that the facticity of Jesus' career (in short, "the historical Jesus," *der historische Jesus*) is meaningless unless one also shares the perspective of Christian meaning-history—its *geschichtliche* aspect, affirming that God acted decisively in "the Christ of faith." Bultmann's students feel that he has separated the historical Jesus too sharply from the Christ of faith, and consequently a large body of literature has accumulated around the problem of the historical Jesus and many attempts have been made to reformulate Jesus-research (the "new quest of the historical Jesus"[29]).

Theology and Anthropology   Several of the *geschichtliche* elements of Bultmann's program are evident in the way he developed his understanding of theology and anthropology.* In theological jargon, anthropology refers to a focus upon the question, What is the nature of man? just as christology* focuses upon the understanding of Christ's effectiveness, pneumatology upon the nature of the spirit, etc. Bultmann feels that the interpreter should be oriented toward anthropological rather than strictly theological questions, since the basic pre-understanding centers around the meaning of human existence. When interpretation is centered on texts such as those of the NT, however, the horizons of discourse also expand to include not-man, namely "God."

[28] *Worldly Theology*, pp. 77, 81. See also W. Fresenius, "Geschichte und Historie," *EvangelTheol* 27(1967), 624–627, and Will Herberg, "Five Meanings of the Word 'Historical,'" *ChristSchol* 47(1964), 327–330. Carl Braaten, in introducing his translation of Martin Kähler, *The So-Called Historical Jesus and the Historic Biblical Christ* (Philadelphia: Fortress Press, 1964), p. 21, nn. 25–26, distinguishes the adjectives *geschichtlich* and *historisch* by translating the former as historic (that which is important in history) and the latter as historical (referring to events of the past).

[29] The historical Jesus problem can be pursued in any recent study of Jesus, the new quest especially well in James M. Robinson, *A New Quest of the Historical Jesus* (London: SCM Press Ltd., 1959) and his subsequent articles and reviews of exegesis. Further reference to the new quest will be made later.

* See Glossary.

Remember that we have seen that Bultmann directs the interpreter to seek out the *meaning* of mythic language. He now tries to show that the presence of seemingly mythic words like "God" does not necessarily imply myth but may be understood anthropologically. When, in the early Christian religious language, we come across phrases such as "God acts," we do not necessarily have to assume that they can only be understood in terms of traditional theological language. Indeed, theology and anthropology are but alternate sides of the same coin. To speak about God is to speak about man, and vice versa.[30] We must speak of God. But we should be clear that such speaking does not actually give us a grasp on God's being. At best we speak analogically: God's action is taken "as an analogue to the actions taking place between men."[31] According to Bultmann's hermeneutic, therefore, we are not forced to speak of God as the necessary precondition to interpretation of texts that include religious language. In fact we should be especially cautious about approaching texts with "religious" questions.[32]

Revelation   For Bultmann, as a consequence of his position on the necessary interrelation between theology and anthropology, no special spiritual exegesis is permitted, no separate "holy" hermeneutics can be justified.[33] But the Christian texts are not neutral texts for the Christian interpreter, since the NT comes to him with a long history of interpretation within the church. The church claims that in some sense the scriptures are intimately bound up with the Christian interpretation of God's communication with man through Jesus Christ. In short, God's Word has been discovered in the NT and Christians speak of God's Revelation in Scripture.[34]

[30] The classical formulation is in the Epilogue to the *Theology of the New Testament*, Vol. II, 239: ". . . an existential understanding of myself which is at one with and inseparable from my understanding of God and the world . . . I am I in my particular existence inseparably bound up with God and the world."

[31] *Jesus Christ and Mythology*, p. 68.

[32] Fritz Buri and Schubert Ogden criticize Bultmann for not going far enough in this direction of non-religious interpretation. Herbert Braun has most consistently followed through the implications of this position; see especially "The Problem of a New Testament Theology," *JournTheolChurch* 1(1965) 169–183; "The Meaning of New Testament Christology," *JournTheolChurch* 5(1968) 89–127; "Gottes Existenz und meine Geschichtlichkeit im Neuen Testament," in *Zeit und Geschichte*, ed. Erich Dinkler (Tübingen: J.C.B. Mohr [Paul Siebeck], 1964), pp. 399–421. This volume of essays honoring Bultmann on his eighteenth birthday is to appear in English translation.

[33] "The Problem of Hermeneutics," p. 240; "The Problem of a Theological Exegesis," pp. 238, 252; "The Significance of 'Dialectical Theology,'" pp. 150–151.

[34] "God's Word is hidden in the Scriptures as each action of God is hidden everywhere," *Jesus Christ and Mythology*, p. 71; see also "The Concept of Revelation," pp. 60–65; "The Historicity of Man and Faith," p. 100, "The Case for Demythologizing," p. 192.

To some extent, then, the hermeneutics of the Christian interpreter is not exactly the same as that of the interpreter of classical texts. The Christian interpreter has certain anticipations about what he will discover. These anticipations need not intrude upon the fairness of the interpretation; they indicate a preliminary rationale, a reason why Christians work out of the texts of the Bible, and not other sources. Christian interpretation uses the same tools and places the same questions as secular interpretation, but the Christian interpreter's beginning position differs because of the church's designation of these writings as Holy Scripture. This, for Bultmann, means that NT exegesis should proceed with a sense of obedience to the decisive *address* of God through these texts.

New Testament Theology   It is his attention to this element of being addressed by God that marks Bultmann as a strongly religious continental Lutheran theologian. For him the self-understanding expressed in the NT is *believing* self-understanding—the expression of faithful existence before God.[35] Now we see why the Christian interpreter is so concerned with interpretation of the NT: he seeks to understand what it means to be authentically human (using anthropological terms) or what God wills for man (using theological terms). When the Christian interpreter explicates what he has found, "New Testament Theology" is the result; NT theology is the articulation of the way in which God works a new self-understanding through Jesus Christ. Again Bultmann refers to the interrelation of theology and anthropology:

> Knowledge of God is first of all a knowledge which man has about himself, about his limitedness; God is the power who breaks through this limitedness and thereby elevates man to his proper being.[36]

The tasks and contours of NT theology include interpretation. This theology, however, is not just interpretation and not just proclamation (preaching) itself, but "indirect word," the basis upon which the address-character of the text becomes the address of the church's contemporary proclamation. Theology as such is always directed both to the past experience in which God has been known and witnessed in the scriptures and to present ways in which God may be known.[37] The work of biblical,

[35] "The Problem of a Theological Exegesis," pp. 251 ff.; "On the Problem of Demythologizing," p. 43; Epilogue to *Theology of the New Testament,* Vol. II, 237; "New Testament and Mythology," pp. 26–33.

[36] "Die Frage der natürlichen Offenbarung," p. 86; see also *Theology,* Vol. II, 75. Bultmann relies to a great extent upon the Augustinian belief that a longing search for God is present in all men; the "Word of God" to which Bultmann has continued recourse, and especially its "address-character," are to be understood as God's responses to the problems of human existence.

[37] "The Problem of a Theological Exegesis," pp. 253 ff.; "Preaching: Genuine and Secularized," p. 237; *Theology,* Vol. II, 238.

systematic, and historical theologians is not ultimately separable, since each moment in the theological process is oriented toward one aspect of the process by which God's Word becomes God's Word Today:

> All that has been said hangs in the air unless it is made clear how such turning back to history can really disclose to us the possibilities of our own existence, and how it is really possible to reach an understanding of an alien—in this case of a past—understanding of existence.[38]

It is the task of preaching to join effectively the present situation to the address of God: "Through the word of Preaching the cross and the resurrection are made present: the eschatological 'now' is here. . . ."[39] In the church the interpreter's task is fulfilled when he brings the eventfulness of God's scriptural revealing of himself into the present in such a way that it becomes a living challenge. The challenge is to answer to the questioning placed upon the individual by the text in such a way that the text's meaning becomes that which gives meaning to the individual's existence.

We have come full circle: for Bultmann, the "paradox of theology" is that its work must be done in language and in conceptualities of language that can be easily understood. Theology must objectify faith and God even while confessing the insufficiency of objectifying language. The paradox is the claim that "the eschatological process which sets an end to the world became an event in the history of the world, and becomes an event in every true sermon, and in every Christian utterance."[40] The fulfillment of this eschatological process will be the culmination of relationship with God, or what Christians regard as true humanity—in which case communication will presumably be direct and one should have no need for studying hermeneutics!

For Bultmann hermeneutics includes a wide range of study. It is more than merely the descriptive theory of interpretation. Hermeneutics means primarily interpretation, and it is a concern not just of theology, but of scholarship itself; but theology has a special stake in the *logos* of theology (*theos-logos*), and interpretation is not pursued in theology for merely humanistic gain. Theology in its broadest meaning concerns not only the study of ancient texts but also the history of the way these texts have been interpreted and the way their meaning is communicable today. For Bultmann, theology is fundamentally hermeneutics.

[38] "The Significance of 'Dialectical Theology,' " p. 155; see "Antwort on Ernst Käsemann," p. 192.

[39] "New Testament and Mythology," pp. 42 f. "The eschatological now" may be paraphrased with "the ultimate decision."

[40] "The Case for Demythologizing," p. 193.

We have seen that Bultmann suggests that it is sufficient to take the primary NT formulation of God's acts in behalf of man through Christ—the kerygma*—pretty much as *that* which is to be transmitted (the fact *dass, that* God has acted, rather than its *wie*, or *how*, in the sense of details about Jesus' career). Those who follow him suggest that the central message of the NT itself calls for interpretation by demythologizing; others criticize Bultmann's use of the concept of myth; still others take their departure from Bultmann's particular understanding of the nature and function of language. The last group of theologians go beyond Bultmann to speak of "the linguisticality of existence," of theology as the "language school of faith," and of God's entrance into and participation within human linguisticality as "language event." These post-Bultmann directions are discussed in the next chapter.

Here it only remains to be said that for all Bultmann's attempts to develop hermeneutics as a modern science of interpretation, he himself goes beyond analysis for the sake of analysis. Willing to reinterpret much of primitive Christian mythology, his own constructive theology arising out of his interpretation remains firmly tied to the primitive Christian kerygma as an irreducible minimum of belief. This kerygma itself, however, remains for Bultmann beyond criticism; he does not seem to be willing to admit that—on his own terms—the kerygma itself is thoroughly mythological.[41]

---

* See Glossary.

[41] I am using the term mythological here precisely as Bultmann used it in "New Testament and Mythology," p. 10, n. 2 (quoted on p. 115).

2

The New Hermeneutic:
New Testament Language as Eventful

It would be difficult to deny to Rudolf Bultmann the title "father of contemporary NT studies," if "father" can be understood as indicating immediate progenitor. Few issues in this contemporary debate were not anticipated or precipitated by Bultmann's own extensive writing. The way success ought to be measured, however, is not so much by how widely a scholar is copied as by the extent to which his ideas and research become the basis for work going beyond his own. Bultmann's influence is enormous, but not so much today in terms of Bultmannian devotees as in "post-Bultmannian" schools of thought that arose in reaction and response to his work.

In this chapter attention will be focused on the attempts to clarify and go beyond Bultmann's hermeneutics (the movement awkwardly called the new hermeneutic) rather than upon the methodology of Jesus-research (the new quest of the historical Jesus). Then the reaction to the early post-Bultmannians will be discussed, including the response from the recent "theology as history" movement.

FROM HERMENEUTICS TO HERMENEUTIC

The post-Bultmann emphasis in interpretation known as the new hermeneutic began, as had the movement known as the new quest, with the attempt to correct and clarify aspects of Bultmann's hermeneutical program. The new quest[1] is the product of those students of Bultmann who were dissatisfied with his emphatic disjuncture between the historical Jesus and the worshipped Christ.* The new quest scholars argue that it is legitimate after all to ask about the historical Jesus, because there was a continuity between Jesus and the Christ—a continuity either in terms of the substance of the early kerygma or in terms of the continuing community of the earliest Christian disciples. The tendency of new quest research, therefore, is to affirm the theological importance of the historical Jesus—in other words, Jesus' importance for Christian faith. To be sure, Christianity centers on God's acts through the christic events, but, the new quest argues, the career and teachings of the historical Jesus are included in these events.

Since both the new quest and the new hermeneutic developed in response to Bultmann's work, it is not coincidental that the scholars pursuing the new quest are often pursuing the new hermeneutic as well. Because the new hermeneutic focuses on broad, overall questions of procedure, it would logically come before the new quest's focus upon the historical Jesus; actually the two movements developed at the same time, during the 1950s and 1960s, and the new quest was recognized before the new hermeneutic as a definite scholarly trend.[2]

The new hermeneutic moves beyond Bultmann when it criticizes his understanding of the way language functions. The new hermeneutic reflects the new understanding of the function and nature of language that has developed in this century, especially by British and Continental schools of linguistic analysis and phenomenology.* Kinship is claimed with the "later Heidegger" rather than with, as in Bultmann's work, the "earlier Heidegger," a shift that follows Heidegger's turn toward a more poetic frame of reference. The new hermeneutic seeks to elucidate the poetic aspects of language; it sees language not just as representing certain external "objects," but as language itself being a performer. This richer

---

[1] This approach to Jesus-studies is "new" by contrast to the "old" quest analyzed by Albert Schweitzer, *The Quest of the Historical Jesus: A Critical Study of its Progress from Reimarus to Wrede* (London: Adam & Charles Black, 3rd English ed., 1963). See the book by Robinson cited in Chap. 1, n. 29.

* See Glossary.

[2] The articles of Ernst Fuchs and Gerhard Ebeling, for instance, may be taken as illustrations of the new quest from one perspective, and of the new hermeneutic from another. James Robinson points to this double-faceted situation in describing Jüngel's *Paulus und Jesus* ". . . not as an effort to ground faith in historical science, but to *interpret* the content of faith (the kerygma) by drawing into view its ground (Jesus' word), that is, as a hermeneutical enterprise." ("The New Hermeneutic at Work," *Interp* 18 [1964] 351, a review article of Eberhard Jüngel, *Paulus und Jesus. Eine Untersuchung zur Präzisierung der Frage nach dem Ursprung der Christologie* [Tübingen: J.C.B. Mohr (Paul Siebeck), 1964, 2nd ed.].)

view of language in the new hermeneutic turns away from attempts to verify the truth or falsity of statements ("constatives") toward attempts to elucidate how language performs, acts, and sets into motion. Language comes to be seen (at least on occasion), as *acting*—as being charged-with-existence, not just as that which describes existence.

Once underway, the new hermeneutic created its own independent patternings (especially in the work of Gerhard Ebeling and Ernst Fuchs†), and incorporated philosophical and theological problems and issues only mentioned in passing by Bultmann. It will be best to back-track a bit to bring out the importance of this new direction in hermeneutical theory.

In modern theology the study of hermeneutics (in the classical sense of the theory of interpretation) was gradually assimilated to systematic theology or in many cases simply ignored, since historical criticism was established throughout theological research. It was to correct the one-sided emphases of historical criticism that Bultmann, following Dilthey, stressed the limitations and biases of the person doing the interpretation. Bultmann correctly noted that it was not possible for the historical-critical researcher to evolve a reconstruction defined in ways other than those of scientific "objectivity," but that in most cases, such a supposedly objective reconstruction was really a projection of the interpreter's own interests. He further emphasized that we do not pursue the meaning of ancient texts out of an antiquarian interest alone; rather we seek answers through these texts to existential questions we already have.

A subtle shift took place when Bultmann reached this position and in the succeeding period of re-interpretation. Up to the time of Bultmann, the assumption had been made that it was the *text* that was to be interpreted that required interpretation; the text was thought to be the object of the subject's interrogation. From the historical analysis of the historical-critical methods, however, it began to be apparent that the primitive Christian texts are, precisely like any other texts, composed of human language and therefore culturally conditioned. It was a short but impor-

---

† Gerhard Ebeling (b. 1912) and Ernst Fuchs (b. 1903) are important figures in German-speaking NT scholarship of this century. Ebeling has worked as an historical theologian and as a systematic theologian, but he conceives of all theological and biblical study as centered in hermeneutics. His most important writings in English translation include *Word and Faith* (1960, ET 1963), *Theology and Proclamation* (1962, ET 1966), *The Problem of Historicity in the Church and its Proclamation* (1954, ET 1967), and *The Word of God and Tradition* (1964, ET 1968). Ernst Fuchs is mainly a NT scholar, who also sees hermeneutics as having primary importance for our generation. His important *Hermeneutik* (1954) has not been translated; several essays have been translated in English language journals, and a volume of essays as *Studies of the Historical Jesus* (ET 1964). Paul J. Achtemeier intends *An Introduction to the New Hermeneutic* (Philadelphia: The Westminster Press, 1969) to be partly an introduction to both Ebeling and Fuchs.

tant step to the realization of the impact of this insight upon the concept of revelation: the conclusion was drawn that the NT is only a relative and indirect formulation of the Word of God.

The force of Barth's commentary on Romans also drove home this relativity. If the text is a human word and therefore conditioned by the cultural circumstances in which it was written, it is not the text that is the Word of God, for the text itself is already an interpretation of the Word of God. Hence Barth's early methodology, as he set it out in the commentary on Romans, was to live with the text until it disappeared and the divine Word itself confronted the interpreter.

Barth's critics pointed out that in such a method the ultimate object of interpretation is not the text (such as the biblical canon) but the Word of God itself. Christian theology has always affirmed, however, that the living Word of God is not available for man's scrutiny, no matter how carefully he works. Just such a blind alley led to Bultmann's suggestion that we can only speak analogously of God's acts.[3]

Finally, there is the remarkable conclusion of the new hermeneutic that, strange as it may sound, it is not the Word of God that is interpreted but it is the Word of God that interprets. It is indeed ultimately the Word of God with which interpreters are concerned, but since this Word cannot be seized, since it is not something that can be specified, labeled, and passed around, it is more appropriate to speak of God's Word reaching out and seizing the interpreter.

With this insight the traditional understanding of the direction of movement between interpreter and text that had dominated biblical criticism was reversed, and hermeneu*tics* in the traditional sense becomes hermeneu*tic*, the effort to allow God to address man through the medium of the text. We might put it this way: traditional theological hermeneutics was concerned with developing theory *about* the text as its object; the new hermeneutic is concerned with God's Word coming *in* and *through* the text's own life.[4]

For the new hermeneutic, the text is primary. The substance of what the text intends is what encounters us. We do not have a situation in which we have mastery over something, but in which something masters us. Robinson puts it this way:

> . . . . The flow of the traditional relation between subject and object, in which the subject interrogates the object, and, if he masters it, obtains

[3] See above, p. 17, and Ernst Fuchs, *Hermeneutik* (Bad Cannstatt: R. Müllerschön Verlag, 3rd ed. 1963), pp. 211 ff.

[4] Hence Ebeling contends that "the primary understanding of language is not understanding *of* language, but understanding *through* language." ("Word of God and Hermeneutics," *Word and Faith*, p. 318—there with different emphasis.)

from it his answer, has been significantly reversed. For it is now the object—which should henceforth be called the subject matter—that puts the subject in question. This is true not simply at the formal level, in inquiring as to whether he understands himself aright, i.e., is serious, but also at the material level, in inquiring as to whether the text's answers illumine him.

In dealings with the text, *its* being interpreted by us turns into *our* being interpreted by the text.[5]

The change in the hermeneutical concept has wide ramifications within theology as well as the study of history and the study of cultural and artistic expression. A similar view is propounded in literary criticism by the "new criticism"; there too the intention is to allow the text its own voice rather than to pursue the text with previously determined psychological, sociological, or aesthetic conceptions.

The relationships between theological and non-theological literary criticism have not been explored to the extent that they should be; anyone familiar with the new criticism will recall similar attempts to judge the literary work on its own merits and independent integrity, similar emphases on tone, context, style, and structure. Since the dominance of the new criticism throughout the first half of the twentieth century, other types of criticism have developed—and again there are analogues to the new hermeneutic. To portray the entire scene would take us too far afield; I would just like to point to the first two articles in Susan Sontag's *Against Interpretation* as examples of contemporary non-theological literary criticism that stress many of the same points stressed by advocates of the new hermeneutic.[6]

The understanding that it is the *text*, not the interpreter, that should determine the interpretation is found in Sontag's argument "against interpretation," for example in her argument that modern criticism too often intrudes its own perspectives upon the literary work. We need, she suggests, to allow the literary work its own holy wholeness—we ought to allow it to speak its own "self," and not take it as a formal pointer to content behind the form identified by a particular theory of interpretation.

For the new hermeneutic, we are no longer to suppose that the text in and of itself is the referent of interpretation, but indeed that the text is also a hermeneutical aid, which, like the interpretation, leads to en-

[5] Robinson, *NF* II, 23–24 and 68. See also Ernst Fuchs, "Translation and Proclamation," p. 206, and "What is a 'Language-Event?' " p. 212, in *Studies of the Historical Jesus,* trans. A. Scobie (London: SCM Press Ltd., and Naperville: Allenson, 1964), and Ebeling, *Word and Faith,* pp. 93–96, 109. See also Via, *The Parables,* pp. 56–57, nn. 90–91, in which he questions the fairness of calling this a step beyond Bultmann, and of accusing Bultmann of taking the text purely as an object.

[6] "Against interpretation" and "On style," in *Against Interpretation and Other Essays* (New York: Dell Publishing Co., Inc., 1961–1966), pp. 3–36.

counter with the substance of the text. In light of the contemporary problem of revelation, the reformulation has more than academic overtones, for it concerns not just any thought coming to expression, but God's Word.

Gerhard Ebeling and James Robinson have most adequately related the philosophical discussion, especially in Martin Heidegger's writings, to theological interpretation. Just as traditional theological language speaks about God un-veiling himself in language, so Heidegger speaks of the disclosure of Being in language (we are given such poetic phrases as the "silent tolling of Being," language as the "house of Being," or language as the "arrival of Being itself"). Heidegger emphasizes "primal thinking," that which is called forth from man as his response to Being itself. Being speaks through beings, unveiling what and how they "are." Robinson notes that "Language, like thinking, is rooted in *Dasein* [concrete existence] as the place where being clears and becomes perceived. . . . for the later Heidegger this means that language does not originate in man as his activity; man's language is his response to being's call upon him."[7] Ebeling relates traditional theological concerns about God to Heidegger's language about Being in terms of God's disclosing truth in his (God's) language. Or, put graphically,

> When God speaks, the whole of reality as it concerns us enters language anew. God's Word does not bring God into language in isolation. It is not a light which shines upon God, but a light which shines from him, illumining the sphere of our existence. If God's countenance shines upon us, the world has for us another look.[8]

Scholars following the new hermeneutic are aware that the real intention of language may be hidden by the ways in which language becomes deformed or decayed (a theme emphasized by Bultmann). An author may find that what he thinks he has said is heard in quite different ways. Of course an author does not intend that his language will reflect his culture's linguistic defects; he intends his language as interpretation, as his expression. But only the rare and truly creative writer is able to avoid language that has become opaque; and the interpreter's task is to teach us how to decide when this has or has not happened.

Interpretation has to do with translation in the obvious sense; but it

[7] *NF* I, 49–50; see also *NF* II, 47–48, with reference to Heidegger's later writings. In Heinrich Ott's work, there is a related emphasis upon language itself speaking through men rather than emphasis upon man, the speaker. See also Heinrich Barth, *Existenzphilosophie und Neutestamentliche Hermeneutik*, ed. G. Hauff (Basel and Stuttgart: Schwabe & Co., Verlag, 1967).

[8] *The Nature of Faith*, p. 190. See also the article "Word of God and Hermeneutics," *Word and Faith*, 324 ff., one of the clearest early expositions of the new hermeneutic.

also has to do with analyzing the peculiar ways in which language is combined and conformed in a particular period, as it moves from the level of primary, immediate expression to the level of fossil-language. If we are not aware of the affective ranges of linguistic expression, we may be mired down in dead language without knowing it. If we are unaware of the specific ways in which language is being used, we may understand every word in the text and yet not be able to grasp the significance of what the author is saying.[9]

Language itself is interpretation: the act of expression forces one to speak in culturally determined words. When a writer deliberately sets out to speak in words of his own self-determined patterns, as does James Joyce in *Ulysses* or *Finegan's Wake*, the reader requires hermeneutical cribs to enable him to understand the language. Or the deformation process must be overcome; we must "unlearn" what we have taken as the only truth. In the history of the interpretation of Jesus' parables, for instance, it can be seen how quickly parabolic language became deformed and sterile. Phrases such as "good Samaritan" or "faith like a mustard seed" are now so distorted that it is difficult to use them seriously without preliminary notice that they are *not* being used according to their twentieth-century man-on-the-street meanings.

Historical-critical studies pointed out the influence of the historical context upon the way a word is used. Now we are learning that it is not enough to understand the words' contexts, but we must also be able to distinguish the way in which language is related to intention within the same text.[10] And even more: we must learn to recognize the layers of use when more than one hand or more than one generation passes along the

[9] An illustration is found in the way the popular political philosopher, Herbert Marcuse, is subjected to ideological simplification by the New Left in American student politics. See Andrew Hacker's review of *Negations: Essays in Critical Theory*, a translation of articles by Marcuse, published in German in the 1930s. "Conditions, Not Problems," *The New York Times Book Review* (June 30, 1968), p. 6. © 1968 by The New York Times Company. Reprinted by permission. Hacker points out that while this collection of writings has reference to events and movements familiar to most of us today, it is written from the perspective of dialectics. Dialectical thinking is easily understood in a European frame of reference, but it is at odds with the American tendency to think of historical movements as problems-to-be-solved. "But," notes Hacker, "the dialectic is far more than a method to be taught in a classroom. It is rather an entire attitude of mind, giving full form to one's perception of social reality." The problem of understanding Marcuse is not that we do not have equivalents for the German words he used, but that in America the whole mind-set of our use of language complicates their true understanding: "Our culture and our history not only prevent us from seeing ourselves as we really are, but they also preclude the possibility of adopting an alternative vision."

[10] See John Macquarrie, *God-Talk. An Examination of the Language and Logic of Theology* (New York and Evanston: Harper & Row, Publishers, 1967), p. 112: "Following the later Wittgenstein, [language] analysts tell us that the meaning of language is to be sought in the way it gets used."

materials of a text. This is so because ". . . in a new situation the old language itself means something different."[11]

When the new situation is separated from the original situation by many hundreds of years, it is especially difficult to regain the original intentions and meanings of texts. The interpreter must be extremely watchful that he does not substitute a contemporary meaning that the original did not intend; we are always tempted to say "what is being said" before we have really listened to the text[12] or before we have comprehended the influence of those who transmitted and shaped the texts.

The interpreter must try to understand how those who transmitted the original texts modified them as they secured the texts for future readings. This alteration of materials by transmitters will be discussed in the next chapter. What we often do not recognize adequately is that the "translation" or transmission of the originals took place in ways that caused the original formulations to be "frozen" as the only ways of stating the points of the texts.

Robinson notes, for example, that the language in which the early Christian kerygma was stated soon became thought of as being the only way to express the kerygma: the words of the first kerygmatic statement became part of the kerygmatic message itself. The translation of the kerygma (moving with the meaning of the kerygma into secondary situations) pulled along with it the original statements of the kerygma in such ways that "the kerygma" now looks like one or more of the stages in the history of stating the kerygma.[13]

What the interpreter has to ask now, therefore, is how adequately the original linguistic formulations of kerygma still convey the original kerygmatic intentions. May it not be, for instance, that "resurrection," or "descent from David," which were important in the early kerygmatic formulae, represent only necessary linguistic forms in which kerygma had to be expressed *in primitive Christianity?*

Failure to acknowledge the way in which linguistic expression is intimately bound up with the original situation's linguistic horizons leads to mistranslation. Or, in theological terms, one way to describe the failure to continue the process of full translation into new linguistic contexts is to speak of heresy. Heresy (leaving aside for the moment the question

[11] James M. Robinson, "Kerygma and History in the New Testament," in *The Bible and Modern Scholarship,* ed. J. Philip Hyatt (Nashville and New York: Abingdon Press, 1965), p. 119.

[12] This is a problem throughout literary criticism. The noted literary critic, I. A. Richards, complains that too often ". . . a judgment seemingly about a poem is primarily evidence about a reading of it" by the later interpreter. ("Fifteen Lines from Landor," repr. in *The Critical Performance;* S. E. Hyman, ed.; New York: Vintage Books, 1956, p. 112.)

[13] "Kerygma and History . . . ," p. 131.

as to what constitutes heresy or orthodoxy—to be discussed later) is faulty translation, an insistence that one's own statements are the only relevant and admissible means of expression. But if translation means to express correctly the *intention* of the text rather than merely to repeat the text's own words, then the translation may have to be into words that, in later times or in different contexts, appear to contradict the original formulations.[14]

The above discussion may help non-theological onlookers to understand the continued battle between religious liberals and fundamentalists today. Liberals claim that holding to the words of the original biblical formulations does not represent authentic movement from the NT to the contemporary situation, as the fundamentalists assert. Repeating the original formulations is for the liberals a sign of failure to take up the gesture of the texts themselves and to move into new situations with adequately new language. Translation, theologically understood, is not just a process of "finding the right words," as the ineptness of much contemporary folk liturgy and religious art demonstrates.

Translation is not just a process in which word equivalents are sought. Actually such a one-to-one substitution of old word: new word may be more misleading than it is helpful, for it fails to do justice to the full sphere of intention that comes only partially to expression in individual words. Robert Funk has such deeper dimensions in mind when he writes:

> Preoccupation with how language is heard . . . tends to obscure what language intends. In fact, precisely this preoccupation may give rise to nonunderstanding. If attention is riveted on what is being said, on the discourse itself, and thus on how it is to be heard, what the discourse is attempting to bring to expression is lost wholly or partially to view.[15]

It is the "difference between language and the intention which calls forth the expression" (W. Pannenberg) that is the root of the problem of translation. The new hermeneutic recognizes this, and attempts to deal with it by directing attention to the "point being scored" in a linguistic expres-

---

[14] John Dillenberger gives an example in his discussion of the debate over trinitarian formulae: terms necessary in the church's defense against dualistic gnosticism (an early heresy) had to give way before other terms so that Christianity would not fall prey to the monistic interpretation of the trinity. (See *NF* II, 153.) Dillenberger puts the issue in sharp terms: "A proper hermeneutic means that formulations must be abandoned the moment in which theological attention shifts from their intentionality to the formulations themselves." (*Ibid.*, p. 159.)

[15] *Language,* p. 302. See also Manfred Mezger, "Preparation for Preaching—The Route from Exegesis to Proclamation," *JournTheolChurch* 2(1965), 166: "Translating does not mean simply to substitute one word for another, but to seek and find at once the place at which this text, without detriment to its historical individuality, meets us."

sion,[16] or by focusing attention on the "world" or con-text of the expression.[17]

The concept of "world" must receive our immediate attention for a moment. Some of our idiomatic expressions point to the significance of "world": What in the world is going on? is asked by the person whose perception of a situation is unclear; What world were you born in, Mister? is put to someone whose discourse has failed to make sense to us. We also speak of world-view or of the state of world affairs. In each case "world" indicates more than a spatial area, more than a location; world refers to the total sphere of meaning in which we are or are not at home.

"World" is the total set of perception and participation in which we exist, the locus of historical being. In Martin Heidegger's terms, world is pre-reflective, which means that in world subject and object are one. It is in "world" that I understand my existence and my self-understanding —in others words world, language, and understanding are correlative.[18] In fact understanding is "not a tool for doing something (like communicating) but the medium in which one exists," and hence language may be called "the repository of a thematized way of seeing the world."[19]

Our attempt to understand the world of the text must not only include clarifying our own exegetical intentions but also seeking to stand alongside the full intention—the drive or thrust—of the text itself, and for this task the concept of "world" may be a more adequate concept than the Bultmannian "self-understanding." Language world is the real world, the actual context of acting.

Language, notes Edward Sapir, ". . . powerfully conditions all our thinking about social problems and processes." One is "at the mercy of the particular language which has become the medium of expression" for

[16] Robinson, "A Critical Inquiry . . . ," p. 22, and throughout his recent writings.

[17] There is a similar emphasis upon "gesture" in Roger Sessions, *The Musical Experience:* ". . . the gesture . . . is in the foreground. . . . the essential musical fact lies precisely in the gesture which animates and not in the idea or context which defines our feelings." According to Sessions, music too "is a language," a "means of communication," but in music the gesture is direct and immediate, whereas in spoken language the point comes through the words. From Roger Sessions, *The Musical Experience of Composer, Performer, Listener* (© 1950 by Princeton University Press; Princeton Paperback, 1971), pp. 27 and 29.

[18] "World" can also mean simply context of meaning, the area of mutual understanding, as in Ernst Fuchs' use; see *NF* II, 47–48, 49f. Via, *The Parables,* p. 40, gives references demonstrating the broader view in Bultmann, Robinson, Ebeling, and Ott.

[19] Richard E. Palmer, "Theses on Hermeneutics and Theology," 1968, manuscript quoted by permission. See also Paul Achtemeier, *An Introduction to the New Hermeneutic* (Philadelphia: The Westminster Press, 1969), Chap. 5, "Language, Perception, and Reality," in which there is an excellent summary of the ways language molds perception.

his society. "The fact of the matter is that the 'real world' is to a large extent unconsciously built up on the language habits of the group." Language *is* world, or in Sapir's term, language is "the *symbolic guide to culture.*" Hence to understand a text's language, interpretation must involve "not merely an understanding of the single words in their average significance, but a full comprehension of the whole life of the community as it is mirrored in the words, or as it is suggested by their overtones."[20]

By and large, we have taken the concept of world too simply, ignoring the complex interaction between language and its context. We have often assumed that language is just arbitrarily made up, created in order to reflect an idea-state or some external fact of life. Actually, however, language and world are coterminous: we experience world *in* language; language brings world to expression, and is itself part of world.

One important aspect of this unified view of language and world has to do with the ways interpreters represent historical phenomena, such as the history of primitive Christianity. Using this approach, the historian or interpreter will avoid the attempt to present a history of the way the religion developed in a straight line, from, let us say, Jesus to the author of the Apocalypse. He will not so much talk about the role of the creative individual thinkers as to trace out the interactions between the ways in which "world" is experienced and the languages arising out of those experiences. He will attempt to represent the religious phenomenon by charting the possibilities, and then by showing how particular paths through the possibilities are taken by this or that theological tendency. He listens as carefully as possible to the complex sociological, political, economic, and other perspectives on world that take language forms, in order to fully comprehend what the language forms are all about.[21] He will especially try to note the horizons at which our language world and

---

[20] Edward Sapir, *Culture, Language and Personality: Selected Essays,* ed. D. G. Mandelbaum (Berkeley and Los Angeles: University of California Press, 1966), pp. 69–70. Originally published by the University of California Press; reprinted by permission of the Regents of the University of California. See also Eberhard Güttgemanns, *Offene Fragen zur Formgeschichte des Evangeliums: Eine methodische Skizze der Grundlagenkrisenproblematik der Form- und Redaktionsgeschichte* (Munich: Chr. Kaiser Verlag, 1969), Section #9, 4.

[21] See James M. Robinson, "World in Modern Theology and in New Testament Theology," in *Soli Deo Gloria: New Testament Studies in Honor of William Childs Robinson,* ed. J. McDowell Richards (Richmond: John Knox Press, 1968), pp. 88–110, 149–151. According to Robinson, the future task of NT theology lies both in gaining perspective on the arbitrary ways in which world has been ignored, and in ". . . the tracing of world as it comes into language." (P. 104) This "tracing of world" is done by sensing what Robinson calls the "trajectories" of theologies; a trajectory is ". . . a gradual change in cast emerging within a language tradition" (p. 105).
To the trajectory model, I prefer the analogy of a force moving through electrical fields: it enters with its own impetus and is deflected or attracted as it moves.

the language world of the text intermesh. The current development of this approach is discussed in the first part of Chapter 4.

Along with the necessity of penetrating the full dimensions of the original linguistic situations and subsequent contexts, the interpreter must also heed the ways language *functions*. He must seek to comprehend the levels of linguistic activity in the text (see Chapter 4) and he must be aware that comprehension of an event is complete only when he knows the future to which it gives rise. It makes good sense to say that whoever wants to understand the NT, for instance, should understand the subsequent decades of the early church. (Students often ask why Christianity in the Roman Empire "succeeded" when other perfectly viable options did not. For such students, the question of the political and cultural futures to which the NT language gave rise is very important in their attempt to understand the language of the NT itself.)

The interpreter's interrogation does not just seek the chronological sequence of events but also the effectiveness of certain language events or language traditions. Ebeling presses this point:

> So we do not get at the nature of words by asking what they contain, but by asking what they effect, what they set going, what future they disclose. How much words belong to man and, like human life, are historical, may be seen in the fact that the discussion of words becomes a discussion of their future, and thus of man's future.[22]

In Ebeling's writings, the careful respect for the effectiveness of language that characterizes the new hermeneutic is evident; in Ernst Fuchs' work, such care leads to linguistic formulations that strike most readers as unusual or even odd.

For Fuchs, Jesus as *the* language event functions not so much to announce and disclose some object of belief as to tell us the right time. The future to which Christian faith gives rise is not just a vague dimension that may some day come to pass, but it is that which determines our present "time." Because of our usual associations with such phrases as "what time it is," it is difficult for most of us to comprehend the extent to which ordinary language is reshuffled for Fuchs' purposes. But this reshuffling is itself an important aspect of the understanding of the linguis-

---

Hence primitive Christianity's development can be understood as an original set of forces moving through a series of attracting and repelling religious forces.

Whichever model one chooses, there is a significant step away from earlier historical approaches that suggested that the development of Christianity was monolithic, unilateral, and basically untouched by the worlds in which it took shape.

[22] Appendix to *The Nature of Faith*, p. 187. The relevance of inclusion of the future to which language gives rise has been stressed more recently in the "theology of hope" movement.

tic nature of existence in the new hermeneutic: we are directed to the ways in which ordinary reality, ordinary language, is made to serve more immediate and profound purposes than usual.

Fuchs' special use of time is explained in a major article, "Jesus' Understanding of Time;"[23] here and elsewhere Fuchs states that Jesus' language was not something that just pointed beyond itself to a new idea but was intimately related to his whole mission:

> Jesus' preaching is exactly like his conduct, his whole appearance: it is quite simply *the announcement of time itself*, the *new* time of the king-dom of God.[24]

This means that Jesus did not bring a new program; it means that Jesus did not intend to change the nature of the world but to intensify existence in the world. According to Fuchs, Jesus tells us that the "time" we live in is not neutral time; Jesus shares with us the courage that he reads back from his understanding of the future of God's actions on man's behalf. The Christian believer shares this perception, and Christian language is that language which is "at home" with God's new time. Hence Fuchs emphasizes that language is not to be understood as the objectification of events, but rather that language announces, that it speaks the *right* time:

> What is distinctive about language is not the content of the individual words, not the thought or the designation, but rather its use, its applica-tion, its concentration upon the time and thus upon the distinction of times. . . .
> So this is what language announces. It does not create something new, but it announces what it is time for.[25]

We see then that Fuchs locates the primal speaking that Heidegger praises in Jesus' language of love, "the language of grace." This language is the authentic language man has constantly sought but seldom found. Fuchs however, in distinction from Heidegger at this point, speaks of a "christological understanding of language" that enables us to understand and participate in "the time of grace."[26] Similarly, Ebeling refers to God's

[23] In *Studies of the Historical Jesus*, pp. 104–166.

[24] "The New Testament and the Hermeneutical Problem," in *NF* II, 128–9.

[25] *NF* II, 125, 126, there in italics. See Joseph C. Weber, "Language-Event and Christian Faith," *TheolToday* 21(1965), 449–457, a negative evaluation of Fuchs' ontology, and G. C. O'Collins, "Reality as Language: Ernst Fuchs' Theology of Rev-elation," *TheolStud* 28(1967), 76–93, a negative evaluation of the historicity of revelation in Fuchs.

[26] *Hermeneutik*, pp. 71, 72, 78. Paul J. Achtemeier, in "How Adequate is the New Hermeneutic?," *TheolToday* 23(1966), 105, paraphrases: "The language of faith is therefore the language of existence which understands itself." Achtemeier's *An Introduction to the New Hermeneutic* contains extensive discussion of Fuchs' thought.

Word as "simply the Word—the pure and true Word, in which the real
life and purpose of the Word is realized."[27]

The new hermeneutic can be distinguished from previous hermeneutical scholarship by its emphasis upon the active directness of language
and by its conception of language as that which unveils or discloses.
What is disclosed is not something "out there" that has merely to be described and defined in order to be understood, for language itself is regarded as performing and disclosing. Much is made, for instance, of the
naming phenomenon familiar to students of primitive cultures: when the
name of something is pronounced, it is understood to be called into being.

The new hermeneutic also has a more poetic frame of reference than
we are accustomed to. It directs us less to the traditional logics of predication and objectification and more toward the poetic modes of saying-
but-not-specifying. The indirectness of language is emphasized, as in
Funk's exposition of the metaphoric character of the parable, or in the
"thick" quality of Ernst Fuchs' personal writing style.[28] In emphasizing
the unmediated happeningness of language, those following the new
hermeneutic attempt to create a linguistic atmosphere in which language
may be as lively as possible and in which there are few decayed words
and as few meaningless generalizations as possible.

We may not find such indirectness familiar, but it is also not as distant from us as we may think. Though not common in theological writing,
the contemporary poem and novel portray a similar sense of disjunctive-
ness and a similar heaping of statements, metaphors and images, one
upon the other, without the accustomed connective tissue or the customary resolution of all tensions. I think especially of a group of superrealist
novelists that includes John Hawkes (*The Lime Twig,* 1961; *Second Skin,*
1963), William H. Gass (*Omensetter's Luck,* 1969), and Robert Coover
(*The Origin of the Brunists,* 1966; *Pricksongs and Descants,* 1970). The
list could be expanded a great deal, moving beyond novelists to essayists
and short-story writers (Norman O. Brown, John Barth, Gary Snyder,

---

[27] Appendix to *The Nature of Faith,* p. 189. Also *Wort und Glaube,* p. 318,
quoted by Robert T. Osborn, "A New Hermeneutic?" *Interp* 20(1966), 404–5: "Jesus
is not one whom a hermeneutic must understand, but is himself a hermeneutic that
leads to self-understanding, to an understanding not in theory but in deed of existence as faith—as speech-event. 'The task of Christology is now nothing but this,
to bring to speech that which has come to speech in Jesus,' and that is of course,
faith."

[28] As an example, the following passage from Fuchs, "What is Interpreted in
the Exegesis of the New Testament?", in *Studies of the Historical Jesus,* p. 101.
"However, if for Jesus' hearers sin consisted of the choice of *need,* because the man
who despaired of history held on to need as his criterion for the interpretation of
history or for his self-understanding, then all the circumstances are changed. The
word itself now became the power which Jesus opposed to need, and the question
was—or is—whether I choose *need* or the *word* as the criterion for the self-understanding or the interpretation of history."

Flannery O'Connor, Kenneth Patchen, especially Jorge Luis Borges), but I find what I call the "disintegrational synthesis" in all of them—use of surreal time and place references, multi-perspective and parallel narration, post-Freudian sexuality, fantasy, inextricability of situation, mystery, and self-made worlds.

According to Fuchs, as we have seen, we know that there is such a phenomenon as perfect language because we know of Jesus' speaking. This talk about "perfect language" represents quite a development from Bultmann's emphasis upon the distorting role of language. In the new hermeneutic there is not so much discussion of the ways language distorts as there is recognition that "It is language itself which brings the obscure to clarity, the important question being, not what the author intended subjectively to say, but what makes itself visible in the text."[29] The emphasis is upon understanding that is brought in language, rather than upon understanding that comes through language.

Perhaps the best way to describe what happens when such understanding takes place is through further discussion of the term word-event, a term used by both the new and the old hermeneutics. Bultmann originally made use of a term common in theology at the beginning of this century, *Heilsgeschichte* ("saving" or "salvation" history),* but he rejected it in his later writings, because he felt that the term carried too many overtones of having access to God's plan of salvation. Instead, Bultmann tends to use either *Heilsgeschehen* or *Heilsereignis* (either means the event or occurrence of salvation). In order to stress the active role of language in comprehending God's actions, however, Fuchs and Ebeling prefer not to speak of the event of *salvation* but of the event of *language*. Fuchs generally prefers *Sprachereignis*, "language event," and Ebeling *Wortgeschehen*, "word-event."[30]

Language becomes event for Fuchs when language becomes more than just talk, when language is understood as the genuine disclosure and the depth revelation of meaning, and when "language itself becomes event," in the sense that it is "world-forming and world-destroying." Ebeling emphasizes the relational quality of communication in the phrase

---

[29] Via, *The Parables*, p. 34; see also James M. Robinson, "Jesus' Parables as God's Happening," in *Parable, Myth, and Language*, ed. Tony Stoneburner (Cambridge: The Church Society for College Work, 1968), pp. 48–50.

* See note on p. 45.

[30] See Bultmann, "History of Salvation and History." The actual term or its provenance is not of great importance; Via, *The Parables*, p. 55, n. 83, points out the occurrence of the concept, if not the term, in C. H. Dodd, *The Parables of the Kingdom* (1935), and in T. W. Manson, *The Teachings of Jesus* (1931), in discussion of Jesus' parables. Via also calls attention to the fact "that literary critics speak of language becoming an event, and of a poem, novel, or story testing a reader and having the power to move him into a new state of being or into the experience of a new horizon" (p. 56, with reference to literary critics in nn. 86–87). See also Funk, *Language*, Chaps. 2 and 3, which have as their main-titles "Language as Event."

word-event; in speaking of the Word of God, he notes that "Word is therefore rightly understood only when it is viewed as an event which—like love—involves at least two."[31] Furthermore, "where word happens rightly, existence is illumined," and hence it can be said that the "precise purpose which the word is meant to serve is, that man shows himself as man."[32]

Since the new hermeneutic holds that hermeneutic itself is interpretation, not just theory of interpretation, it can be said that what happens in the eventful, hermeneutical situation is that the original situation is revitalized and revisited, and that the original situation is revoiced. This has always been the professed goal of interpretation, of course, and it is not easily attained.[33] The new hermeneutic is one of the best-formulated attempts to hear the original dimensions of expressions of antiquity; it has its problems, especially insofar as much work is needed to give substance to its theories, but then as Ebeling noted in one of his earliest works,[34] a perfect hermeneutic remains an eschatological entity!

RESISTANCE AND REORIENTATION

Responses and reactions to the program of the new hermeneutic developed quickly, although the very complex and detailed manner of argumentation used by the German writers and the general lack of emphasis upon hermeneutics in English-speaking countries have restricted widespread discussion here.[35] Three major types of reaction and response can be sketched. The first is the most substantive and also the

---

[31] *Word and Faith*, p. 326.

[32] *Ibid.*, p. 327, there partly in italics.

[33] See Benjamin Jowett (1817–1893; quoted by E. C. Blackman (*Biblical Interpretation* [Philadelphia: The Westminster Press, 1957], p. 206): "The true use of the interpreter is to get rid of interpretation and leave us alone in company with the author"; and T. S. Eliot (in "Andrew Marvell," repr. in *The Critical Performance* [S. E. Hyman, ed.; New York: Vintage Books, 1956], p. 47): "To bring the poet back to life—the great, the perennial task of criticism . . . ."

[34] *Evangelische Evangelienauslegung: Eine Untersuchung zu Luthers Hermeneutik* (Munich: Ev. Verlag Albert Lempp, 1942), pp. 102–3. See also the very important work by Ray L. Hart, *Unfinished Man and the Imagination: Toward an Ontology and a Rhetoric of Revelation* (New York: Herder & Herder, 1968), p. 99.

[35] The most convenient discussion for American readers, NF II, *The New Hermeneutic*, grew out of the first Drew University Consultation on Hermeneutics in 1962. The first volume in the same series, NF I, *The Later Heidegger and Theology*, consists of papers debated at the San Francisco Theological Seminary in 1961; some of the papers from a third Drew consultation in 1966 have been edited by Stanley Romaine Hopper and David L. Miller, *Interpretation: The Poetry of Meaning* (New York: Harcourt Brace Jovanovich, Inc., 1967). Two additional consultations I have attended, at the Institute for Antiquity and Christianity, Claremont Graduate School, 1968, and at Syracuse University ("Ontology as Utterance"), 1970, also produced important papers, which are being published in various places.

most important: the German "theology as history" school, centered around Wolfhart Pannenberg, which represents an attempt to change the entire course of recent theological studies. It is critical of the new hermeneutic even though it does not bypass recent hermeneutical systems in its own formulations.[36]

A second type of response shares the desire to point out the weaknesses of the new hermeneutic, although it is not so much a school of thought as a general characterization of recent studies that sense a weakness in the new hermeneutic's lack of emphasis on human values and social structures. A third type of response replies critically but appreciatively to the new hermeneutic, and is primarily characterized by its inclusion of non-theological hermeneutical theory, especially contemporary literary criticism. This third response is treated in the first part of the next chapter, following the exposition of what the term literary criticism has meant in classical NT studies.

Theology as History   Pannenberg undertakes an expansion of hermeneutics to correct the excessive individualism that he feels existentialist interpretation imported into hermeneutics. He does this by introducing the historical transcendence of universal-history (*Universalgeschichte*) into the theological field. He contrasts the approach of the new hermeneutic with his own approach as follows:

> Both reach from the text to the interpreter's present, and both draw the interpreter into the interpretation of the text. However: the hermeneutical approach apparently moves exclusively between the past text and the present interpreter, whereas the universal-historical approach first of all

[36] In addition to the set of programmatic essays edited by Pannenberg, *Revelation as History*, trans. David Granskou (New York: The Macmillan Company, and London: Collier-Macmillan, Ltd., 1968), his christology, *Jesus—God and Man*, trans. L. L. Wilkins and D. A. Priebe (Philadelphia: The Westminster Press, 1968), and several articles are now available in English: "Appearance as the Arrival of the Future," *JournAmerAcadRel* 35(1967), 107–118; "Did Jesus Really Rise from the Dead?", *Dialog* 4(1965); "Redemptive Event and History," in Claus Westermann, ed., *Essays on Old Testament Hermeneutics*, trans. J. L. Mays (Richmond: John Knox Press, 1964), pp. 314–335; "The Revelation of God in Jesus of Nazareth," *NF* III, 101–133; and the article referred to above (p. 14), "Hermeneutics and Universal History."

Again we are in the debt of James M. Robinson and John B. Cobb, Jr., for editorial creativity in bringing together a series of essays around a major new direction of interpretation: *Theology as History* (*NF* III, 1967). The "theology as history" group consists primarily of Pannenberg, Ulrich Wilckens, Dietrich Roessler, Klaus Koch, Rolff and Trutz Rendtorff, M. Elze, and August Strobel. There is a sympathetic analysis of the movement by Carl E. Braaten, *History and Hermeneutic* (Philadelphia: The Westminster Press, 1966). See also Daniel P. Fuller, "A New German Theological Movement," *ScotJournTheol* 19(1966),160–175; and a negative evaluation of the school's use of apocalyptic by William R. Murdock, "History and Revelation in Jewish Apocalypticism," *Interp* 21(1967),167–187.

goes back behind the text, and considers the occasion or the event which gave rise to the text in the context of its universal-historical significance, a context which includes the interpreter's own historical epoch. The universal-historical method of approach therefore takes a detour, the detour of going behind the text to the event which underlies it, the event to which it points, in order that by means of this detour a bridge may be built to the time contemporaneous with the interpreter (or the historian).[37]

Pannenberg's formulations are close to those of the hermeneutical theories we have been discussing: the new hermeneutic also seeks to penetrate behind the text, and it also emphasizes the current situation as part of the language history of the original text. Pannenberg attempts to "rescue" the "historical approach," however, and so exaggerates the differences between himself and his opponents.

There is more at stake here than is immediately apparent. In the theology as history school there is an attempt to regard historical events in such a way that we might speak once again of the "objective historicity" of some event as having normative meaning. The appeal to universal history is an attempt to bring the event into a framework valid for all times, not just valid within the experiencing of the text in interpretation.

To theologians whose theological teeth were cut upon such meaty stuff as Bultmann's rejection of Oscar Cullmann's concept of salvation history,† however, this can only sound like a return to a previously discarded position. Upon closer examination, the issue is not all that simple. Pannenberg's criticism is really more allied with that of Karl Barth, since Pannenberg attacks, as did Barth, existentialist interpretation's "anthropological narrowing of the question, of the pre-understanding."[38]

To escape this narrowing of theology into anthropology, Pannenberg replaces the crisis-quality of the interpretive encounter (when the text and the interpreter are locked in engagement) with a conception of history-as-interconnection (universal history). And it is this universal history that alone provides the comprehensive frame of reference for Pannenberg (even including that which is "behind" the text). The individual finds his-

---

[37] "Hermeneutics and Universal History," p. 124.

† Salvation history (or "redemptive history" or "saving history," *Heilsgeschichte* in German) refers to the faith posture that affirms that God works out the events of men according to his own purposes. An event of ordinary history—say the Israelites' escape from Egypt—can become salvation history to those who understand it not as an accidental happening but as a means by which God intervened in history. A classic statement of this point of view was argued in Cullmann, *Christ and Time: The Primitive Christian Conception of Time and History,* trans. Floyd V. Filson (Philadelphia: The Westminster Press, 1950). Cullmann affirms that the purpose of the Old Testament salvation history was to prepare for the Christ event, which event then became the mid-point in God's plan for the world and established the church as the place of God's Lordship until the Parousia (end of time, return of the Christ).

[38] "Hermeneutics and Universal History," p. 152.

torical events meaningful, according to Pannenberg, insofar as they are related to the whole past, the future, and also the present:

> Only within the context of universal history can the past of the text be bound to the present of the interpreter in such a way that their temporal, historical difference is not eliminated, but is rather, in the context of events that binds the two together, preserved and at the same time bridged over.[39]

Pannenberg's emphasis upon what enables us to bridge the distance from the past to the present and the future indicates that the theology as history school and the new hermeneutic are not very far apart in their aims: in each case the main problem is how to move meaningfully from our own context into that of the text and how this informs our present reality. But the ways the common aims or concerns are realized differ greatly. Pannenberg, for example, is quite disenchanted with the line of thought evolving from the use of Heidegger in theology; he desires that theology be less linguistically than historically oriented.

According to Pannenberg, we are not just dependent upon the faith-witness of those who recognized the Christ in the period following the crucifixion, since the resurrection itself can be established as a historically verifiable occurrence.[40] In order to establish that the resurrection took place, Pannenberg's argument proceeds referentially:

> Now, precisely because the resurrection of a single man was quite un-familiar to the apocalyptic tradition, we must suppose that a special event underlay the apostolic Easter message, an event that caused so decisive a change in the traditional expectation of the End. Evidently something had happened to the witnesses of the Risen One for which their language had no other word than that used to characterize the eschatological expecta-tion, i.e., resurrection from the dead.

In the very next sentence Pannenberg states that "This expression is a *metaphor*," and goes on to speak of "that *parabolic* word of eschatological

---

[39] *Ibid.*, p. 148. Note that an important part of the argument has been devel-oped in theological concentration on *Traditionsgeschichte,* the history of the trans-mission of the traditions (discussed later). This is expressly stated by Pannenberg (Postscript to *Offenbarung als Geschichte,* 139, quoted by Robinson, *NF* III, 81): "The problems of hermeneutic have been taken up in the concept of universal history as the history of the transmission of the traditions, i.e. [hermeneutic] is preserved as one aspect and also left behind as a whole."

[40] Robinson interprets Pannenberg's objective as trying "to create a situation in which faith can rest on historically proven fact." From certain "historically verifiable facts man can gain knowledge of God, if such facts are not seen in isolation but in a context of traditions that speak of God in an 'understandable way.'" (*NF* III, pp. 29, 41.)

expectation: resurrection from the dead."[41] The general line of interpretation is not structured in terms of metaphor and parable, however; instead Pannenberg argues that "in principle, every event has its original meaning within the context of occurrence and tradition in which it took place and through which it is connected with the present and its historical interest."[42] Even though the whole idea of resurrection is incompatible with modern thought, it is not so odd in the context of Graeco-Roman Hellenism—and so, he argues, it has much more probability.

Especially when such a phenomenon is comprehended as significant within the totality of time (its universal-historical significance), it may have what Pannenberg considers significant historical foundation-character today. In this sense meaningful events of the past are not so much to be interpreted or translated into contemporary understanding as they are to be revered as essential to faith itself. Pannenberg's remarks about the history of Jesus illustrate this aspect very well:

> One can understand the history of Jesus only if one understands the future salvation of mankind as having already appeared in and with him, and as having been made accessible through him. In the history of Jesus a future was anticipated that has not yet appeared in its general bearing. Therefore those who penetrate the meaning of Jesus' history will inevitably be led to God's not yet accomplished future, which nevertheless is held to have appeared already in and with Jesus when one speaks of his resurrection from the dead. Hence through knowledge of Jesus' history they are led to faith, to trust in God's future.[43]

Pannenberg's universal history and his attempt to revive the status of "historical" events as foundational for Christian faith are attempts to found theology upon the theological approach of the Bible itself. Certainly the attempt is more satisfactory than the type of salvation history developed earlier by Oscar Cullmann, which also sought a biblical model for contemporary theology. But what remains to be seen is whether or not this approach is satisfactory for a contemporary theology that is *fully* contemporary—that is, a theology that takes into account our sense of the radical disparity between the periods of history, our feeling of absolute lack of continuity between events, and our disenchantment with any system that would arbitrarily re-supply the connective tissues.

Bultmannian theologians are accused of saying that "it really doesn't matter what happened, because of the fact that a certain group of people

---

[41] "The Revelation of God in Jesus of Nazareth," *NF* III, 114–115, my emphasis.
[42] *Ibid.*, p. 127.
[43] *Ibid.*, p. 130.

experienced the actuality of the resurrection in their own lives, and that's enough." Pannenberg attempts to guarantee that "it really did happen," and he demands that we have only to understand and share the perspectives of those who anticipated and then reported the event—something demanding that we share the faith perspectives of the first Christians. His school is making a major contribution to theological precision by forcing renewed discussion of the relationship between historical events and their interpretation, but it may be asked if we have not only been given another very religious way of viewing the course of human history at a time when it is precisely the "religious" dimension of life that seems most in question.

Social Criticism   There have been a number of criticisms of the new hermeneutic's lack of emphasis upon the social responsibilities and contexts of theology. As in Pannenberg's program, the continued influence of theological existentialism is criticized. There is always the danger of what Carl Michalson called "existentialist rape"—the tendency to isolate the world's meaning in terms of one's own experience—and this danger has been especially appreciated in American circles owing to the sustained criticism of ideological individualism by theologians Richard and Reinhold Niebuhr.[44]

In New Frontiers in Theology, Volume II, John Dillenberger, Robert W. Funk, and Amos N. Wilder further emphasize the importance of the historical context in approaching theology. These scholars stress the community responsibility for interpretation—the need to encounter and work out the horizontal dimensions of a theology as it affects the entire social order. Dillenberger, for example, emphasizes the transitory nature of heuristic tools (for example the way interpretive and educational models tend to change). The existentialist analysis, according to Dillenberger, must not be regarded as some form of ultimate method. Understanding is always historically conditioned understanding:

> . . . There is no such thing as a final analysis of existence itself. Existence is as fluid as the cultural forms that give us life, and that is why all the configurations of history must continually confront and reshape us.[45]

[44] See also Hans Jonas' rejection of his former teacher Heidegger, not less significant because of Jonas' moral repulsion of Heidegger's acceptance of the Nazi regime. See the revision of Jonas' address at the second consultation of hermeneutics at Drew, "Heidegger and Theology," Chapter 10 in *The Phenomenon of Life: Toward a Philosophical Biology* (New York: Harper & Row, Publishers, 1966).

[45] *NF* II, 161. See also Claus Westermann, "The Meaning of Hermeneutics in Theology," *The Drew Gateway* 33(1963),127–141.

Amos Wilder attacks the "unsatisfactory anthropology" of interpretation in the new hermeneutic. It results, he thinks, in a "kind of generalized *Anthropos* [man]" that contributes little to the question "to what is man saved?" and that results in an aesthetic and cultural vacuum. Consequently man is asked to make the decision of faith as a matter of his will alone, and all that we associate with man's reason and imagination is neglected—"the Word of God has no structure, and there are no human structures to which it is meaningful."[46]

Such criticisms as these have been made before, especially in evaluations of existentialist interpretation. But the intensity of criticism of the new hermeneutic is greater, and I suspect that one reason may be that the jargon of the recent discussions (which could not be entirely avoided here) sounds esoteric indeed. When a typical interchange of those following the new hermeneutic is overheard, the language may be so abstract as to be almost meaningless; or the obverse may be the case: only one writing or poem may be discussed, and the listener wonders how the discussion might be more generally applied. Some of this indirection may have been necessary in the initial shaping of new directions; since the most helpful contribution of the new hermeneutic is its concentration upon the historical situation in which a text was composed (see Chapter 4), we may expect that, with the working tools honed, future interpretation will speak more concretely in terms of the present level of comprehension into which the interpretation is to be spoken.[47]

The need to have greater respect for the dimensions of historical community (what we are accustomed to calling the moral or ethical aspects) is also the basis of criticism of the new hermeneutic in a lively article by Jürgen Moltmann entitled "Toward a Political Hermeneutics of the Gospel."[48] That we are once again dealing with one basic set of

[46] *NF* II, 204, 205, 209.

[47] There is a parallel in Funk's criticism of Ogden and van Buren: he feels that they have not taken seriously enough the "secular man" for whom they supposedly were writing. It may be noted that religion is taught in the German school system, and that there are several popularly-oriented books which may be used by the German school teacher to convey the applications of the new hermeneutic in class. The criticism that the new hermeneutic is only a matter for the rarified atmosphere of scholarly debate, unrelated to the "needs of the church," and hence of little value for future American biblical study, is voiced by Brevard S. Childs, *Biblical Theology in Crisis* (Philadelphia: The Westminster Press, 1970), pp. 80–81.

[48] *UnSemQuartRev* 23(1968),303–323. See also Moltmann's *The Theology of Hope: On the Ground and the Implications of a Christian Eschatology*, trans. J. W. Leitch (New York and Evanston: Harper & Row, Publishers, 1967), and articles discussing this new theology of hope, pp. 79 ff., in Martin E. Marty and Dean G. Peerman, eds., *New Theology No. 5* (New York: The Macmillan Company, and London: Collier-Macmillan, Ltd., 1968).

hermeneutical and historical issues is well illustrated in the following quotation from that article:

> . . . The question becomes how the past can be brought into the con-
> sciousness of the present so that the freedom of the present for the future
> can be maintained or increased without being limited by the prejudices of
> tradition or subordinated to an ideology of history (p. 305).

While Pannenberg was influenced by Hegel's concept of history-as-a-whole, Moltmann is influenced by Wilhelm Dilthey and Karl Marx in speaking of the *futurity* of reality. We are directed by Moltmann to God's promise in Christ: what is important is not just the whole framework of history, but the directions and goals, the eschatological orientation of Christianity.

Once this is established, important consequences follow for the task of hermeneutics. Moltmann is impatient with traditional hermeneutics and criticizes the passivism of hermeneutics-become-theology: "Hermeneutics falls into the danger of formalism when it only seeks in retrospect for an understanding of the past under the conditions of the present." (p. 315). Rather, he argues, a legitimate hermeneutics "must seek changes of the present conditions." This is indeed a call for moving out of theological ghettos: ". . . Theological hermeneutics is abstract as long as it does not become the theory of practise, and sterile as long as it does not make 'the entrance to future truth' possible." (p. 315.) Moltmann then begins to develop a "political hermeneutic," using political in the Aristotelian sense of involvement with the full dimensions of life's concerns. Hermeneutics does not just have to do with texts, but with the ". . . political configuration of the church and the ethical form of the Christian life. . . ." (p. 318.)

In coming years, both the theology of hope of Moltmann and the theology as history of Pannenberg will be further refined and developed. We are still affected by the impact of twentieth-century existentialism, and each of these reactions seeks a contemporary way to keep the contributions of existentialism without surrendering either the traditional Christian affirmation of the importance of history or Christian social involvement. Pannenberg's school desires to clarify the senses in which Christianity is "historical," and Moltmann seeks to relate the scholarly discipline of theology to more activist political involvement. In either case, interpretation of hermeneutics is vitally important, since all theology builds upon the patterns that emerge in its use of and care for language. Whether or not contemporary formulations of the process and dimensions of interpretation will be sufficient in the future is not really as important as that the complexity and the difficulty of adequate translation have come fully into view. And they will not be quickly cast to the side.[49]

[49] Part of what is at stake is the particular articulation of theological formulations that make sense in the American context. Theology in the United States has most often reflected European models; when individual American theologians have worked vis-à-vis major American thinkers, they have been treated as "irrelevant" or as bowing before the worst of American pragmatism and Social Gospelism. Space prohibits delineation of alternatives, but some indications of resources for student reading may be indicated.

Argument that there are unique contributions from the American tradition to face the future "sociotechnical" inevitabilities of our culture is made by Herbert W. Richardson, *Toward an American Theology* (New York, Evanston, and London: Harper & Row, Publishers, 1967). The first three chapters of this book, while difficult reading, lay out the need to get beyond existentialist individualism and work toward a theology that is adequately responsive to sociotechnics ("management," "cybernetics"); the remaining chapters are much more difficult, and require some background in philosophical theology.

Langdon Gilkey, of the University of Chicago Divinity School, sustains an excellent critique of the excessive futurism of the theology of hope movement in "The Contribution of Culture to the Reign of God," in *The Future as the Presence of Shared Hope*, ed. Maryellen Muckenhirn (New York: Sheed and Ward, 1968), pp. 34–58. (The same volume has a very basic introduction to Moltmann's thinking, "'Behold, I make all things new': The Category of the New in Christian Theology," pp. 9–33.) See also Gilkey's major work, *Naming the Whirlwind: The Renewal of God-Language* (Indianapolis and New York: The Bobbs-Merrill Company, 1969), a widely-reaching survey of current "secularist" approaches and Gilkey's response.

The first 87 pages of Brevard S. Childs, *Biblical Theology in Crisis* lay out the American reactions to the "biblical theology movement" in the first sixty years of this century.

3

The Search for Proper Methods

A comprehensive theory of interpretation must be built around factors such as the function of understanding, the nature of religious language, and the problems involved in either interpretation or communication. In the broad sense, interpretation also includes the aims, the directions, and the specific methodologies of criticism. In this chapter attention is directed to methodological questions, beginning with literary criticism and form criticism,* and continuing with critical approaches developed out of and in response to form criticism. Because so few NT introductions or handbooks discuss form criticism in any detail, I have given more than a brief sketch of this important method. And finally, the components that might be found in a "typical" exegetical study today are discussed in outline.

LITERARY CRITICISM

Within NT studies, literary criticism (*Literarkritik*) usually refers to matters of source analysis,* to questions of the authenticity of texts, and to the interrelations between NT materials. The "literary question" of the eighteenth century, for instance, was primarily a question about the origins of the gospels; such great scholar-theologians as Griesbach, Lessing, Eichhorn, Herder, Gieseler, and Schleiermacher pursued *Literarkritik* as a type of source analysis, seeking to identify the exact sources of the gospels.

* See Glossary.

This type of detective work was pursued so rigidly, however, that the main insights of literary analysis—observations about the function of the literary form or its place of origination in the community—were often lost. The making of detailed and minute divisions in the biblical texts according to hypothetical sources took so much concentration that no one seems to have had any energy left to develop broader aspects.[1]

As an important aspect of historical criticism, literary criticism was expected to develop biblical studies into a scientific and historical discipline on a par with other burgeoning sciences such as physics and mathematics. In its attempt to establish the "personality" of an author or to determine the earliest and most basic gospel (the *Urevangelium*) or the authenticity of the epistles, scholars pursuing literary criticism sought to do their work as scientifically as would be possible in any other field of scholarship. No matter how scientific or historical was the announced intent of such criticism, however, dogmatic motifs and concerns still dominated the actual research.

We see in J. G. Eichhorn's five-volume introduction to the NT, for instance, that interests of dogma were controlling. Eichhorn stated that "the *content* of a NT writing should have decisive say in determining its authority," which indicates that he was not really critical in terms of primarily listening for what was actually in the text; indeed he indicated elsewhere that "content" was basically that which he and his churchly colleagues agreed it was.[2]

The attempt to make biblical studies into an "objective" discipline is found throughout the literary-critical work of the nineteenth century. Of primary concern was the determination of the exact date a text was written, the extent of editing, and the relationships of the editors to one another (note the development of redaction criticism* in Old Testament studies during this period), the picture of the authors' and editors' personalities (note the growing awareness of psychology in the latter part of the century), and the types and extent of the sources that had been used.

---

[1] A classic example from H. Holzinger's work is given by Klaus Koch: Joshua 5:4–8 was attributed to no fewer than five sources—vv. 4 & 7 to P, v. 5 to R[JE], v. 6a to JE[S], v. 6b to D[s], and v. 8 to the original source. Klaus Koch, *Was ist Formgeschichte? Neue Wege der Bibelexegese* (Neukirchen-Vluyn: Neukirchener Verlag des Erziehungsverein GmbH, 1964), p. 76, n. 9; see also *The Growth of the Biblical Tradition: The Form-Critical Method*, trans. S. M. Cupitt from the 2nd ed. (New York: Charles Scribner's Sons, 1969), p. 76, n. 88.

[2] See Werner Georg Kümmel, *Das Neue Testament: Geschichte der Erforschung seiner Probleme*, 2nd, revised and enlarged ed. (Freiburg/Munich: Verlag Karl Albert, 1958), pp. 88–104. The quotation is on p. 103. The ET of this important historical encyclopedia by Kümmel is now being completed by Howard C. Kee.

* See Glossary.

Hermann Gunkel, a literary critic of the end of the century, dismantled much of the work that had been done under the literary criticism banner by showing that the working concept of the literary originality of an author (so important to our way of thinking, and hence presupposed of the writing practise of antiquity) failed to do justice to the extent to which biblical materials were reworkings of traditional materials. Most of the books of the Bible, suggested Gunkel, were not the products of individual "authors" as much as they were the end-results of traditional materials being passed along through a long period of oral development.

Gunkel's insights represented a necessary reorientation insofar as it began to be seen that there was a much richer relationship between individual authors and traditions than that suggested by a simple process of writing and later editing. It began to be evident that the biblical materials were codified or organized around interests, insights, and requirements of various situations in the life of the religious and secular communities, and that "authors" were mostly collators and organizers ("redactors")* of particular sets of traditions.

Yet another presupposition of literary criticism began to seem less and less tenable, owing to Gunkel's type of analysis—namely the evolutionary schema of the late eighteenth and early nineteenth centuries. J. Wellhausen (in OT studies) and F. C. Baur (in NT studies) had pointed to the *Tendenz* of the author—to his "tendency" to write in such a way as to reflect his own times or to argue for a certain point of view. Accordingly, the typical picture of Israelite and early Christian religious writings that emerged was something like this: various writers, each reflecting the historical and theological developments of his own background or school, portray the progressive evolution of religion from fetishism (animism) through polytheism to monotheism, with Christian messianism as the supreme point of development. For such a schema, scholars now began to substitute an approach that allowed each statement its own weight, without prejudicing the argument by deeming it either primitive or advanced.

The late nineteenth century also saw the development of the school of *Religionsgeschichte* (literally, history-of-religion, but we are more accustomed to speaking of this approach as comparative religions). This school focused its research upon the large number of materials from ancient oriental and Hellenistic religions that became available at this time, and so began comprehensive comparison of ancient Israel and early Christianity with their contemporary analogues.

Now that it was seen that neither Israel nor Christianity could claim to be the absolute high point of religious development, the interrelations

* See Glossary.

and mutual influences between Israelite-Christian materials, and materials from the other religions of antiquity were studied, and the result was the final dissolution of the evolutionary chain-of-development theories. These studies also broadened the horizons of research, since now analysis of non-Christian texts had taken into account a much wider range of situations (worship, festivals, etc.) than had previously been studied in historical analysis of Israel and Christianity.

At the start of the twentieth century, the final springing of the rigid literary-critical framework was carried out by the philologian Eduard Norden, in his literary analysis of forms of religious writing in antiquity, by Hans Lietzmann (1875–1942) in his presentation of the various types of Christian literature in relation to Hellenistic literature, and by Paul Wendland (1864–1915) in his summary of the various forms of early Christian literary production. Rudolf Bultmann, in his dissertation,[3] sought to show how the literary-critical approach should be modified by giving greater attention to the literary genre* (*Gattung*) as such, after which the scholar could attempt to show how biblical writings modified traditional genres in a creative or an imitative way.

It would be wrong to give the impression that once the weaknesses of literary criticism were established the method itself was totally discredited. While it is true that today few biblical scholars would characterize their main work as "literary-critical analysis," there are many aspects of such analysis that are not to be discarded. The problem of gospel sources, for example, is not a problem admitting of any final solution, and we may not lightly ignore the problems of the interrelations between strata of the traditions. We will probably never reach a final verdict as to the indentification of the source Q, and debate on the problem continues.

Some of the questions of literary criticism were continued by form criticism, as we shall see; other aspects, in modified forms, are very much at issue in other types of research, such as the concentration on levels of tradition in redaction and tradition criticism.* But by and large literary criticism has become one aspect of the total range of methodologies employed by the biblical scholar, rather than the designation of the whole direction of studies. This is commendable, since contemporary criticism is open to the use of several complementary methodologies and should not fall again into the trap of lifeless fragmentation of the text and the pedantic exegesis that was representative of classical literary criticism at

[3] *Der Stil der paulinischen Predigt* . . . , esp. pp. 1–5.
* See Glossary.

its worst. Present literary-critical analysis is marked by attempts to evaluate the significance and influence of the larger units of the materials, the genres, as we shall see in Chapter 5.

Especially in the American university context, which places value on interdisciplinary approaches, biblical criticism is informed by contemporary non-theological literary criticism. Amos N. Wilder has made outstanding contributions to the ongoing dialogue between literary critics and biblical critics.† His recent book, *Early Christian Rhetoric: The Language of the Gospel*,[4] was an attempt to relate aspects of the new hermeneutical approach to such biblical genres as the dialogue, the parable, the story, the poem, and the anecdote. I do not know of any similar attempt to combine a theological perspective with attention to literary and rhetorical modes. On the other hand, William A. Beardslee's *Literary Criticism of the New Testament* has suggestively analyzed the ways in which literary criticism may open up perspectives on the early Christian literature by relating literary forms and impulses to the life style and vision of the religion.

The Parables . . . , a book by Dan Otto Via, Jr., is a recent contribution to a particular area of the discussion; probably no other volume has so canvassed the resources of non-theological literary criticism to confront a biblical genre. Richard E. Palmer's *Hermeneutics* concludes with "A Hermeneutical Manifesto to American Literary Interpretation," which proposes that the insights of hermeneutical theory be directly applied to criticism in all types of literary criticism. Following Palmer's exposition of the development and contours of hermeneutics, and especially

---

† Terminology has again become problematic: it is difficult to find the phrase that would describe biblical literary criticism concerned especially with "regular" (i.e., non-theological) literary criticism. To describe its working sessions on such matters, the Society of Biblical Literature simply designates the sessions "Biblical Criticism and Literary Criticism." Because of my own conviction that contemporary biblical criticism has so much to gain from cooperation with nontheological literary criticism, I am grateful to the Society for Religion in Higher Education for a postdoctoral fellowship for cross-disciplinary study to pursue this subject full time in 1971–72.

[4] Cambridge: Harvard University Press, 1971, orig. ed. 1964. Information on the other titles in the following paragraphs: William A. Beardslee, *Literary Criticism of the New Testament* (Philadelphia: Fortress Press, 1970); Dan Otto Via, Jr., *The Parables: Their Literary and Existential Dimension* (Philadelphia: Fortress Press, 1967); Richard E. Palmer, *Hermeneutics: Interpretation Theory in Schleiermacher, Dilthey, Heidegger, and Gadamer* (Evanston: Northwestern University Press, 1969); Ehrhardt Güttgemanns, *Offen Fragen zur Formgeschichte des Evangeliums: Eine methodische Skizze der Grundlagenkrisen-problematik der Form- und Redaktionsgeschichte* (Munich: Chr. Kaiser Verlag, 1969).

The response of a literary critic to the lack of methodological discipline in previous studies is found in Roland M. Frye, "A Literary Perspective for the Criticism of the Gospels," in *Jesus and Man's Hope*, Vol. II, ed. Donald G. Miller and Dikran Y. Hadidian (Pittsburgh: Pittsburgh Theological Seminary, 1971), 193–221.

his attention to Martin Heidegger and Hans Georg Gadamer (a contemporary German philosopher of language), the Manifesto seeks to elicit discussion of basic hermeneutical questioning in literary critical operations to an extent comparable to that experienced in twentieth-century theology.

Finally, we may mention a work not yet translated, Ehrhardt Güttgemann's "open questions about the form criticism of the gospels." This work, with the long subtitle "a methodological sketch of the problematics of the fundamental bases of form and redaction criticism" relies upon linguistics and literary sociology to clarify and improve upon these methodologies. Güttgemanns argues that form criticism especially was developed without adequate reference to the canons and experience of traditional literary criticism, and that concentration upon these methodologies without methodological acuity has contributed unnecessary confusion to recent analyses.

Contributions to biblical literary criticism often come from seminary and university professors working in the sub-field usually identified as "Religion and Literature"; hopefully more of these scholars will devote attention to biblical materials as well as to contemporary literature. Within a discipline dominated by the methodologies of German scholarship, however, we must remember that the term literary criticism is usually understood to refer specifically (narrowly) to source analysis and to tracing the literary relationships of biblical writings to one another.

An introduction to biblical methodology by Heinrich Zimmermann reinforces this restriction, as does the sketch of "Old Testament Exegesis" by Otto Kaiser, in *Exegetical Method: A Student's Handbook*.[5] Kaiser's sketch of exegetical method places literary criticism between textual criticism and metric analysis (analysis of the metres, rhyme schemes and so forth); his following outline of what literary-critical analysis should include provides a convenient summary of literary criticism understood in the traditional, technical sense.

First the text is to be carefully studied and each part classified ac-

---

[5] See Heinrich Zimmermann, *Neutestamentliche Methodenlehre: Darstellung der historisch-kritischen Methode* (Stuttgart: Verlag Kath. Bibelwerk, 1968, 2nd ed.), p. 85: "On the whole, literary criticism has to do with the so-called introductory questions, but is directed specifically to source-criticism." These "introductory questions" include questions of authorship, date, provenance, sources, and the like, and are treated in the German *Einleitung* ("introduction"; we catch the nuance better in "handbook"). The best such technical handbook now available is Werner Georg Kümmel, revision of Paul Feine and Johannes Behm, *Introduction to the New Testament*, trans. A. J. Mattill, Jr. from the 14th rev. ed. (Nashville and New York: Abingdon Press, 1966). The material by Kaiser is from Otto Kaiser and Werner Georg Kümmel, *Exegetical Method: A Student's Handbook*, trans. E. V. N. Goetchius (New York: The Seabury Press, 1967). Used with permission.

cording to the point of view from which it has been composed, or according to its function. Then ". . . the train of thought expressed in the text is to be traced from sentence to sentence and examined for possible inconsistencies. By working through the text repeatedly in this way, doublets, secondary glosses, alternations between poetry and prose, stylistic deviations, omissions, shifts in thought and direct contradictions are brought to light. . . ."

After this dissection, the "real work of literary criticism follows"—obvious additions and glosses are to be eliminated; the main strands of the narrative are to be identified; subordinate sources or stages in the process of revising or passing on the text are to be noted. Further, commentaries, monographs, and other research tools are consulted in order to familiarize oneself with previous literary solutions and with the history of exegesis. Examination of the "linguistic usage of the source documents, narrative strata, prophetic oracles, and the like must be made with great care . . . ," and the use of key words is to be explored. Linguistic statistics will be of relevance in some cases; certainly a concordance should be consulted. Analysis of the "joins" with the immediate context of the material as well as attention to the wider contexts in which the editor-author has placed the material should take place; and finally characteristic use of language, including theological terms, and the types of discourse should be noted.

While I believe Kaiser includes more in his sketch of literary criticism than should properly be included (see the last part of this chapter), his suggestions provide a reminder that literary-critical analysis in this technical sense remains as an important, if somewhat tedious, aspect of proper exegetical method.

FORM CRITICISM

The specific type of literary analysis with which the contemporary biblical interpreter is most familiar is undoubtedly form criticism. Since the form-critical method is so widely established today, it is essential that it be understood both in its application and its immediate historical contexts. Broadly defined, the form-critical method involves identification of the units ("forms") in which traditions tend to be conveyed; it seeks to discover how these forms arise in the oral period preceding the literary stage, and it attempts to relate the use of the forms to the sociological settings in which they arise. Typical forms* are the parable, the simple saying, the short narrative, the healing story.[6]

---

* An overview of forms with examples will be found in Appendix 1.

[6] William G. Doty, "The Discipline and Literature of New Testament Form Criticism," *AnglTheolRev* 51(1969)257–321. The article treats in greater detail the

The Initial Impact We should have to go back quite a way to pick up all the threads that were eventually woven into the fabric of form criticism. The method was developed as a means of treating the synoptic materials (the contents of the first three gospels), and hence was devoted to an important concern of NT scholars since the beginnings of Enlightenment criticism. David F. Strauss, the most famous of the early nineteenth-century scholars, focused the problem in ways that became normative for all subsequent research. He emphasized the importance of evaluating separate gospel passages one at a time; he established the contrast between the synoptic gospels and John, and the necessity, for historical reconstruction, of choosing between them; and he showed how the actual sequence of events in the primitive Christian history had been systematically reworked into a conceptually coherent (Strauss would have said into a "mythological") framework.

By the end of the last century biblical scholarship, especially in the form of literary criticism, had reached a standstill. There was widespread recognition that multiple sources had contributed to the creation of the gospels, but wide disagreement on how to understand their interrelations and the ways individual gospels had eventually been composed out of the mass of individual passages. Wilhelm Wrede's analysis of the messianic-secret motif in Mark† found wide acceptance and led to great distrust of the synoptic chronology.

The advance that led to the development of a comprehensive form-critical approach to the NT materials, however, took place within studies of the Old Testament. Hermann Gunkel's suggestion that biblical literature was the product of combined traditions, each of which had a long period of oral growth behind it, was used by Julius Wellhausen to portray the development of the oral traditions behind the gospels. Gunkel had

---

historical development of the method, and lists over 238 form-critical studies; parts of this section appeared in the article, and are used in revised form by permission of the journal.

See also Edgar V. McKnight, *What is Form Criticism?* (Philadelphia: Fortress Press, 1969); and Robert M. Montgomery and W. Richard Stegner, *Forms in the Gospels:* I. The Pronouncement Story (Nashville and New York: Abingdon Press, 1970), II. Allegory and Parable (forthcoming)—these are programmed learning devices.

† According to Wrede's theory, which is accepted with modifications today, Mark (in contrast to Matthew and Luke) has Jesus tell his disciples the secrets about the Kingdom of God—as for instance the inner meaning of the parables—but then tells them to keep silent. This was Mark's way of explaining how people so missed the significance of Jesus that they murdered him—at least according to Wrede. Theodore H. Weeden shows that Mark was dealing with a problematic theological problem among his own fellow Christians, and that he casts the disciples into the role of those who disagreed with him! When we hear Jesus chastising the disciples for their understanding of his role and status, Weeden feels we ought to hear Mark chastising his own contemporaries whose christological beliefs Mark disputes. See "The Heresy that Necessitated Mark's Gospel," *ZeitNTWiss* 59(1968),145–158.

analyzed such a process of traditional growth in Israel's legendary materials, with special attention given to the search for the originating context of the materials (the *Sitz im Leben**); Axel Olrik and others formulated rules of development which various types of popular literature seem to have followed.

And then, in the study of the primitive Christian literature, three remarkably similar works appeared almost simultaneously (1919–1921). These were studies that sought to clarify the processes by which the Christian materials had taken shape from the period of oral transmission down to their final written collation and publication.

It was under the express rubric of literary criticism that the first work of this new twentieth-century methodology appeared. Karl Ludwig Schmidt's book, *The Framework of the History of Jesus* carried the subtitle *Literary-Critical Investigations of the Ancient Jesus-Traditions*.[7] Schmidt demonstrated that it was necessary to expand the classical two-source theory for the gospels to take account of a large body of orally transmitted materials. Schmidt directed his scrutiny primarily to the framework within which the life of Jesus was set by the evangelists. He suggested that the gospels consist for the most part of a series of short episodes, of which Jesus is the subject, and in the majority of cases such episodes are complete in themselves—vivid, terse, and compact. As one of the first organizations of these materials, the Gospel of Mark linked units of tradition (by a series of bridge passages) into a chronological scheme, by means of which one is able to follow the ministry of Jesus from the preaching of John to the crises of the final week.

Schmidt utilized the old image of D. F. Strauss that the pre-gospel stories of Jesus are like a handful of pearls for which there was no connecting string; he thought that the connecting string—the framework—had been supplied by Mark himself, although before Mark's time some of the stories had already coalesced into small groupings, collected for the needs of the early Christian communities. By careful reconstruction of the early gospel-making situations, we are brought back to the earliest stages of the formation of the gospel tradition.

A few months after publication of Schmidt's work, Martin Dibelius published his *Die Formgeschichte des Evangeliums*, 1919 [Form Criticism of the Gospel].[8] This work contained a six-element classification of the synoptic materials, and was responsible for setting the tone of much

---

* See Glossary.

[7] *Der Rahmen der Geschichte Jesu: Literarkritische Untersuchungen zur ältesten Jesusüberlieferung* (Berlin: Trowitzsch, 1919; repr. Darmstadt: Wissenschaftliche Buchgesellschaft, 1964).

[8] Translated from the second edition by B. L. Woolf, as *From Tradition to Gospel* (New York: Charles Scribner's Sons, n.d.).

subsequent form-critical work. Dibelius believed that the writers of the gospels worked as compilers or redactors rather than as authors (in the sense of the older literary criticism): their work consisted mainly of grouping and reworking the traditional materials. The evangelists' theological understandings of that material are seen in the ways they performed their editorial tasks. The form-critical point of view developed by Dibelius is therefore consciously anti-individualistic and sociological:

> The individual personalities disappear here behind the materials, and so we do not have to do only with noting their idiosyncracies, but must also pay attention to the levels of the transmission which are glimpsed through their reports.[9]

Furthermore, Dibelius showed that it was important for NT criticism to free itself from the clutches of theories used to explicate classical literature in order to comprehend the true spirit of the gospels. He felt that the gospels should be judged by the standards of popular or folk literature rather than by the standards of classical writers.[10]

Independently of Dibelius' work, Rudolf Bultmann, just installed as professor at Marburg, published the first edition of his *Die Geschichte der synoptischen Tradition* [The History of the Synoptic Tradition] in 1921. Bultmann's work was the first comprehensive and systematic presentation of his own methodology, the result of several years of teaching and research. A large number of synoptic passages are analyzed and discussed, a final part reviews the process of redaction by the synoptic evangelists, and a brief conclusion displays some of the historical insights that Bultmann gained from his analysis.[11] Later scholarship has taken Bultmann's analysis as its central structure; much work has been focused on refining Bultmann's categories, although not one has yet attempted an equally comprehensive treatment.

The Contours of the Method　As in the famous case of the elephant described by five blind men, each of whom reported his experience of the animal according to the part he encountered, form criticism has been described from many different starting points. It has also been used with

---

[9] "Zur Formgeschichte der Evangelien," *TheolRund* N.F. 1(1929),188.

[10] "The Structure and Literary Character of the Gospels," *HarvTheolRev* 20(1927),151–170, and K. L. Schmidt, "Die Stellung der Evangelien in der allgemeinen Literaturgeschichte," in *EUCHARISTERION für H. Gunkel* (Göttingen: 1923), II, 50 ff.

[11] These insights are also evident in his small *Primitive Christianity* of 1949 (ET 1956), and in even more precise and schematic form in Karl Kundsin, "Primitive Christianity in the Light of Gospel Research," translated and printed with Bultmann, "The Study of the Synoptic Gospels," in *Form Criticism*, ed. F. C. Grant (New York: Harper & Row, Publishers, 1962).

quite a number of different aims in mind: to certify Christian faith by determining the bedrock of faith's witness; to provide "neutral" access to the early Christian literature and hence to the community bound up with it; to determine which materials are original and which secondary; to provide a solution for the problem of synoptic sources; and for contemporary theological exegesis. It may be that form criticism is so widely acknowledged and utilized today because the method has something to contribute when used for any of these purposes; it would be difficult to specify any one exhaustive definition of the aims of the method. Definitions seem to grow when aims, purposes, and methods are pressed into one another, but a preliminary definition might be:

> Form criticism is a systematic, scientific, historical, and theological methodology for analyzing the forms, and to some extent the content, of the primitive Christian literature, with special reference to the history of the early Christian movement in its reflective and creative theological activities.

The definition reflects the close relationship between the particular situations in the life of the communities and the literary materials coming from those situations. The form critics introduced the use of the term *Sitz im Leben* into theological discussion to indicate this relationship: in the analysis of a literature we reason from the final literary form to the situational source of the author or community that produced it. *Sitz im Leben,* or "sociological setting," refers to that source, the context in which a type or a form of literature is produced. This situation must be established by use of a circular methodology: "The form of the literary tradition must be used to establish the influences operating in the life of the community, and the life of the community must be used to render the forms themselves intelligible."[12]

Two examples of passages in their sociological settings may clarify this concept. The first is a floating saying used in no fewer than four settings: "he who humbles himself will be exalted." It appears as a means of ending a parable (Lk 18:9–14, the parable of the Pharisee and the publican), is associated with becoming a child to enter the Kingdom (with changed wording, Mt 18:4), is used in conjunction with determining places of honor among disciples (Mt 23:12), and as part of a section on places of honor at a wedding banquet (Lk 14:11). In each case, the saying's meaning is heightened according to the types of situations in the evangelist's minds; generally speaking, we hear overtones of early Christian problems of justifying the developing church structures and offices with the egalitarian teaching of Jesus. We are directed to the

---

[12] Bultmann, *History,* p. 5.

sociological setting by the concern with status in the saying; knowing this concern, we are able to understand how the saying functions, and what needs it met, in the gospels.

The second saying is more obvious; Mt 16:18–19, "And I tell you, you are Peter, and on this rock I will build my church. . . . I will give you the keys of the kingdom of heaven, and whatever you loose on earth shall be loosed in heaven." Regardless of the claim that it stemmed from the career of Jesus of Nazareth, the saying is clearly included (by Matthew only) because Matthew and the leaders of the church in his time clearly understood the important role of Peter. Many scholars, accepting this sort of sociological referent, claim that Matthew has created this saying in order to elevate the position of Peter and of Christian church leaders. Our purpose here is simply to show how a saying can be related to a particular life situation in primitive Christianity—in this case, the debate about status and official structure.

By concentrating on the classification of synoptic materials, the early form critics attempted to get behind the literature as we now have it in order to reach into the period in which the oral traditions were being crystallized and formed. The forms in which literature appear are of great importance as a sort of forecast of what we are to hear or read, since linguistic forms are the record-in-language of some part of life that is specified or emphasized in a particular way. Forms are the agencies for binding traditions.

The early form critics were also concerned with the questions of the authenticity of the gospel materials and they went beyond literary analysis to make historical judgments. They valued the authenticity of the sayings materials (logia*), for instance, more highly than they did the more developed legendary narratives. Second- and third-generation form critics have also stressed the importance of the *content* of the form, as is indicated in my definition. The traditional Aristotelian-Kantian distinction between form and content is no longer viable, and instead of speaking of a certain content expressed in a number of forms, contemporary critics emphasize that certain forms are the only way some content can come to expression. The situation is like that in the interpretation of poetry: we may specify what every line of a poem "means," but what the poem means cannot be reduced to an intellectual exposition and still live as a poem.

Comprehensive presentation of all the details of the form-critical method is out of the question here; in Appendix 1 I have provided a chart of the main features of the method as practised by Bultmann and Dibelius, and in the following discussion I have tried to draw out aspects

* See Glossary.

of the method by comparing specific features of Bultmann's and Dibelius'
analysis.

Bultmann—Sketch of Entire Synoptic History   The fact that Bultmann entitled his work *The History of the Synoptic Tradition* is significant, for it indicates that his work is more than just form criticism in a
narrow sense, whereas Dibelius' book was specifically entitled *The Form
Criticism of the Gospels* (ET, however, is *From Tradition to Gospels*).
Bultmann is indeed a representative of form criticism, but his work is
more than just an exercise in the description of the forms of the gospels.
It is a history of the entire synoptic tradition, and is therefore involved
with sketching the development of the primitive Christian materials by
means of all available methodologies, with the entire sweep of the developing tradition in view.

Dibelius—Greater Refinement of Form   Dibelius was hardly un-
concerned with the wider question of the interrelations of synoptic
traditions, but he placed greater working emphasis upon refining a few
inclusive forms. Since Bultmann did not devote much space to justifying
the forms he used, giving his attention directly to the materials themselves, much of the criticism that greeted his work focused on the demand for clarification and better definition.

Constructive vs. Analytical Methods   Bultmann preferred to begin
with an analysis of the material actually at hand and thence "to draw
conclusions from the material of the tradition, as to its *Sitz im Leben,* its
point of origin and conservation in the community. . . ." (*History*, p. 11.)
This "analytical" method was contrasted to Dibelius' "constructive"
method. Dibelius "reconstructs the history of the synoptic tradition from
a study of the community and its needs," whereas Bultmann proceeds
from "the analysis of the particular elements of the traditions." (*History*,
p. 5.) Dibelius defended his procedure by saying that while he made his
own historical conclusions evident as he began, Bultmann made a similar
set of conclusions the hidden agenda of his work (although of course such
conclusions do appear, following Bultmann's analysis of the phenomena).

Form vs. Historical Reconstruction   The procedural difference
should not be overstressed, because in the early period of form-critical
work, as Bultmann notes, the two scholars are "engaged in mutually
complementary and corrective work."[13] Indeed these are but alternative
starting points in what is the essentially circular procedure of all historical
analysis. The process of criticizing the synoptic traditions must keep the

---

[13] *History,* p. 5. Bultmann was disappointed that Dibelius did not choose, in
subsequent editions of the latter's own work, to enter into dialogue with him.

two poles of "form" and "historical reconstruction" in view while working within the immediate proximity of either factor.

Literary vs. Literary, Historical, and Content Judgments   A more substantive difference is apparent in the extreme to which analysis is taken for the reconstruction of the primitive Christian history. Here Bultmann appears as the radical skeptic compared to the more conservative Dibelius. Bultmann held to the necessity of making judgments concerning the actual historical phenomena of early Christianity, whereas Dibelius restricted his judgments primarily to matters of literary style.

Bultmann therefore made historical evaluations concerning whether or not a passage was "genuine," or whether a text originated in the earlier Palestinian community or in the later, non-Palestinian (Bultmann: "Hellenistic") communities. Consequently he defined the aim of form criticism as determining: (a) "the original form of a piece of narrative, a dominical saying [a saying of Jesus] or a parable," in the process of which determination (b) "secondary additions and forms" are to be excluded, leading (c) "to important results for the history of the tradition." (*History*, p. 6.)

Dibelius rightly saw that Bultmann's work had to do in this instance with judgments going beyond the specific technical phase of form-critical analysis (on into the realm of content-exegesis, as discussed in Chapter 1). Dibelius found it repugnant that Bultmann made judgments of content and of historical probability, both because many of those judgments were negative with respect to their original relationship to Jesus and because many adverse criticisms against the form-critical method he defends were occasioned by this theological aspect of Bultmann's procedure.

The Sociological Setting   Bultmann distinguished his use of the term *Sitz im Leben* from Dibelius' concentration upon one specific and all-inclusive situation in life, namely the preaching of the early church:

> To say that preaching is the starting-point of all the spiritual products of early Christianity, that it was preaching that begat the tradition, seems to my mind a gross overstatement that endangers the understanding of numerous items of the tradition. . . . Apologetics and polemics, as well as edification and discipline must equally be taken into account, as must scribal activity. (*History*, pp. 60 f.)

Dibelius did accept a wider interpretation of "preaching" by suggesting that these other activities are not antithetical to preaching but are included therein, although he often seemed less inclined to modify his position in his actual exegesis. It appears that for Dibelius the *Sitz im Leben* concept functioned primarily with respect to the sociological setting of the tradition as a whole; Bultmann's more concentrated concern was determining the sociological setting of the passage under discussion at any particular time.[14]

The form-critical work of Bultmann and Dibelius concentrated upon the materials of the synoptic traditions, although Dibelius also contributed studies of Acts, and Bultmann developed a very influential literary interpretation of John. Since the period of their work, form-critical studies have multiplied the classifications of the materials and have sought to clarify and improve the definitions and characterizations of the forms. Specific parts of the traditions that have been analyzed in greater detail include the legendary materials, the passion narrative, the parabolic materials, credal and hymnic fragments, and the gospel prologues. Outside the synoptic gospels, work has been done on the book of Acts (especially on the speeches, as begun by Dibelius), apocalyptic materials, and the epistles. In general it may be said that the literary aspect of form criticism has come to the forefront: the concentration of today's criticism is upon how the forms are present and what using a particular form meant rather than upon the earlier search for the oral period behind the gospels. Other specific developments are discussed below.

Reaction and Criticism   The form-critical method received its full share of negative criticism almost from its beginnings. In Bultmann's program especially, critics were bothered by a skeptical orientation toward recovery of any genuine Jesus-traditions, and they challenged the form-critical historical results as well as the method's procedures and presuppositions. Here I can only note in summary form some of the most helpful criticisms of the method.[15]

Role of Jesus as a teacher. Some critics feel that form criticism does not take seriously enough the possibility that Jesus consciously formulated his sayings in ways that would secure their careful transmission. Hence the form critics, who emphasize how the Jesus-materials have been formed according to the needs of the primitive Christian communities, are seen as falsifying the original situation. Those who stress

---

[14] The concept must now be developed in a more comprehensive way: traditional form criticism put too much emphasis upon identifying the sociological setting of the material and not enough emphasis upon the linguistic situation in which material is at home. Ehrhardt Güttgemanns, *Offene Fragen zur Formgeschichte* . . . (see Chap. 2, n. 20), relies upon Malinowski (*The Problem of Meaning in Primitive Languages*) and C. K. Ogden and I. A. Richards (*The Meaning of Meaning*) to develop an interpretation of the sociological setting that is itself linguistic. In what he would prefer to call a "sign-situation," we look for the context that is not merely a matter of social relationships but is also linguistically developed.

[15] Some of the critical articles are conveniently gathered as Chapters 1, 2, 4, 5, 6, 29, and 30 of Harvey K. McArthur, *In Search of the Historical Jesus* (New York: Charles Scribner's Sons, 1969).

Jesus' role as an authoritative Teacher argue that most of the forms in which the Jesus-materials are found originated with Jesus himself. (I think the argument can be easily reversed, however: given contemporary models of how an authoritative teacher formed his teachings, the primitive church then cast Jesus-materials into the "standard," expected forms.)

Role of eyewitnesses. Some critics are dismayed by the way form critics rule negatively when evaluating the historical accuracy of the gospels in ascribing materials to Jesus. These critics stoutly defend the historicity of the synoptic materials by referring to the possibility that the traditions were secured for the early communities by eyewitnesses. They point to the possibility that first-generation Christians were either still living and could check the "publication" of the materials, or had carefully passed on their first hand experiences to the compilers of the gospels.

Allied with this criticism is the complaint that the form critics over-emphasize *the creativity of the early communities.* They question speaking of "creative communities" as we speak of creative authors and suggest that the form critics assign too active a role to various church traditions in the development and even in the creation of synoptic materials. The designation of the years A.D. 30–50 as "the tunnel period" represents the conservative view that we will never gain full knowledge of the actual process; those who apply this phrase, however, support the view that it is more correct to refer to the creativity of individual inspired authors than to a corporate and anonymous creativity.

Kerygmatic dominance of the gospel materials. Some critics argue that the primitive church, from its beginnings, was interested in more than kerygmatic witness to the Christ, and that it also sought to satisfy biographical interests. According to this point of view, the gospel compilers were interested in the *bios* (life, as in biography) of the historical Jesus as well as in the kerygmatic witness, and in reporting such materials were less free in elaborating than they would have been if kerygma were the only concern.

Motivation to gospels. The "preaching" sociological setting has been greatly expanded by some critics to portray additional motivational factors leading to production of gospels. Aspects of the life of the communities, especially their activity in missionary work, has been emphasized. This type of criticism has led to important insights into the life of the early church as it consolidated itself for purposes of mission, and especially for catechesis (instruction of initiates). In fact Gottfried Schille takes this line of interpretation so far as to suggest that it is only by accident that we have the synoptic gospels at our disposal. Schille supposes that the gospels were developed around a kerygmatic outline to serve catechetical and missionary purposes for specific regions, churches, or occasions, and were not intended to last beyond their immediate use in those situations.[16]

Nature of forms used by form critics. Here attention is concentrated upon attempts to justify or disprove the adequacy of the form-critical categories, and upon attempts to refine the categories used.

By far the most substantive negative criticism of the school has been initiated only recently by two Swedish scholars, Harald Riesenfeld and Birger Gerhardsson.[17] The chief concern of this reaction is the concept of Tradition. Riesenfeld and Gerhardsson start from the assumption that Jesus' words functioned as "holy word" or as "oral Torah," and that strict procedures of passing these words along were developed. The Christian communities, according to this hypothesis, functioned less as creators of the synoptic traditions than as guardians of the holy tradition, and the forms in which the materials now appear indicate that the materials were organized for the purposes of rote memorization for community instruction and edification.

Against the "pneumatic [spiritual] democracy" suggested by Bultmann and Dibelius' reconstruction of primitive church order, Gerhardsson and Riesenfeld suggest that the materials from the Dead Sea sect at Qumran should alert us to the presence of a firmly structured community organization in which certain men were recognized as doctrinal authorities. If Bultmann and Dibelius consider the men around Jesus to have been *idiotai* (grk., unlettered laymen), Gerhardsson and Riesenfeld consider them to have been rabbis.

The two men have made an important contribution to the form-critical perspective, parts of which they are concerned to refute. In the future we shall have to pay much greater attention to the aspects of Jesus' teaching that seem to have been shaped in a conscious attempt at easily remembered patterns. We shall also have to continue our study of the role of tradition in the early church and late biblical Israel.

[16] "Bemerkungen zur Formgeschichte des Evangeliums," *NTStud* 4(1957–58),1–24, 101–114, 5(1958)1–11, and *Anfänge der Kirche: Erwägerungen zur apostolischen Frühgeschichte* (Munich: Chr. Kaiser Verlag, 1966).

[17] Riesenfeld's programmatic essay at the 1957 International Congress on the Four Gospels, *The Gospel Tradition and its Beginnings: A Study in the Limits of 'Formgeschichte'* (London: Mowbray, 1957), was followed by Gerhardsson's dissertation in 1961, *Memory and Manuscript. Oral Tradition and Written Transmission in Rabbinic Judaism and Early Christianity,* trans. E. J. Sharpe (Lund: C. W. K. Gleerup, 1961), and then by Gerhardsson's response to attacks on their common proposals, in *Tradition and Transmission in Early Christianity,* trans. E. J. Sharpe (Lund: C. W. K. Gleerup, 1964). We now have an illustration of their exegetical method by Gerhardsson, *The Testing of God's Son (Matt. 4:1–11 and par.): An Analysis of an Early Christian Midrash,* trans. John Toy (Lund: C. W. K. Gleerup, 1967).

It is not easy to understand the roles of innovation or tradition in the formative period of Christianity. We must avoid the common post-romantic conception that authors of antiquity were lone individuals, manufacturing whole cloth out of their minds. Equally incorrect is the opposite approach that denies any personal creativity to authors, seeing authors as merely group functionaries who only pass along shared information. We are only beginning to have methodologies such as redaction criticism to evaluate adequately the total author-material-text situation. The reactions to form criticism as well as form criticism itself have forced us to consider as never before the shared information and the community traditional materials.

SUBSEQUENT DEVELOPMENT

Form Criticism and the New Quest   One of the close alliances that developed in the first half of this century was that between theological thinking focused on the importance of the kerygma (emphasizing the "thatness" of God's having acted in the "event" of Jesus Christ) and form-critical methods of interpreting the NT. The two, representing a theological model and a methodological model for biblical interpretation, were often at work in the scholars trained by Bultmann. The alliance of form criticism and kerygmatic theology led to the conclusion that one could justify separating the "historical Jesus" from the "kerygmatic Christ"* on both exegetical and theological grounds.

The movement James M. Robinson named as "the new quest of the historical Jesus" was directly related to the underlying concerns and concepts of the form-critical method; indeed its members were trained within schools in which form criticism and kerygmatic theology were strongly represented. In some ways, however, the new quest is a conservative reaction against the extreme historical skepticism promoted by the form-critical picture of early Christianity.

Followers of the new quest (and it ought to be understood as a designation of a tendency within NT scholarship rather than as a formal school) emphasized that the radical disjuncture can be pressed to such an extent that the essential relation between the historical Jesus and the kerygmatic Christ is hopelessly obscured. Hence, operating with historiographical methods that focused especially on the intentionality and behavior of Jesus, they sought to detail the continuity between Jesus and the proclaimed Christ. This took the form of analysis of Jesus-traditions (Robinson, "The Formal Structure of Jesus' Message"), or of suggestions

---

* See Glossary.

about the relationships between the disciples' fellowship with Jesus and the subsequent church fellowship.[18]

What is important for our purposes is the way form criticism is used in the new quest. If form criticism and kerygmatic theology seemed to go hand in hand, the new quest and the new hermeneutic are similarly paired, and the representatives of the one are often the representatives of the other, as noted above. The emphasis upon language means that the new questers' critical studies concentrate upon the ways Jesus' speaking related to his self-understanding and his mission. Especially the parables and the sayings-materials are explored with respect to what they may disclose about Jesus' own linguisticality. The connection between the pre- and the post-Easter communities is sought less in terms of whether or not Jesus operated as a typical rabbi—whether or not he self-consciously formulated his words with a view to their eventual preservation—than in terms of whether or not that faith to which Christianity gave expression was grounded in the experience of Jesus' career. Instead of arguing whether there was or was not a sociological continuity in the communities involved, the contemporary focus is upon the more important question of whether or not there was a *material* continuity. Eberhard Jüngel, for instance, finds such a continuity in the eschatologically-fused form and content of early Christian faith.[19] This possibility will be explored in Chapter 4.

Redaction Criticism   Form criticism has been dominant in studies of the gospels in this century. Form-critical concentration upon the individual passage and its transmission has contributed insights so profound that even today most scholarly research is directly influenced by this way of asking about the inner life of biblical materials. Already within early form criticism, however, it was soon realized that attention to the specific forms, while very important in understanding the synoptic traditions, could be overemphasized and could lead to the same sort of tedious analysis practiced by the earlier literary critics. And so the consequence of applying form criticism is a return to questions posed initially by Wil-

---

[18] Eberhard Jüngel, "Eschatologie und Formgeschichte," in *Paulus und Jesus;* Heinz Schürmann, "Die vorösterlichen Anfänge der Logiontradition: Versuch eines formgeschichtlichen Zugangs zum Leben Jesu," in *Der historische Jesus und der kerygmatische Christus,* H. Ristow and K. Matthiae, eds. (East Berlin: Evangelische Verlagsanstalt, 1962), pp. 342–370; see also Schürmann's *Nachwort* to his collection of *Worte des Herrn* (Herder Bücherei, 1961).

[19] The amount of literature is already immense; I can only refer again to Robinson's book for a survey of the earlier debate (*A New Quest . . .*), and to a later survey for a wider public, Heinz Zahrnt, *The Historical Jesus,* trans. J. S. Bowden (London: Collins, ET 1963). I do not mean to imply that this movement is a thing of the past, but discussion among biblical scholars is no longer as tightly centered around "the problem of the historical Jesus" as it has been in recent years.

helm Wrede and Karl L. Schmidt: To what extent were the evangelists involved in forming and shaping the traditional materials into the contexts of their own theologies? To what extent did the form "gospel" itself influence the choice of materials and the presentation of materials? How are we to grasp the theological points of view of the evangelists and where do they come into sight?

Redaction criticism (*Redaktionsgeschichte*) takes up these questions, emphasizing once again the process of editing (or redaction—but not in the purely mechanical sense of "assembling" as it was used by the early literary criticism). In comparisons of materials found in several sources, the role of the evangelists are newly identified: the way Matthew and Luke present the substance of the Sermon on the Mount, for example, is directly related to their understandings of the significance of Jesus and their understandings of what a "gospel" should do. Matthew takes great care to have Jesus ascend a mountaintop where, as in the traditional view of Moses giving the Torah, he promulgates a new Christian Torah. "Mountain" functions differently for Luke, however, and his composed "Sermon" takes place not "on the Mount," but on the plain, the locus of Jesus' encounters with the lowly, the poor, and the outcast. So in Matthew the anthology of Jesus sayings (the "Sermon on the Mount") is presented as a New Law, whereas much of the same material becomes, in Luke's gospel, teachings directed to the down-and-out, to whom Luke thought contemporary Christian preaching should be directed.

The process of redaction was briefly reviewed by both Dibelius (Chapter 8 of *From Tradition to Gospel*) and Bultmann (Section III of *History*),[20] but neither scholar analyzed the theological positions of the evangelists in depth. Redaction criticism, on the other hand, is primarily concerned with such positions. It seeks to understand the broad lines of thought that underlie the gospels and how the evangelists have been able to impress their own theologies (or the theologies of their communities) upon the traditions. If form criticism has sought the discrete units of tradition—the forms (the pebbles embedded in a stream bed)—redaction criticism is now more interested in how the entire gospels took on shape and

---

[20] Later writings show that Dibelius, especially, was moving toward the more comprehensive view of redaction history; Joachim Rohde, *Rediscovering the Teaching of the Evangelists*, trans. D. M. Barton (Philadelphia: The Westminster Press, 1968), pp. 32–33, quotes examples from Dibelius. The need for redaction history was also acknowledged in the work of Gunkel, Gressmann, and Bousset (references in Klaus Koch, *The Growth of the Biblical Tradition*, trans. S. M. Cupitt [New York: Charles Scribner's Sons, 1969], pp. 64–65), but the redaction-critical questions tended to be posed in theory, then forgotten in actual practice. Norman Perrin's *What is Redaction Criticism?* (Philadelphia: Fortress Press, 1969), as the third volume in a series that also includes volumes on form criticism and literary criticism, is a competent introduction to redaction history for English-speaking audiences.

form (the course of the stream bed and how it channels the water flowing through it).

The first self-designated study in redaction history, by Willi Marxsen, *Mark the Evangelist: Studies on the Redaction History of the Gospel*,[21] has only recently been translated into English. Marxsen introduces his work with the observation that no one questions the anti-individualistic and sociological orientation of form critical research, with its judgment as to the anonymous character of the synoptic traditional materials. Redaction critics do not believe, however, that the actual composition of the gospels was merely the final stage of an anonymous process of tradition-building. The aim of the redaction critics is to identify and clarify the functional roles of the individual evangelists precisely at the points of the transition from free-floating synoptic traditions into the synoptic gospels.[22]

The redaction critics seek to discover the roles of the evangelists as redactors; but they do not conceive of these roles in romantic personalistic ways, as earlier literary criticism did. Rather they seek to discover the individual characteristics of the evangelists as they operated in *transmitting* the traditions.

Thus the question of the individual contributions of the evangelists, which had been by and large canceled out by the anti-individualist tendency of the form critics, is reintroduced. From form criticism, redaction criticism learned to treat the evangelists not as lone, "creative" authors as much as representatives of certain formal theological patternings (even schools) of primitive Christianity.[23] A recent commentator, Klaus Koch, gives a sketch of the way the redactor's work is now conceived:

> Through their compositional work, [the biblical authors] have furnished their texts with *themes* (*Leitideen*); they have *eliminated* from the tradition what according to their understanding was misleading, and have added clarifying *comments*. In many cases the individual sections have received, in this process, a completely new meaning—without the author

[21] The book was first published in 1956; 2nd ed. 1959, trans. J. Boyce, D. Juel, W. Poehlmann, with R. A. Harrisville (Nashville and New York: Abingdon Press, 1969).

[22] *Der Evangelist Markus. Studien zur Redaktionsgeschichte des Evangeliums* (Göttingen: Vandenhoeck & Ruprecht, 1956, 2nd ed. 1959), pp. 7–8, with references to Bultmann, *Geschichte*, 1931-2nd ed., p. 347. See also Hans Conzelmann, *The Theology of St. Luke*, trans. Geoffrey Buswell (New York: Harper & Row, Publishers, 1961); Günther Bornkamm, Gerhard Barth, and Heinz Joachim Held, *Tradition and Interpretation in Matthew*, trans. Percy Scott (Philadelphia: The Westminster Press, 1963); and David G. Buttrick, ed., *Jesus and Man's Hope*, Vol. I (Pittsburgh: Pittsburgh Theological Seminary, 1970).

[23] The most emphatic argument that a formal school tradition lies behind the creation of a gospel is made by Krister Stendahl, *The School of St. Matthew and its Use of the Old Testament* (Philadelphia: Fortress Press, 1968). His book was first published in Europe in 1954.

being aware of it. The redactors remove the materials from the continuous transformation caused by the oral transmission, and at the same time freeze it through the pen of the individual.[24]

So the evangelists' own viewpoints, and the characteristic interests of each must be taken up into our study. Marxsen suggests that Mark, for instance, was centrally concerned with the primitive Christian preaching, Matthew with giving an account of the development of the churches, and Luke with the ways the Holy Spirit was creatively active within the church—and that these interests had a major influence upon the ways Mark, Matthew, and Luke shaped the outline and the contents of their gospels.[25]

So too, Hans Conzelmann's study of Luke demonstrates how extensively Luke's conception of history as divided into three theological epochs shaped his materials, and how Luke used this perspective to explain the development of primitive Christianity. The difference in the perspective of redaction history from that of the earlier form criticism is seen in Bultmann's statement that Luke did not "permit his dogmatic conceptions to exercise any essential influence upon his work. . . . We can speak of any leading ideas only to a very limited extent."[26]

Redaction criticism now pays specific attention to the ways such "leading ideas" have been influential, and as it is presently pursued, it refines and seeks to explain factors uncovered in earlier stages of literary analysis. Before a reading of the theological emphases of an evangelist (or other biblical writer) can be proposed, the specific editorial and literary characteristics of the writer must be carefully charted and analyzed for their role in expressing the author's ideas.

Such questions as the following[27] must be addressed to the text:

[24] Koch, *Was ist Formgeschichte?*, p. 62 (see ET, p. 58). See Richard L. Rubenstein, *The Religious Imagination: A Study in Psychoanalysis and Jewish Theology* (Indianapolis, Kansas City, and New York: The Bobbs-Merrill Company, Inc., 1968), pp. 31–42, for reference to contemporary studies of the process of transmission by the psychologists Gordon Allport and Leo Postman. Allport and Postman (*The Psychology of Rumor*, New York: Henry Holt and Co., 1947) trace three types of distortion: leveling and shortening of the account for easier comprehension, selective sharpening according to the teller's interests and drives, and assimilation or contemporanizing. Rubenstein applies this analysis to Jewish haggadic legends.

[25] Willi Marxsen, "Bemerkungen zur 'Form' der sogenannten synoptischen Evangelien," *TheolLitZeit* 81(1956),345–348. See also Howard C. Kee, *Jesus in History: An Approach to the Study of the Gospels* (New York: Harcourt Brace Jovanovich, Inc., 1970), Chaps. 4–6.

[26] *History*, p. 336; see also Ulrich Wilckens, "Interpreting Luke-Acts in a Period of Existentialist Theology," in *Studies in Luke-Acts* (Festschrift for Paul Schubert), L. E. Keck and J. L. Martyn, eds. (Nashville and New York: Abingdon Press, 1966), pp. 60–83, esp. p. 77, n. 8.

[27] A more extensive development of these items will be found in Heinrich Zimmermann, *Neutestamentliche Methodenlehre*, pp. 221–230. See also Bultmann,

Why has an author applied stylistic improvements? Are there characteristic omissions or additions to his use of common traditions? How has he modified images, and why? (Zimmermann refers to Mt 7:24–27 and Lk 6:47–49, where Mt speaks of the *ground* upon which the house is built but Lk refers to the *foundation* of the house built upon this ground.) If the author rearranges materials by transposing them into a different context than they have in the source, or if he rearranges events within a single passage, does he do this because of a theological scheme that includes topographical features? (Zimmermann cites Mt 4:1–11, where the sequence is desert-Jerusalem-mountain, while Lk 4:1–12 has the sequence desert-mountain-Jerusalem.) How and why has the evangelist expanded a passage or inserted materials into an earlier sequence? (See Mk 4:10–12, which is inserted between the "parable" of the sower, 4:3–8 and its "interpretation," 4:13–20.) What reasons does the evangelist have for shortening his sources or for substituting one source for another?[28]

Further, even more inclusive questions must be asked: How did an evangelist reach a balance between his conception of the life and career of Jesus of Nazareth and his conception of what a "gospel" should include?[29] How has the evangelist thought out a geographical and chronological framework into which he can organize his presentation? Christological and ecclesiological questions must also be put to the text: How does the evangelist conceive of Jesus? To what extent does he think of the church as a divine institution?

Redaction criticism is not interested in redactional procedures just out of historical or literary curiosity. It is much more a matter of determin-

---

History, and the now classical presentation of rules of transmissional changes in the parables, Part III of Joachim Jeremias, *The Parables of Jesus,* trans. S. H. Hooke (London: SCM Press Ltd., 1963, rev. ed.). These rules are summarized and criticized by Frank W. Beare, "Concerning Jesus of Nazareth," *JournBibLit* 87(1968),125–135.

[28] Even items we understand fairly well—such as the way Matthew and Luke omitted materials found in Mark—must be examined anew in light of purpose and motivation. May it not be the case, for instance, that Matthew and Luke shortened Mark not just because they had additional traditions to fit into place and were bound by the physical length of one scroll, but because they sensed a difference in perspective between their own situations and Mark's? If Matthew, especially, was writing out of a developing "school," he would have wanted to include more legal materials than were necessary or relevant in Mark's circle.

[29] With respect to the question of the historical situation of the gospel as a whole, we touch a methodological circularity corresponding to that found in form-critical analysis. See Marxsen, *Der Evangelist Markus,* p. 14 (*Mark the Evangelist,* p. 25): "Finally we must refer to the circularity in which redaction criticism also takes part. The form of the gospels should offer us inferences as to the conception of the author and as to the situation of his church, just as redaction criticism, which brings us directly to the form, can on the other hand lead us to greater clarification of these two dimensions. Both the analytical and the constructive approaches have their value."

ing *why* such redaction has been carried out, and patterns of redaction provide important clues to the discovery of the evangelists' theologies. The synoptic gospels and John provide us with an unusual phenomenon in the literature of antiquity insofar as they are several editions of the same basic store of events and teachings. Hence we can follow the course of development and modification as we see how these individuals forced their own points of view upon the materials. And in this interplay between the tradition and its transmission we are able to sense the theological development of primitive Christianity. Such exploration is now being extended beyond the synoptic gospels into the epistles. Perhaps Norman Perrin is correct when he asserts that, thanks to redaction-critical work of the foreseeable future, we will soon be able to write the first truly comprehensive history of primitive Christian theology.[30]

The Kerygma Anew: Tradition History   Another development from literary and then form criticism is the approach that can be adequately translated into English only with the phrase "the history of the transmission of the traditions." This phrase contains all the implications of the German term, *Traditionsgeschichte*, and is preferable to briefer translations such as "tradition history" or "tradition criticism."[31]

The approach was developed in the early part of the century in studies of Israelite literature by Hermann Gunkel. Unlike form criticism and redaction criticism, the history of the transmission of the traditions means different things to different scholars, and we shall have to trace the strands of usage. For Gunkel the term referred to the process of studying the ways traditional materials were handed down. According to the first basic meaning of "tradition history," then, it can be compared with form or redaction criticism as being a method for exploring the ways a form or tradition is used in specific instances.[32] Initially, therefore, tradition-historical work is part of the literary-critical analysis: after the form is located in the history of literature, the critic traces the specific concrete instances in which the form has been used.[33]

The second main way of using this approach was developed by two

---

[30] See also James M. Robinson, "On the *Gattung* of Mark (and John)," in *Jesus and Man's Hope*, Vol. I, ed. David G. Buttrick (Pittsburgh: Pittsburgh Theological Seminary, 1970), 99–129; on pp. 99–101 Robinson suggests that "editorial history" conveys the intent of *Redaktionsgeschichte* better than the usual "redaction history."

[31] See James M. Robinson, *NF* III, ix–x, for discussion of the more extended translation. "Tradition history" is also used to translate *Ueberlieferungsgeschichte*.

[32] Already in 1937, when "form criticism" was not yet widely acknowledged, Kendrick Grobel (in *Formgeschichte und Synoptischer Quellenanalyse*) suggested that a similar term, *Ueberlieferungskritik* (transmission criticism) would have been a better term than "form" criticism.

[33] See Koch, pp. 45, 54 (ET pp. 38, 50–51). For Koch tradition history is, with the history of the genre (*Gattungsgeschichte*), part of the work of form criticism.

Christian scholars of Israelite theology, Gerhard von Rad and Martin Noth.[34] These men point to Israel's use of its historical traditions as "kerygmatic"; they suggest that not just theological affirmations but the sheer eventfulness of historical moments in Israel's history were revered. Israel pointed not to a vague abstract divine principle but to a Yahweh who was known to enter history decisively. Tradition history in this sense, then, refers to the theological weighting of historical traditions within a religious group; in order to understand the theological significance of an event, the event must be understood within the entire history of traditions of the group.[35] ". . . The study of the dynamic historical process by which Israel transmitted her credal testimonies to the acts of God," becomes an important aspect of theological reflection.[36]

Similarly, in contemporary NT scholarship, James M. Robinson advocates the full translation, "the history of the transmission of the traditions." He wishes to emphasize the ways historical traditions were, for many early Christians, "kerygmatic," insofar as historical traditions about Jesus became important as theological affirmations that Jesus of Nazareth was the Messiah of God.

In explicating the ways in which the theological concept of kerygma became binding ("fateful") for research into primitive Christianity, Robinson finds that the primitive Christians were not concerned with the historical Jesus per se, but primarily with the historicity of the transmission of the traditions about this Jesus. These traditions—and here Robinson speaks of the tradition history in the way it is now being used in study of Israelite theology—became themselves "a kind of kerygma." We pursue such traditions not out of idle curiosity, but "to see what the kerygma had

---

[34] Two of Noth's books include the term in their titles, *Ueberlieferungsgeschichtliche Studien* (Halle: 1943; Tübingen: 1957, 2nd ed.), and *Ueberlieferungsgeschichte des Pentateuch* (Stuttgart: 1948; 1960, 2nd ed.).

[35] Especially in the school around the contemporary German Protestant theologian, Wolfhart Pannenberg, the term is now assimilated into a concept of theology parallel to the concept of universal history discussed above. Rolf Rendtorff relates the event and its significance as follows: "We are confronted with the task of tracing the entire course from the first event to the final form of the tradition, in order that thereby we may make clear the historical significance of the event and its history. . . ." Quoted by Braaten, *History and Hermeneutic,* p. 114, from Rolf Rendtorff and Klaus Koch, *Studien zur Theologie der Alttestamentlichen Ueberlieferung,* p. 89. From *History and Hermeneutics,* New Directions in Theology Today, Volume II, by Carl E. Braaten. Copyright © MCMLXVI, W. L. Jenkins. The Westminster Press. Used by permission.

Koch is now considered one of the Pannenberg circle, but in his *Was ist Formgeschichte?* p. 117, he carefully contrasts his use of the term from the "wider sense" in which *Traditionsgeschichte* is used by Rendtorff.

[36] Braaten, p. 114; see also p. 146. From *History and Hermeneutics,* New Directions in Theology Today, Volume II, by Carl E. Braaten. Copyright © MCMLXVI, W. L. Jenkins. The Westminster Press. Used by permission.

to say and how it stood in relation to the kerygma [i.e., that other kerygma] of cross and resurrection."[37]

In probing the way the Gospel of John differs from the synoptic gospels in using traditional materials, for instance, we become aware that "the missionary purpose, the point, intended by such transmission of traditions could vary . . ." (p. 139). The history of the transmission of traditions, pursued as a method of exegetical analysis, will be concentrated on the points made, on the reasons why and how only certain historical traditions remain at the focal center of a particular religion.

If on the one hand the term tradition history represents a methodology—a necessary step in the process of letting the text do its own speaking —it also becomes a theological tool by means of which some theologians wish to scrutinize the nuances of the biblical writings. It is a very sophisticated tool—so much so that we are just now learning to use it well —but it is one of those perspectives that, once grasped, informs our interpretation in every respect. We begin to see, for instance, that one uniform "kerygma" hardly defines all that characterized primitive Christianity. We begin to sense that alongside the kerygma, defined in terms of a standard outline of saving events centered in the cross and resurrection, there were other formal statements of what was considered crucial, and that the transmission of these traditions had an important place alongside the traditionally conceived kerygma. Part of the subtlety of this approach is that it provides a way into the heart of the texts by listening not only for explicit formulae (such as the kerygma) but also for implicit ones (such as "implicit christologies," or often-repeated series of sayings of Jesus).[38]

The various methodologies we have been studying will reappear at specific points in the next section, which sets out a pattern for full exegetical analysis. Here is a summary of the specific methodological procedures we have discussed:

Literary Criticism has two foci: (a) it deals with specific relationships between biblical writings, asking for instance how materials in the Gospel of Matthew are related to those in the Gospel of Mark and to other

---

[37] "Kerygma and History . . . ," pp. 118, 135.

[38] I have not introduced into the discussion a third way of using *Traditionsgeschichte*, namely as a designation for the work of a Scandinavian school of exegesis headed by Ivan Engnell. This school focuses upon the means and the processes of transmission of Israelite traditions on the one hand and upon the identification of patterns and concepts on the other—all in a much more limited and technical way. Helmer Ringgren, in "Literarkritik, Formgeschichte, Ueberlieferungsgeschichte. Erwägerungen zur Methodenfrage der alttestamentlichen Exegese," *TheolLitZeit* 91(1966),641–650, prefers to call this method *Motivforschung*, but he does refer to the way *Traditionsgeschichte* investigates "the milieu and the cultic and religious traditions which form the background and the presuppositions of the prophetic preaching." The first part of Chapter 5 gives a brief tradition history of primitive Christian literature.

sources; (b) in an expanded sense, it concerns the large units of biblical tradition (epistle, gospel) and how they are composed and function as literature.

Form Criticism (a) identifies smaller units of oral and literary tradi-tions, (b) relates such "forms" to their probable sociological setting (*Sitz im Leben*), (c) analyzes the ways traditional material is modified or ex-panded for such contexts, and (d) evaluates the claims of such materials to come from particular strata of the primitive church.

The History of the Transmission of Traditions probes the reasons why certain historical and religious materials are highlighted and trans-mitted, primarily in specific instances; it notes which materials were the most widely respected and valued.

Redaction Criticism studies the ways the materials are finally com-posed into a literary work according to the theologies or interests of the eventual "authors."

To varying extents, all of these methodologies are concerned with tracing the paths of traditional materials within the primitive Christian communities. The methodologies will have been seriously misunderstood if they are thought to be "putting down" the primary creativity of the primitive Christian religious phenomena, or to be relegating them to utterly-sociological, cause-effect models. Rather the various modes of con-temporary NT literary criticism seek to expose the inner dynamics and exquisite sensitivities of a powerful development in the history of man. They intend to open up the complexities of primitive Christian literature and religious formulation in ways that will enable fully comprehensive appreciation of the beginnings of Christianity.

EXEGESIS: THE MOVEMENT FROM TEXT TO INTERPRETATION

It would not be helpful to provide at this point a neat passage or two put through certain exegetical hoops to the tune of a "helpful guide to exegesis." Exegetical study usually includes making pages and pages of notes and locating a great deal of material that is not used in the final edition. It would also take too much space, and would take away some of the delight rightfully belonging to the interpreter.[39]

Instead of a full comprehensive exegetical study we can present a sketch of the methods, the analyses, and the processes included in com-prehensive exegetical study. The average student comes to biblical studies from contexts in which the range of methodologies is usually not nearly

---

[39] Abbreviated examples of exegesi ·are available in "New Testament Exegesis," Kaiser and Kümmel, *Exegetical Method,* and Chap. 3, "Redaction Criticism at Work: A Sample," in Norman Perrin, *What is Redaction Criticism?*

as comprehensive; he or she frequently discovers references to stages in the exegetical process without having a sense of the inner logics of exegesis. This can lead to some sad results, as in the case of a student who worked out all the theological implications of the Great Commission (Mt 28, concluding with the command to "Go therefore and make disciples of all nations . . .") only to conclude, just before submitting her paper, that on text-critical as well as form-critical grounds, she could no longer accept the passage as being important to her argument about Jesus' sense of mission.

Other students fail to distinguish judgments of historical probability based on style-critical evidence from those based on redaction criticism or history-of-religions evidence. There is further complication because the terms employed by contemporary authors are the German theological terms to which they have been accustomed, and the student can find little aid in dictionaries. To get from *Traditionsgeschichte* to "the history of the transmission of the traditions" requires more than a one-for-one translation, as we have seen, and there are many other examples in which the scholarly theological use is unrelated to the non-compounded everyday forms.

The following chart provides an overview of the process of exegesis, and lists the usual German equivalents. It should be noted, however, that the German words are not always used consistently: for example *Sachexegese* (exegesis in terms of the "content" or "theological exegesis") is often replaced by *Sachkritik* (content or theological criticism); and *Geschichte* is given variously as "-history" or as "-criticism." The German terms in the second column are therefore only roughly correlated with the English terms.[40]

Anyone who has ever attempted exegetical study is aware of one fact that puts the lie to the logic of this chart, for the process of exegesis is more complex than it appears in any such presentation. Also, few of us have the time to sift through working materials (concordances, lexica, encyclopaedia, commentaries, and the like) in order to note before we begin just where each step is discussed. Anyone who performs an exegeti-

---

[40] The student who reads German should have a look at the brief resumé by Erich Dinkler, "Bibelkritik, II. Im NT," *RGG* I(1956/57, 3rd ed.)1188–1190; English-speaking students will find some help in Kaiser and Kümmel, *Exegetical Method,* and in the handbooks and introductions to NT studies. A very helpful beginner's guide to exegesis with extensive use of textual illustrations is available in Zimmermann, *Neutestamentliche Methodenlehre,* but I know of no good English parallel. Fred L. Fisher, *How to Interpret the New Testament* (Philadelphia: The Westminster Press, 1966) will be somewhat helpful, and there is a brief outline in Eduard Heller's "On the Interpretive Task," *Interp* 21(1967)158–166. John Reumann, "Methods in Studying the Biblical Text Today," *ConcTheolMonth* 40(1969),655–681, presents a sequence and exposition similar to mine, but directed to the specific tasks of preaching and theologizing.

I. LITERARY-HISTORICAL ANALYSIS

1. Establishment of the *Text*
   a) Initial reading and translation (or choice of translation)
   b) Textual criticism — *Textkritik*
   c) Source criticism; determination of authorship — *Quellenforschung; Verfasserfrage*

2. Identification of the *Form* and its History
   a) Literary criticism (including style analysis and literary sequence analysis) — *Literarkritik, Stilkritik, Schallanalyse*
   b) Form criticism (including the history of the form and its sociological setting) — *Formgeschichte, Gattunsgeschichte*

3. Determination of the *Context*
   a) History of the transmission of this text (incl. secondary sociological settings and frequence of occurrence) — *Traditionsgeschichte (narrow sense)*
   b) History of the transmission of the tradition — *Traditionsgeschichte, Ueberlieferungsgeschichte (wide sense)*
   c) The process and influence of redaction and composition — *Redaktionsgeschichte, Kompositionsgeschichte, Zusammenhangsexegese*

II. HISTORICAL-THEOLOGICAL ANALYSIS

1. Survey of the Contextual Thought-World of the Text; History of the Period — *Religionsgeschichte, Kultgeschichte, Zeitgeschichte*

2. Evaluation of the Significance and Influence of the Situation or Persons Addressed

3. Religious and Theological Explication (incl. motifs, concepts, theological sequence analysis) — *Motivgeschichte, Begriffsgeschichte, Sprachgeschichte, Sachexegese*

4. The Text's Life Today—Theological or Interpretive Translation

cal analysis must have his overall organization in mind at the outset—and then begin and carry through his research as it takes on its own patterns. This is especially true when consulting commentaries, since commentators frequently interrupt the sequence of their exegesis to discuss matters of historical or theological background, relationships between passages, and the like.

Use of such a chart, therefore, is to be understood as portraying the overall framing logic of exegesis; in actual practice the process of exegesis may move rather differently. At the same time, however, there is an inner logic that must be followed in one's final correlation of the results of his exegetical study, since there is nothing more exhausting than an analysis that jumps about from word-studies to form criticism to textual criticism, all intermingled with references to "what the text says today." Since most recent exegetical studies have concentrated upon illuminating a text from the point of view of the one particular methodology for which they are arguing, it is not surprising that this disjointed approach is often found.

We also have to deal with the fact that biblical scholarship has not taken adequate account of the ways in which the various moments of the contemporary exegetical enterprise fit together; some of the same exegetical studies are classified by different reviewers under different categories.[41] In general the process of exegesis is organized here around two foci: first the Literary-Historical Analysis and then the Historical-Theological Analysis. In the actual work of exegesis, however, these two are not always easily separated; furthermore it is usually necessary to keep two or more of the subdivisions in sight when working on a particular verse or passage; and of course not every passage needs to be studied with all the methodologies.

I. LITERARY-HISTORICAL ANALYSIS

The Literary-Historical Analysis deals primarily with the external features of the text, namely its most well-attested ancient text, its form, and the situation in which the text has been placed by the biblical author/s.

1. Establishment of the *Text*. There are several guides to textual criticism available; the student whose working tools do not include Greek must be satisfied with choosing several translations and paraphrases and using commentaries, attempting to determine which are the most successful literal or free translations. The work must begin with a careful, slow and thorough reading of the text; an initial outline should be devised. Great care should be taken to enter into the inner logic of the text. Source analysis is employed, especially in those texts where multiple sources are recognized (such as the synoptic gospels and John, and in such specific cases as Jude and II Peter). Questions of authorship and provenance* (place of origin) must be raised.

---

[41] Klaus Koch, *Was ist Formgeschichte?* and Joachim Rohde, *Die redaktionsgeschichtliche Methode,* assign some of the same articles to form criticism (for Koch this is the all-inclusive term) and to redaction criticism (for Rohde this is the advance beyond form criticism).

* See Glossary.

2. Identification of the *Form* and its History. The literary-critical analysis comes at this second stage, and is composed of three aspects:

—the stylistic analysis, including literary sequence analysis (How is the thought organized? How does the passage do its job?)
—the form-critical analysis (What is the form in which the passage appears? What stylistic characteristics are representative of this form? What is the relationship of this passage to the sociological setting out of which it originates, its *Sitz im Leben?*)
—the history of the use of the form (How did the form originate? How frequently does this form appear and for what purposes? What other forms are related to it? In what ways does this form usually change in appearance in the process of being transmitted?)

The study of the literary forms themselves seems at first glance to be of much greater importance for the analysis of the Old Testament than of the NT, and it is true that within the OT we have the opportunity to observe the changes, developments, and/or decline of forms in a way not possible in the NT. Even though NT studies cannot work with a period of some generations of oral transmission, however, there is a similar movement of traditions, both in their oral stages and in their later literary stages. We must differentiate between the identification of a form and the history of the way this form was transmitted.[42]

3. Determination of the *Context*. The "context" refers both to the narrow framework in which the passage has been framed by the original or the final author or editor, and to the wider framework of the passage in the whole life of the early church. Attention to the way the passage was used illuminates the form itself by informing us of the situations (the levels of the transmission) in which it has been transmitted; concentration on this aspect is the task of tradition history.

A shift in the use of the passage may come about when a form becomes more or less important and hence is given special attention (as we see in the selections of portions of the gospels inscribed on personal amulets) or is assimilated into wider contexts (as when originally independent liturgical materials are incorporated into the early Christian literature).

Koch shows how this part of the analysis may be pressed to the advantage of exegetical richness in the case of the beatitude form (the makarism) in the NT. We learn, for instance, that the makarism makes its comparatively late appearance in the NT not in the form of a series of

---

[42] Albertz and Bertram showed how the work of Bultmann and Dibelius needed amplification since they did not take this latter factor of transmissional change sufficiently into account. Koch (p. 20; see ET, p. 17) notes that *"no form of literature* remains *unchanged* over a long period of time," and suggests rules of change (pp. 24–26; not translated in the ET). See esp. André Jolles, *Einfache Formen* (Tübingen: Niemeyer, 1930; 1965, 3rd ed.), and Joachim Jeremias, *The Parables of Jesus.*

statements familiar to us in the NT "Sermons" (Mt 5–7, Lk 6:20–49) but as brief single sayings such as those of Ps 2:12 ("Blessed are all who take refuge in him"), Ps 84:5, and Isa 30:38, or in the NT, in Lk 1:45 ("Blessed is she who believed that there would be a fulfillment of what was spoken to her from the Lord"), and John 20:29b ("Blessed are those who have not seen and yet believe"). In late biblical Israel beatitudes were arranged sequentially (II Enoch 51, see I Enoch 130:5), and their earlier content—the generalized praise of the values of the faithful life—has given way to concern with the "faithful expectation of the end of the time of this world, with *eschatological* hope."[43]

In this particular instance analysis of the form's history of use supplements analysis of the form itself (which of course is rather easily sighted in the makarisms) as well as the overall history of the form. Such analysis yields important consequences for understanding the role of the beatitudes and their function in the primitive Christian communities: "in the primitive Christian makarism, the usage of late-Israelitic apocalyptic is continued" (Koch, 21). The history of the use of the form alerts us to the interaction of two theological matrices and at the same time enables us to understand the modifications of this form in the synoptic gospels: the introduction of direct address ("blessed are you"), and the stress upon the paradoxical eschatology of primitive Christian hope (he who is poor will be rich, etc.).[44]

The interpreter asks, then, how the passage under study is related to its overall context and to its immediate context. He attempts to determine if it has been modified by being situated in these contexts, either by gaining or by losing special significance. If in form criticism the special concern is to identify the original sociological setting, interest at this stage focuses on whether or not subsequent sociological settings must be accounted for. We need to be specially sensitive to the way the material fits into its immediate environment—whether it appears in an obvious grouping of similar passages or is used to establish a concluding or summarizing point. Literary forms are not sterile static entities, but tend both to have their own contours changed and modified and to be grouped with related materials.[45]

[43] Koch, p. 21, his emphasis.

[44] See further Koch, esp. pp. 21–22, and James M. Robinson, "The Formal Structure of Jesus' Message," in *Current Issues in New Testament Interpretation,* W. Klassen and G. F. Snyder, eds. (New York: Harper & Row, Publishers, Inc., 1962), pp. 91–110, 273–284; this article makes available in English the supplement to the German ed. (1960) of Robinson's *A New Quest* . . . .

[45] See Koch's remark: "Language does not live in an immense number of antiseptically-distinguished categories; rather language loves to bring literary forms into a narrower or broader relationship to one another as soon as they are used." (P. 27; ET, p. 23.)

The redactional analysis completes the first part of the exegesis and leads naturally into the second. As we have seen above, the place of redaction criticism in contemporary biblical studies is no longer located under "literary criticism," where it had only to do with identifying characteristic speech-patterns, favored vocabulary, or place names, but is pursued today as a means for understanding the mostly implicit theological concerns that guided our authors.

II. HISTORICAL-THEOLOGICAL ANALYSIS

The Historical-Theological Analysis is more difficult, but at the same time more important for the eventual interpretation than the literary-historical analysis, even though it is dependent for its success upon the quality and thoroughness of the earlier work. The first level of analysis is primarily that concerned with the external appearance of a text—its linguistic features or its relationship to other literary forms—whereas the second level attempts to penetrate into the text's own inner life, to comprehend just what it is that happens in this text.

In order to do this, the widest historical context in which the text appears is studied (1. Survey of The Contextual Thought-World of the Text) and parallels to the text's contents are explored, especially where literary analysis has discovered parallels in the use of literary forms. We must be alert to see if the form is used in similar or in different situations, and for similar or different purposes. Historical leads offered by our passage must be pursued, especially any specific mention of events, movements, persons, or concepts of antiquity; and the historical relationships of persons, movements, or locations must be determined (2. Evaluation of the Significance and Influence of the Situation or Persons Addressed).

More is involved in 1. and 2. than simply finding parallels between biblical and non-biblical writings. In most cases there are few direct cross-references, and so the real task involves establishing whether or not *any* relationship exists and whether or not our text deliberately and cleverly misrepresented the actual situation—as when an author has disguised or misrepresented his opponents for the sake of an argument. Since there is usually little evidence of direct assimilation of nonbiblical materials, the biblical interpreter must seek to understand not only possible derivations of ideas and concepts but also the ways such materials have been modified, adapted, and brought into context by the biblical writer.

In pursuing the nuances of our text, its theological vocabulary must be carefully analyzed (3. Religious and Theological Explication). Since the first parts of the exegesis lead to awareness of the general linguistic usage prevailing, we now take key concepts or words of the text and analyze their linguistic background and their philological derivations, the frequency and range of usage of the word (in our author and elsewhere), and ask how the word or concept attains a special or a general meaning by its use in the particular contexts of the Bible or of this passage.

The task of evaluating the context is a very difficult one; we have recently been forced to admit that even the extensive analyses of the six-volume *Theological Dictionary of the New Testament,* edited by Gerhard Kittel and Gerhard Friedrich, do not always give full and sufficient recognition to the influence of the particular context or to the author's own theology in the specific ways theological words have been used. Of course the provenance of a word is of great importance, but of more determinative importance is how our author or his traditions have understood the word's connotations, and how the word has actually been put to work in the service of concrete theological expression.

The theological explication of a text is hardly exhausted in the study of its vocabulary, however, even when this necessitates extensive research in itself. Theological explication concerns the whole patterning of the passage: it concerns the way in which everything learned about the text and its author up to this point is brought together in a meaningful whole. It involves checking with major theological studies of the whole NT as well as with monographs and articles, and it involves the determination of whether or not certain motifs or characteristic religious nuances are present.

Finally (4. The Text's Life Today—Theological or Interpretive Translation) the interpreter tries to conjoin what he has learned with his own situation. If interpretation is pursued for the sake of religious preaching or doctrine, such concerns are especially present at this point—but there is a danger (which I find present in most discussion of exegesis) in assuming that these are the only concerns that motivate an interpreter.

The logical consequence of the exegetical process outlined to this point would seem to be that pattern of exegesis-before-interpretation that has been popular in this country (and incarnated in the format of the *Interpreter's Bible* series, which prints the "exegesis" above the "exposition" on the same page). If we have been rightly served by our hermeneutical reflections, however, it will be apparent that such a neat distinction is not possible. Logically, or at least schematically, such a distinction can be made; in practice it belies the wholeness of the hermeneutical process, and we shall be moving back and forth all the time. Specific attention to "theological translation" is necessary, in keeping with the nature of the biblical texts. Specific attention to non-theological interpretation is, I would contend, just as important today.

The question of theological or interpretive translation may be put in terms of the question To what future does the text give rise? (See André

Gide, as quoted in the drama section, *The New York Times*, April 5, 1970: "I hold that the best explanation of a work must be its sequel.") Hence we need to consider the immediate impact of the text as well as the impact of the text in the history of exegesis (and these are necessary hermeneutical aspects), and the impact or the "degree of reality" of the text within today's linguistic horizons.

If the contemporary view of hermeneutics is followed, then it will be seen that this last step is not one that can be divorced from the others. And while it can be logically and systematically distinguished from the others, it cannot but enter our study at every stage. It must be emphasized once more that the interpreter who rigidly attempts to exclude any interpretive factors until the very end deceives himself, since weighted categories of understanding influence all parts of his work. It should be the purpose of hermeneutical reflection and training within the study of biblical interpretation to make these perspectives clear.

Our study of interpretation has aimed at disclosing that exegesis is something much more than simply historical investigation of a text of the past. Exegesis becomes hermeneutic—dialogue with the text—and it is especially at this point that we have to ask whether or not the language world of the text is utterly foreign to us—whether dialogue is at all possible. We have to ask whether or not terms that imply a whole "world" in themselves (like Messiah, righteousness, love, resurrection) still ring true. If from time to time we decide that they do not, we have—through the process of our exegetical and hermeneutical study—gained the sense of what they were attempting to do and what they were intended to convey, and the task of full translation has at least been started.

4

Contemporary Perspectives on Authentic Translation

We have now completed a brief sighting of some of the methodological and theological problems that face the interpreter, and can now return in this chapter to discussion of some of the issues raised by the discussions of hermeneutics raised earlier. Specifically we will focus upon revised comprehensions of the levels of activity and language functions in primitive Christianity.

Within our own century, attention is focused on language—not on words alone, and not so much on the Word of God in the older sense, but upon language as the way in which the world is present. The process of translation and interpretation is therefore to be understood as the way the interpreter's world is brought into conjunction with the world of the text receiving his attention. "Form" also comes into sight as the ordering of linguistic expression in such a way that what is being spoken comes through in one formal way alone. We have to speak of the totality—the form-and-content—and we attempt to stand near the dynamic whole where this configuration happens.

The dynamic whole that represents the beginnings is the place of basic creative language. It is especially to the beginnings of the Christian religion, that is, the writings of the NT, that Christians usually go to find their sources of creativity, renewal, promise, and hope. The NT is not the only source of promise, nor is it the only location of sacred Christian traditions; for the Protestant, for instance, there is similar powerful language in the writings of the Protestant Reformers of the sixteenth century. And for the Roman Catholic, pronouncements of the Papal Father, insofar as they create new study and appropriations of belief, often have a similar role.

But for Christian thought as such, the primitive Christian language has a priori importance by reason of its closeness to the foundational event of God's acting in Jesus Christ. Jesus' language therefore receives special hearing; as "The Founder" (as the old liberals were fond of calling him), Jesus gave birth to a language tradition. Contemporary Christian theology suggests that in Jesus' words there was an especially close conjunction of the ordinary (everyday, secular, worldly) dimension of reality and the extraordinary (the eschatological, the transcendent)—but note that the tension is not between the secular and the religious. This language founded a tradition stretching between present reality and possibility—between the given and what might be hoped for.

But since Jesus' words were carefully altered and fitted into the frameworks of the primitive theologies, Christian scholarship has had to place stress upon distinguishing Jesus' own words from the traditions that formed around Jesus and around Jesus-as-the-Messiah. The various types of gospel criticism that we have discussed were formulated in attempts to find that procedure which would best differentiate authentic Jesus-material from what accrued to this material in the very lively and creative Christian communities.

The whole process of tradition-building is a complex subject; we may not speak simply of "kernel and husk," since the situation is much more complicated. Not only are there competing interpretations of the core (or "kernel"), but the subsequent interpretations of the significance of Jesus (the "husks") are often completely intermingled with the primal Jesus-materials themselves.[1] Add to this the rise of those who interpret the interpretations, already within the NT, and we begin to see these levels:

Interpretation of Jesus' words and deeds

Reporting about the first "layer," but also especially *reflecting* upon and *reformulating* it in the light of Christianity's growth as a phenomenon of Graeco-Roman Hellenism.

[1] Kurt Frör, *Biblische Hermeneutik* (Munich: Chr. Kaiser Verlag, 1964, 2nd ed., pp. 62–68, points out that it will not do for us to deplore the elaboration and enveloping of Jesus-materials by the early church, since this process is continued within contemporary churches (for example in the use of sayings of Jesus in church school curriculae). The process begins to look more like an enlarging snowball than a kernel-husk situation. Furthermore, it would be impossible to identify the "core" in terms of the earliest materials, for some of these primitive materials only surface in later writings.

And to complicate the matter yet further, such books as this one are primarily concerned with a subsequent layer:

> *Subsequent refinements* of scholarship, historical method, interpretation, and theology.

The relationships between these various levels will be the primary concern in this half of the book. The contemporary scene is marked by renewed attention to the historical contexts of biblical texts, but in such a way as to take into full account the commentaries of the intervening centuries. We learn from Bultmann and the new hermeneutic the importance of acknowledging our own preconceptions, and such historical review is of great importance in that attempt to gain distance from our texts. Several aspects of the recently renewed historiography and the recently intensified hermeneutics are discussed in this chapter, and attention is given to the increasingly important role of language analysis in approaching the creative worlds of primitive Christian theology.

EMPHASIS UPON "THE HISTORICAL": RECENT EVALUATIONS OF PRIMITIVE CHRISTIANITY

When theological studies began to mature in the period of the Enlightenment, most scholarly attention was upon the historical occasions that gave rise to texts. The "historical" part of historical-critical analysis sought to uncover or reconstitute the original situations; this reconstruction, it was believed, could be accomplished in a critical spirit of inquiry. Actually, however, the particularity of the original situations was frequently overlaid by the concepts and theologies of interpreters; even the nineteenth-century positivists failed in their attempts to recover "what it was really like" or "what actually happened" (Ranke: "wie es eigentlich geschehen ist").

The contemporary scene also manifests an attempt to reconstitute what happened, though contemporary scholars have a much greater awareness of the slanted nature of all historical perspective, and an appreciation of the unconscious influence of their own heritage and training. The early twentieth-century scholars' impatience with idealism and liberal theology marked the start of the movement seeking more comprehensive recognition of the actual historicity of the NT texts; this movement surfaced in the new quest, and now underlies one aspect of the new hermeneutical approach. Generally speaking, most contemporary exegesis seeks to listen as carefully as possible to the original context, despite the fact that there are still interpretations of texts that ignore this historicity, and that could have been written in any of the last several centuries.[2]

There are many cases in which our interpretation of a passage or key phrase has to be completely revamped because our knowledge of the actual historical situations has expanded. The first of this century, for example, saw an unparalleled revision of our understanding of biblical language, largely because of comparisons with the mass of records of antiquity then being published and studied. Gustav Adolf Deissmann (1866–1937) spent many years of his life demonstrating from non-religious Greek papyri just how ordinary and secular were many words used in the NT. Phrases for early Christian officials—for example priest, bishop, shepherd—as well as terms used to identify the Christ—Lord, Savior, Son of God—were placed in their full historical contexts, and their (neutral) pre-Christian meanings clarified. The word "bag," which appears in a saying of Jesus to the disciples ("Carry no purse, no bag, no sandals; and salute no one on the road." Lk 10:4, see also Mk 6:8, Mt 10:10, and Lk 9:3), appears in a non-Christian inscription that speaks of begging for a Syrian goddess. Knowing this context, and the implications of "bag" in the sentence, we should probably translate the saying, "You are not to undertake a preaching trip for recompense, nor to go about begging for money."[3]

The impact of this era of historical scholarship is to be seen in the changed evaluation of NT Greek: one no longer talks about God who, in some mysterious or mischievous manner, speaks a Sacred Language into the ears of the primitive Christian authors; we recognize instead that biblical, *koine* Greek was nothing other than the popular (and not always grammatical) street language of Graeco-Roman Hellenism.

We have learned that when the NT authors spoke of the effectiveness of the Christ in terms of expiation, propitiation, and the like, they were doing nothing more than reaching into their own linguistic worlds to make themselves understood. Even such important Hebraic concepts as covenant, justice, and exodus, were originally neutral or secular. In each case we have to look not only at the derivation of the words but also at how they were employed in the particular text. We have only

---

[2] We have only to glance through any number of popular biblical commentaries, or listen to many sermons, to realize that such interpretations could be plastered onto a number of texts with equal ease. For example, the reading of Romans 13 often issues in the "message" that Paul says we ought always to give the state its due and not buck the establishment: if we are content with ourselves and seek out the best in others, even our politics will be Christ-like. No one has to search very far to discover just such ahistorical, generalizing pap.

[3] See Adolf Deissmann, *New Light on the New Testament from Records of the Graeco-Roman Period,* trans. L. R. M. Strachan (Edinburgh: T. & T. Clark, 1908), pp. 78–84 and 31–44.

begun to grasp the full impact of a word used in a theological formulation when we have determined the original instances of its use. Of much greater importance is its application by a particular writer—and indeed by a particular writer in a particular text, since he may use the word or concept differently as his thought changes.

In fields other than theological vocabulary, similar reexamination and rethinking is necessary. A series of third-century murals in the Christian house at Dura-Europos on the Euphrates River, for instance, has been interpreted as an example of theological concepts such as atonement (the good shepherd painting, the healing of the paralytic), forgiveness (the figures representing Adam and Eve superimposed on one section), and the like. Much careful reconstruction and further exploration and comparison was necessary before it began to be seen that these sketches do *not* illustrate Western, legalistic-oriented themes such as justification, but rather themes of the Eastern type of early Christianity, whose central metaphor was *illumination*. In the East the emphasis was not upon being pronounced righteous, upon attaining a favorable verdict by one's upright moral stance, but upon participation in the "light" of the deity and upon the in-dwelling of the sacred (this theme is represented especially clearly in the mural portraying ten women carrying candles). Hence the Dura Christian house scenes really represent the virtues of the illuminated divine hero and not the moral benefits of the good life. Better knowledge of the actual historical situation of Christianity in this small Syrian town demands recasting of the entire earlier interpretation.[4]

We do have some "better knowledge" at our disposal in contemporary research, but it is not all of such dramatic impact as the new information about Dura or the Dead Sea texts at Qumran or recent archaeological discoveries. Most of this better knowledge is available to us because methodologies are more subtle and because the original situations are more completely in view. Especially by paying attention to the types of language employed and to what we now know about Hellenistic culture, more adequate hermeneutical reflection is taking shape. We are in a better position to comprehend and appreciate texts of antiquity in their historical unity and wholeness. We begin to see early Christian authors as men of their time, responding to issues raised in their own contexts, and speaking in languages conditioned by these contexts.

There is a certain circularity here: excessively dry and tedious applications of historical-critical methods led to Barth's call for attention

---

[4] See *The Excavations at Dura-Europos*, Final Report VII/II, Carl H. Kraeling, *The Christian Building* (New Haven: Dura-Europos Publications, 1967), esp. 178 ff. James Snyder's review of this volume, *JournBibLit* 87(1968)329–332, suggests however that we are not yet able to reinterpret with Kraeling's confidence.

to the deeper dimensions of the texts. Then Bultmann and others concentrated upon meaning-history to such an extent that "facticity" in the usual sense was no longer a vital concern. And now concentration upon the theory of interpretation leads to renewed attention to the historical contexts. The claim being made is that the whole hermeneutical approach has been improved. It is no longer thought to be the case that interpretation has to do with pure witness, kerygma, or pure *bruta facta*—"objective facts"—lying about like objects in a showcase. Neither is the object of attention thought to consist in purely non-specific "meaning" or "self-understanding." Rather the hermeneutical circle operative in interpretation of a particular text has also been operative in the development of contemporary exegesis: questions put to the texts are modified by the texts themselves so that new questions are placed, and the process of exploring the texts begins all over again.[5]

We may illustrate the renewed attention to historical and interpretive factors by making reference to a discussion found in several articles by James M. Robinson (of the Claremont Graduate School) and Helmut Koester (of Harvard University), which concentrate on the contextual nature of the development of early Christian theological language. Here we have a good example of what the fully historical and fully hermeneutical approach may mean in understanding the early Christian history, especially in comprehending the movement of theology in the primitive church. One centralizing concept, the problem usually posed as Heresy-Orthodoxy, has been used to organize the presentation.[6]

[5] An excellent example of this process is found in Gershom Scholem, "The Holiness of Sin," *Commentary* 51(1971),41–70. Scholem, writing on medieval Jewish messianism, notes that as long as Jewish historians were ashamed of mysticism in Judaism, the extensive medieval mystical writings were either ignored or suppressed. In our own period there has been a resurgence in Jewish mysticism, however, and consequently the whole history of medieval Judaism has to be redone, recognizing now the extensive influence of mystics such as Sabbatai Zevi and Jacob Frank upon the mainstreams of theology.

[6] As far as I know, there was no initial plan to coordinate these efforts, although Koester and Robinson are not infrequent discussion partners. Several of the articles are to be brought together in Robinson and Koester, *Trajectories Through Early Christianity*, forthcoming. In this section I have abbreviated references as follows, the italicized words serving as brief titles: James M. Robinson, "The *Formal Structure* of Jesus' Message," 1962 (see p. 83, n. 44); "The *Historicality* of Biblical Language," in *The Old Testament and Christian Faith*, ed. B. W. Anderson (New York: Harper & Row, Publishers, 1963), pp. 124–158; "*LOGOI SOPHON:* Zur Gattung der Spruchquelle Q," in *Zeit und Geschichte*, ed. Erich Dinkler (Tübingen: J. C. B. Mohr [Paul Siebeck], 1964), pp. 77–96; "*Kerygma and History* in the New Testament," 1965 (p. 35, n. 11); "A *Critical Inquiry* into the Scriptural Bases of Confessional Hermeneutics," 1966 (see p. 8, n. 3); "*World* in Modern Theology and in New Testament Theology," 1968 (p. 38, n. 21). Helmut Koester, "*Häretiker* im Urchristentum als theologische Problem," in *Zeit und Geschichte*, 1964, pp. 61–76 (see also "Häretiker im Urchristentum," *Die Religion in Geschichte und Gegenwart* III [1962, 3rd ed.], 17–21); "*GNOMAI DIAPHOROI.* The Origin and Nature of

The accepted picture of the development of the Christian faith was painted by the early church itself. The views of Eusebius (Bishop of Caesarea; 260–340 A.D.) became the dominant way of regarding the progression of the faith: Jesus, it was thought, represented the most pure stage of Christianity, and Paul was highly considered as one who faithfully handed on the Jesus-traditions, but after that there was a weakening of the originative thrust. The terms heresy and orthodoxy were applied to movements of Christian thought according to the view that there was a regressive falling-away from the "pure religion" of Jesus.[7] This "decline" was halted in most places by the development of the Catholic Church's authority, especially as it authoritatively decreed dogmas. Throughout the history of the church, Eusebius' approach to the development of Christianity has been more or less consistently maintained: the heretics were the spoilers.

In 1934, however, Walter Bauer's book *Orthodoxy and Heresy in Earliest Christianity* challenged this paradigm.[8] According to Bauer, Eusebius' historiographical method leaves much to be desired. In place of the pattern of one massive universal church from which there were unfortunate deviations, a more complex situation must be recognized. Bauer suggested that the heretical movements, rather than being "deviations" from main-line Christian development, were actually live options within early Christianity—options that were foreclosed because of the development of the organizational and doctrinal skills of the church at Rome. What came to be labeled heresy was in most cases simply a local form of Christianity,[9] which gave way before the universalizing influence of Roman Christianity.

Diversification in the History of Early Christianity," *HarvTheolRev* 58(1965),279–318 (German ed. with some additions: *ZeitTheolKirch* 65[1968],160–203); "One Jesus and Four Primitive Gospels," *HarvTheolRev* 61(1968),203–247 (copyright by the President and Fellows of Harvard).

[7] Heresy can mean division from that which is *kat' holikos*—"catholic" or universal. In use in early Christianity it is opposed not to the later term orthodoxy (for which the contrast is properly heterodoxy) but to *ecclesia,* church. See Hans Küng, "'Early Catholicism' in the New Testament," repr. in *The Council in Action: Theological Reflections on the Second Vatican Council,* trans. Cecily Hastings (New York: © Sheed and Ward, 1963); and *The Church,* trans. R. and R. Ockenden (New York: Sheed and Ward, 1967); also Heinrich Schlier, "HAIRESIS," *Theological Dictionary of the New Testament* I(ET1964)183.

[8] English translation ed. R. A. Kraft and Gerhard Krodel (Philadelphia: Fortress Press, 1971); see also Georg Strecker's notes on his revision of the first ed. in 1964, "A Report on the New Edition . . . ," *JournBibRel* 33(1965),53–56, and G. Clarke Chapman, Jr., "Some Theological Reflections . . . ," address at the American Academy of Religion, 1967. References are to the typescript provided me by Professor Chapman.

[9] Strecker uses the term "waste-product of orthodoxy" in "A Report . . . ," p. 53.

The impact of Bauer's criticism of earlier historical analysis has not been great, although subsequent studies have reflected aspects of the analysis pressed by Bauer. It is now generally recognized, for instance, that orthodoxy and heresy are relative terms, depending upon which starting point one chooses as he sets out to interpret the history of the early church. If we are presented in Bauer and those who follow with "Eusebius demythologized" (Clarke Chapman's phrase), we are already familiar with the demythologization process from study of the gospels and have only to extend the results of form criticism's portrayal of earliest Christianity to the portrayal of the subsequent Catholicism.

Furthermore, specific studies of early Christianity in some of its geographical areas substantiate Bauer's thesis that the localized forms of Christianity were at least not deliberate deviations from a main-line orthodoxy, but represented early alternative interpretations of Christianity. The role of the Roman congregation has been clarified, and it does look as though "orthodoxy" spread outward from Rome, although Bauer's negative evaluation of this process is not necessarily accepted today. The new historical-theological approach, however, gets deeper into the situation than did Bauer, largely because of the attempt to interpret early Christian development hermeneutically. Just as Gerhard Ebeling applies hermeneutical analysis to the work of Luther and Acquinas, so Koester and Robinson, especially, press hermeneutical questions to the fore in the investigation of the heresy-orthodoxy issue.[10]

Heresy vs. Orthodoxy is sometimes studied as a consequence of History vs. Kerygma, and the opposition of history and kerygma is reflected in most modern theology. We have had or will have occasion to note several ways in which the basic tensions have come to the fore: in the opposition between the gospel and the law (p. 98), in the differences in weight between historic and historical (*Geschichte* and *Historie,* p. 22), and in the necessary distinction between the historical Jesus (history) and the worshipped Christ (kerygma) (see pp. 23, 69 f.). We also saw that the theological weighting of the term tradition history (*Traditionsgeschichte*) emphasizes the ways in which information about Jesus (history) came to have religious importance (kerygma) alongside the basic proclamation that God had acted in Jesus the Christ (pp. 75 ff.).

The distinction is a helpful one, and it reflects the modern ability to distinguish between events that can be proved to have happened by external means and events whose importance has accrued due to faith perspectives placed upon them. Professor Robinson, however, points out

---

[10] Gottfried Schille also emphasizes the necessity to reconsider our historical picture of primitive Christianity, but he still does it only in the traditional history of religions framework of form criticism. See *Anfänge der Kirche,* and "Der Mangel eines kritischen Geschichtsbildes in der neutestamentlichen Formgeschichte," *TheolLitZeit* 88(1963),491–502.

two important aspects of early Christian theology and literature that are not comprehended by the distinction between kerygma and history. The first aspect refers to the development of the high evaluation of the tradition history about the historical Jesus, just recalled. Here we must see that "history and kerygma" do not adequately represent the range of factors in the problematic relationship of theology to the historical events of the early Christian faith, since the NT itself takes recourse both to the historical Jesus and to the kerygmatic preaching. And the "history" as it is usually understood does not refer to the actual historical Jesus as much as to the tradition history about Jesus. So it is false to speak of an absolute antithesis between those interested in history on the one side, and those interested in kerygma on the other. There is no pure, unadulterated, nonhistorical kerygma; rather:

> The event itself includes a process of understanding in terms of given categories. To this extent the saving event cannot be shelled out as a brute fact behind the language witnessing to it.[11]

To be sure, the apostolic preaching "kerygmatized" Jesus. But in doing so, it also kerygmatized the original historical situations in which it was expressed: to speak the kerygma is always to speak one interpretation of it.

This complicates the task of NT exegesis and historical analysis, for it means that not only do we have to reflect upon the relative frequency of use of kerygmatic phrases and vocabulary, but also to look at the historical contexts, and to listen to what was being expressed. As Robinson puts it, we have to look for the point being scored, and this point is not something that can be neatly lifted out with a scalpel:

> To be sure, the language in which the point is expressed is not neatly separable from the point, but the concrete point scored is the total impact of the language. . . . Yet the language used to score a point not only becomes itself part of the concrete point scored; it also stands in some potential tension to the point intended, as that point is translated out of an earlier language into the new language. ("Critical Inquiry," pp. 22–23.)[12]

---

[11] Robinson, in "Kerygma and History," p. 119, noting that the *Traditionsgeschichte* has two functions: it was the *Traditionsgeschichte* about Jesus with which the kerygma was concerned, and it is by *Traditionsgeschichte* that one gains access to these traditions today. The term and its translation were discussed in Chapter 3.

[12] This point is what was meant above when we noted that the traditions about Jesus were taken up into the kerygma. See Hans Küng, *The Council in Action*, p. 207: "It is an oversimplification of truth to suppose that every proposition in its verbal formulation as such must be unambiguously true *or* false. Every proposition can, as far as the verbal formulation goes, be true *and* false, according to how it is aimed, situated, and intended. And how it is intended is a harder thing to discover than how it is said."

We spoke earlier of the sense in which *language world* has to be recognized fully and sensitively; here we see the way in which a text's *point(s)* can only be highlighted when we explore (a) the language world, (b) the specific contents of the text, and (c) the ultimate points that an author or a tradition desire to make by using the text.

The second aspect in which Robinson feels the history-or-kerygma distinction has been overdrawn is in the correlated fact, related to what we have just seen as characteristic of Bauer's analysis, that there was no one primitive, "pure" orthodoxy in Jesus and his disciples; nor can we hold that there was *only one* kerygma. In other words heresy, from one perspective, represents not a decline from a primitive purity, but just as much *one interpretation of the kerygma* as orthodoxy is one such interpretation. The appeal to kerygma can be made with equal justification by almost any of the groups that were later designated heretical. For example, in the relationship between Paul and the Galatian church, or between Paul and the Philippians, the issue was not who had the right to appeal to the earliest kerygmatic traditions but rather how far and in what direction these traditions were to be taken. (See Koester, "GNOMAI DIAPHOROI," pp. 309 ff.) Paul and his opponents seemed to be using the same vocabulary; what was at stake was how these words were to be used. Did they give linguistic expression to the Christ? Were they sufficient manifestations of the "point" of the Christian gospel?[13] Or had they been misused, co-opted for the wrong purposes?

In such situations, it is the criterion for testing right interpretations of the kerygma that gains in importance, as Koester notes. According to Koester, the criterion should be the historical Jesus, but this is not to say "the pure unadorned historical Jesus" as if he were recoverable in some form of direct tape-recording ("GNOMAI DIAPHOROI," pp. 282 f.), since the legitimacy of the church's proclamation and faith "does not depend upon the quantity of genuine Jesus material but upon the degree to which the earthly Jesus was the criterion of the church's proclamation and faith." ("One Jesus," p. 205.) This is so because the gospel or kerygmatic outlines, which provide a framework for the incorporation of sayings and narratives, are important not so much as sources of Jesus-materials, but as they "are actually an extension of the kerygma of Jesus' passion and resurrection." (*Ibid.*, p. 207.) In those early Christian writings

[13] A similar situation is found in the Old Testament, where competing prophetic groups claimed exclusive rights to the same ancient traditions. The differences between the groups appear when it is asked how these ancient traditions are to be appropriated,—realized or interpreted. Since most of the classical prophets were unpopular in their own day, we can assume that popular opinion resisted the way these prophets *interpreted* the ancient Israelite traditions. See Rolf Rendtorff, "Reflections on the Early History of Prophecy in Israel," *JournTheolChurch* 4(1967),24.

not based on the passion-resurrection kerygma, other standards were in effect.[14]

Koester makes a further point relevant to the hermeneutical re-evaluation of primitive Christianity: we must now simply recognize that primitive Christianity was syncretistic ("GNOMAI DIAPHOROI," p. 280). This is an insight of the history-of-religions research that we may no longer ignore.[15] Hence we shall have to be more cautious than to assume that Christianity was as monolithic or as one-minded as it is often presented. The idea that syncretism is to be found within patristic Christianity has been a longstanding judgment; the idea that *primitive* Christianity itself was not "pure" but was rather a complex admixture of religious factors is also accepted in most recent studies.

The phenomenon of primitive Christianity that is now coming into view is a much more widely contoured phenomenon than it has been taken to be.[16] The new evaluations of the history of early Christianity will have to proceed more carefully; they will have to be more sensitive toward the multiplicity of choices being made and toward the processes of choosing, and they will have to include perennial reevaluations both of "known" facts and of categories of interpretation.

At the risk of moving too quickly into "what it all means," the following theses and observations serve to draw together some of the directions in which thinking about Christianity and the early Christian history may now be structured. (The material has been organized into five main sections, and each sub-section is indicated with letters or numbers, as in an outline.)

[14] A fourth- or fifth-century writing giving a supposed dialogue between the risen Christ and the disciples, the Letter of the Apostles (Epistula Apostolorum), for example, used the well-established confessional creed of the early church—not the earthly Jesus—as the criterion of faith. In the apocryphal Gospel of Thomas the teachings of Jesus are expanded, but in general the criterion has also become the church's declarations of faith rather than the earthly Jesus. See Koester, "One Jesus," p. 247, and "GNOMAI DIAPHOROI," p. 318.

[15] A more conservative scholar than Koester, Walter Grundmann, puts the point even more sharply: "There is scarcely a form of presentation and visualization within primitive Christianity and the later church to which history-of-religions analogies cannot be cited, scarcely a conceptual formulation to which history-of-religions parallels cannot be advanced, scarcely a form of manifestation to which related history-of-religions manifestations cannot be exhibited." *Umwelt des Urchristentums*, ed. J. Leipoldt and W. Gundmann (Berlin: Evangelische Verlagsanstalt, 1967, 2nd ed.), I, 417. This is not to say that Christianity was *as* syncretistic as some of its religious counterparts, an observation made by Samuel Laeuchli with reference to later Gnosticism, *The Language of Faith: An Introduction to the Semantic Dilemma of the Early Church* (Nashville and New York: Abingdon Press, 1966), pp. 85, 90 ff.

[16] Gerhard Ebeling rightly observes that "the church has never existed, not even in primitive Christianity, as a demonstrable and undisputed unity," *The Problem of Historicity in the Church and its Proclamation*, trans. Grover Foley (Philadelphia: Fortress Press, 1967), p. 95.

I. Christianity appears as a religion in progress, on the move, in which history is highly valued.

   A. Christianity is radically involved in history. Whether one takes the model of Yahweh's relationship to the people Israel, which early Christianity appropriated, or the model of God becoming incarnate in a man, Christianity grounds its theology in the historical, not in the general and the atemporal.

      1. The Church has a "gospel," and a "kerygma"—but not in such ways that it has control over either one. That there is no single kerygma is evident from the fact that kerygma and gospel remain closely tied to specific events. That is to say kerygma and gospel do not become timeless, eternal ways of God's dealing with man, since each passing-on of the early kerygma meant passing it on into different contexts. No single ". . . instance of the kerygma, however carefully codified . . . was itself not another instance of that hermeneutical linguistic process . . ." by which Christianity took on shape and form. Thus to speak the kerygma is what Robinson calls a "hermeneutical risk," for kerygma is specific and direct, and hence open to the dangers of shifting language.[17]

      2. Also, the tradition history is itself a kind of kerygma, and hence when one places himself within that tradition history, his own situation becomes a situation that may give rise to kerygma.

   B. Just how Christianity is historical, however, is not always clear—and indeed in contemporary theology and philosophy the question as to the "meaning of history" is placed again and again.[18] Christianity lives in the tension between God's freedom and man's insecurities, although Christian thought has frequently foreclosed on God's freedom by presenting God as one whose main activity is establishing normative patterns for human behavior. Then by observing such holy ordinances, men think God can be brought under their sway. This issue is frequently discussed in terms of the tension between the Law and the Gospel; it arose within the primitive Christian communities themselves, where it became clear that what was at stake was not just Jewish Law vs.

---

[17] Robinson, "Kerygma and History," p. 147. Also "Critical Inquiry," p. 31: ". . . Any effort to put the point concretely is always a hermeneutical risk, lest one make concrete not the point of the gospel, but rather just the language of a previous age of which the gospel had made use. . . ." Robinson illustrates this with the instance of Paul's controversy with the Corinthians, pp. 24–25.

[18] See esp. Van A. Harvey, *The Historian and the Believer: The Morality of Historical Knowledge and Christian Belief* (New York: The Macmillan Company, 1966).

Christian Freedom, but that there was also a Christian Law as binding as Jewish legalism.

C. From the first thesis also comes the fact that Christianity's expressions are always temporally conditioned, and as such subject to change and modification. Christianity has only temporary languages. This is not necessarily to suggest that Christianity is but a temporary manifestation in the purview of world religions, but to suggest that if it takes itself seriously it will not claim any era's formulae as ultimate.

D. We may also conclude that if at any time Christianity restricts "true Christianity" to a particular formula or creed, it makes such a formula the object of faith rather than letting the formula serve as a pointer or road-sign to faith. The history of the church is full of its attempts to force conceptual conformity within its own walls (Servetus) and without (the crusades and the holy wars). The history of the church is largely the history of Christians forcing the language of each preceding generation into literal rather than symbolical interpretations.

II. The movement of Christian faith in the apostolic churches was diverse; the patterns of early Christianity appear in a multiplicity of forms.

A. Christianity makes its appearance in the NT as a syncretistic phenomenon. This is not to say that it had no guidelines (it was not eclectic), but its syncretism reflects the creative speech and the opening of theological horizons that characterized the church's agonizing search for self-identity in a cosmopolitan religious atmosphere.

B. Within the communities that produced the literature of the NT, there was a wide range of views on such matters as eschatology, ecclesiology, and christology. Movement is from the more diverse to the more unified, as seen in the pseudo-Pauline† and the catholic† letters, where there is a tendency toward consolidation in terms of reverence for the past foundational epoch of the church and for the present doctrinal and administrative authority of the church-as-institution.

C. The terms heresy and orthodoxy, or more properly, heterodoxy and orthodoxy, were used as a means of identifying deviations from the positions of those having the most authority and power

---

† Letters in the NT which are not from Paul fall into these two groups; the pseudo-Pauline letters (such as Timothy and Titus), which sought to use Paul's authoritative name to buttress their own concerns with structure and authority, and the catholic letters (James, Jude, Peter, Hebrews), which portray the fully developed status Christianity attained as a religious institution in the second common century.

and represented after-the-fact decisions. The concrete shapings of Christianity from place to place were not so much at stake as were fundamental issues and directions Christianity was to assume in its religious milieu (in its language worlds).

III. The question heretical/orthodox? is basically neutral with respect to the "original materials." It was the interpretation of these materials that was at stake.

    A. However negatively regarded a particular heresy may have been, it still represents one possible interpretation of the kerygmatic stances of primitive Christianity. When Paul reasons with the "heretics" at Corinth, he combats the Corinthians' understanding and historical application of traditions that were shared by Paul and others. (The conflict concerned various understandings of the resurrection: evidently some Corinthians thought that its proper interpretation was the view that the final resurrection had already taken place; see I Cor 4, 6, 15.)

    B. Orthodoxy was not so much tested by the specific language or traditions one used as by the ways such terms were used. Again Paul's dialogue with the Corinthians provides an example: both Paul and certain Corinthian Christians used the Greek term for wisdom, *sophia;* but Paul reproves the Corinthians for holding an erroneous view of *sophia* that rebounded into Hellenistic philosophical religions rather than sufficiently conveying the sharp edge of the theology of the cross that Paul stressed.[19] The later battle between Christian orthodoxy and Christian gnosticism* reflects similar issues: nothing sounds more like "Christian language" than some of the language of the gnostics, but when not just the vocabulary, but the theological patternings of this language are studied, the differences are apparent.[20]

    C. Attempts to freeze the tradition into the framework of only one particular world view were truly "heretical," and hence we may say that heresy was a refusal to demythologize or to move fully into a new context or language world where the terms no longer carried the same essential meanings.[21]

IV. The distinctions between heresy and orthodoxy, faith and unfaith, although partly determined by decisions made in the history of the

---

[19] See Funk, *Language*, Chap. 11, "Word and Word in I Corinthians 2:6–16."

 * See Glossary.

[20] This is strongly argued by Samuel Laeuchli, *The Language of Faith*, pp. 73–93.

[21] See Laeuchli, "Christianity and the Death of Myth," in Stoneburner, ed., *Parable, Myth, and Language*, p. 11: the council of Nicea represented "the key act of demythologization if there ever was one in the church. Primitive Christian mythology became heresy."

church, remain essentially matters of theological choice that must be newly made in each generation of believers. The hermeneutics of heresy-orthodoxy has to do with the intimate tension and paradox between that which was once formulated and that which must be formulated today.

A. Since Christianity claims to be rooted essentially in concrete historical events (see #I), the real problem is how these events retain their importance in any modernizing interpretation. There is a ready confusion between the historical and the historic, although neither ought to be regarded as irrelevant.

B. Merely to restate the terms of the early traditions means to incarcerate Christian creativity, to instate a restrictive legalism, and to refuse to take historical change seriously. (The biblicist is the heretic.)

C. Christianity's perennial problems, therefore, are deciding when earlier terms must be relinquished, and how their intentionalities are to be carried forward in contemporary terms. Three examples can be given:

1. "Resurrection" is a concept implying an apocalyptic, and probably a mythic, world view: perhaps its point can only be translated into a contemporary world view with loss of meaning —or perhaps its point can only be represented in other conceptual matrices. It can be demythologized into existentialist categories, but then it may lose its historical rootedness. Or the NT's own polyphony can be respected (what is meant by resurrection also appears as Luke's Pentecost, or as Paul's "conversion experience"), in which case resurrection is understood as the birth of a saving, caring, loving community.

2. A crucial question for the primitive church was: *When* did the eschatological inbreaking of God into history become a reality? In the synoptic gospels, Jesus himself is made to answer: with John the Baptist. This functional view of Jesus' role in the eschaton is portrayed by having John's baptism of Jesus as the Christ designate the time when God began to rule in new immediacy. In other NT interpretations, however, not John's baptism but the Easter events signal the eschatological beginnings. And under the christological aegis of Jesus' preexistence, it had to be said that Jesus' role in the eschatological reigning of God was preshadowed by his eternal presence with the Father. So for John's gospel, the When? is really when the believer personally accepts Jesus as eternal Lord.

No unequivocal answer to the question When? can be

found in the NT. And after the period of the NT, the When? question gave way before the question Who was Jesus?, and so instead of answering to When did the Kingdom begin? the church fathers sought to define the *nature* of Jesus' being (the ontological question). To be sure, this was anticipated within the NT, as when Matthew and Luke included traditions relating Jesus to the beginnings of the human race (the genealogical prefaces) and when John developed the Logos imagery to relate Jesus to the beginnings of time itself. Christological development was such that it became heretical (adoptionist) to claim that Jesus became divine either at his baptism or at his resurrection. A question having chronological dimensions (When?) became a question having ontological dimensions (Who? What nature?).

3. The demand for data of Jesus' life as a model for the pious believer is rejected by Paul (II Cor 5:16, "From now on regard no one according to the flesh: even though we once knew a fleshly Christ, we no longer think that way"); but the gospels and especially the apocryphal* gospels rely strongly on such data. To speak the Christ event in the NT is not to speak a unanimous theological consensus; to speak about the Christ today may necessitate similar ranges of interpretation.

V. The use of the primitive Christian past is also a problem as soon as the issue of "canon" forces itself into the field of theological attention. The issues of canon and of heresy-orthodoxy are related insofar as both involve decisions about which aspects of primitive Christianity are to be given normative value.

A. Attempts to delineate canonical materials go hand in hand with judgments about what is worthy of inclusion and hence "orthodox." The canon sets boundaries: it limits the sources of orthodoxy. Usually the canonizing process is a negative process because it excludes heterodox materials, or materials considered to postdate a period of primary creativity.[22] The process also functions positively insofar as it elevates certain documents (or organized traditions) to the rank of official and orthodox scripture.

B. In certain cases, therefore, the Christian canonizing process took place in such a way as to freeze the free formulation of materials

---

* See Glossary.

[22] The setting of the NT canon is generally regarded as having been a response to the heretics' use of NT materials on the one hand, and as a matter of the authors' having lived in the "apostolic" period as the norm for canonical authority, on the other. Catholic (widespread) use among the churches was also an important criterion for inclusion.

that could be used authoritatively by the church (for example, the closing of the Pauline canon). In other cases, the canonizing took place in such a way as to make normative specific lines of interpretation (for example, Matthew's and Luke's editorial interpretations of the source Q).

1. Robinson points out that the Q collection lent itself to certain gnosticizing proclivities (see "LOGOI SOPHON"), and that "it was, after the waning of the first generation's fervor, really too hot to handle." ("Critical Inquiry," p. 28.) The materials of Q could be used in any number of ways: as we have seen in Chapter 1, the church soon overcame the danger of false use by allowing Q to be used only when imbedded within the framework of the authoritative gospels. Koester suggests that the Gospel of Thomas (a heretical gospel, not accepted into the canon) portrays an early version of Q in which Jesus appears as a more thorough-going apocalypticist and as a wisdom teacher. ("One Jesus," p. 230; see "GNOMAI DIAPHOROI," p. 298.)

2. One logical conclusion is that we may not simply assume that the early church's decisions about excluding certain materials need be ours. We need today to study the apocryphal and noncanonical gospel materials as never before, since these materials are not necessarily (though they are usually) secondary or later developments of the gospel traditions—indeed they may well represent parallel developments. (See Koester, "GNOMAI DIAPHOROI," pp. 279–283, and "One Jesus," pp. 203, 208.) The last generation of interpreters drew into the picture of the historical development of primitive Christianity the group of later Christian writings ascribed to the Apostolic Fathers.* Today we must also include those materials that were not always considered theologically reputable by official catholicism.[23]

C. Those who live centuries after the original canonizing do not share the sense of crisis that made a canon necessary; for them "canon" represents merely a decision made "way back then," although it is still associated with heresy and orthodoxy in a general sense—witness the uneasiness whenever new "secret sayings of Jesus" are published. And actually some sort of a canon-within-

---

* See Glossary.

[23] The boundaries of canon must not be confused with the boundaries of materials available for research. We may recognize in, let us say, the Gospel of Thomas, materials more ancient that those in the synoptics—and yet one would not immediately assume that they are eo ipso of greater theological merit, or vice versa.

the-canon always determines religious positions, and a theological canon (in the sense of a standard or favorite passage or writer) is used as a touchstone to the historical canon (the canonical list of books). Hence the hermeneutics of canon must reflect the extent to which canon is *effective canon.* The decision as to what is truly canonical is a theological decision that must be renewed again and again.

1. Although Protestant churches have a different historical canon from those of their Roman or Eastern Catholic brethren, and although the setting of this canon was an act of reformation, the Reformers did not effectually disturb the status quo of the NT canon (given Luther's well-known distrust of the Epistle of James). In one important way, however, the Reformers did effect a very fateful change: reformation theology championed Paul's concept of justification by faith—emphasizing the individual believer's reactions—over against later NT concepts of ecclesiastical salvation through structure and authority. The subsequent overemphasis upon Pauline justification by faith is now being criticized from within Protestantism itself.[24]

2. A related feature of contemporary exegesis and interpretation further illustrates this point: in recent years Protestant scholars have come to accept the traditional Roman Catholic judgment that "early" or "nascent" Catholicism (the German term in the discussion is *Frühkatholizismus*) is a phenomenon that appears within the NT, not just in the later development of the Catholic Church. But the results of NT research can be developed in two ways. According to the usual Protestant tendency to emphasize Paul and to believe that early Catholicism was a step away from the pristine purity of the church concept in the NT, the presence of early Catholicism (the tendency toward a hierarchical episcopacy, firmly established orders of clergy, etc.) can be simply ignored. By maintaining that Paul's writings are primary, contemporary Protestant churches can continue to emphasize the ideal of a minimally structured church order. Those who are willing to broaden their effective canon-within-the-canon, however, will admit that ecclesiastical development is as normative as its absence, and that such development does not represent something alien to the NT, but integral to it.[25]

[24] See Ernst Käsemann, "God's Righteousness in Paul," *JournTheolChurch* 1(1965),100–110, and Günther Bornkamm, *Paul,* trans. D. M. G. Stalker (New York and Evanston: Harper & Row, Publishers, 1971), Part Two.

[25] See Eduard Schweizer, *Church Order in the New Testament,* trans. Frank Clarke (London: SCM Press Ltd. and Naperville: Allenson, 1961); Ernst Käsemann, "The Canon of the New Testament and the Unity of the Church," in *Essays on New Testament Themes,* trans. W. J. Montague (London: SCM Press Ltd. and Naperville:

3. It is also only fair to ask whether or not the hermeneutical question of canon is adequately placed in advance of basic determinations of scholarly directions in, for instance, the new hermeneutic. Does the canon of the new hermeneutic differ from the traditional Lutheran emphasis upon Paul? Failure to recognize one's implicit inner canon is a failure to clarify properly one's pre-understanding, for what one holds as canon provides a wide-reaching orientation and affects one's evaluation of primitive Christian theology. (See Bultmann on pre-understanding and on revelation in Chapter 1.)

The contributions of the new hermeneutical approach are manifold, but the renewed attention to the actual historical matrices—the attempt to listen to the historical dynamics of the text's own context—is of primary importance for valid interpretation. Insofar as this new historical study allows the text itself greater independence and clarity, modern scholarship continues the aims with which historical-critical exegesis began, and that subsequent research has taken as its continued aim. The discussion of heresy-orthodoxy has shown only one of the areas which are being reexamined and reappraised. We acknowledge sound decisions on the part of the theological enterprise throughout the history of the Christian church, but we do not accept their decisions blindly. And indeed it may often be necessary to challenge the "accepted" viewpoints in order to gain a more accurate and total view of our own.

If, as affirmed above, the NT itself is already interpretation, then it should be even more clearly evident that the theological vantage points and theories of the intervening centuries are also open to free and scientific inquiry. And we should probably anticipate that there will always be new hermeneutics, that subsequent generations will regard our interpretations as being just as quaint as we now consider medieval exegesis to have been.

PRESSING LINGUISTIC BOUNDARIES: LANGUAGE LEVELS AND FUNCTIONS

The new hermeneutical approach has been responsible for greater attention to the full historical dimensions of early Christian texts and it represents a maturation of the historical-critical approach to the NT. The

---

Allenson, 1964); Hans Küng, *The Council in Action,* Chap. 12; Gerhard Ebeling, "The New Testament and the Multiplicity of Confessions," Chap. 7 in *Word of God and Tradition: Historical Studies in Interpreting the Divisions of Christianity,* trans. S. H. Hooke (Philadelphia: Fortress Press, 1968); and Myles M. Bourke, "Reflections on Church Order in the New Testament," *CathBibQuart* 30(1968),493–511.

renewed historiography attempts to listen to the writers of NT texts in their own linguistic worlds rather than forcing upon them the intellectual matrices of later Christianity. In pursuit of this task, the biblical scholar looks to the secular historian for help and guidance, and he utilizes the resources of such allied disciplines as anthropology, art history, linguistics, the psychology and sociology of literature, and archaeology.

Attention has also been focused recently upon how texts themselves actually *function:* along with a renewed appreciation of historical contexts and developments, scholars seek to gain a better sense of the literary and phenomenological dimensions of texts of antiquity, and so turn for guidance to literary critics and to those working in nonreligious hermeneutics and language theory. The impact of philosophical language analysis is felt also, especially since linguistic analysis (first in the form of verificational analysis and then of functional analysis) has shifted attention from identifying types of language to the question of the levels on which language is used.

"Theology" comes from *theos* (god) and *logos* (word; thought; theory) and hence is a shorthand description of the process of theologizing: giving word to man's experiences of the gods. However theology has not always given the linguistic component of theo-logy the sort of self-conscious reflection it gave to the religious component. To be sure, the church fathers had a great deal to say about language, both in terms of interpretation and in terms of the right language for the expression of Christian belief. Augustine, for example, devoted *De doctrina Christiana* (On Christian Doctrine) to the use of language; and in the middle ages Thomas Aquinas was deeply aware of the roles played by types of religious expression (see esp. *Summa Theologica* I,i,Q.1, Arts. 9 & 10). But it is only recently that full attention to theological linguistics has become an integrated part of theological hermeneutics.

Much of the recent discussion was precipitated by Martin Heidegger's extensive analysis of linguistic phenomenology and by the primarily British school of linguistic analysis. The latter has developed from an initial, positivist stage in which religious statements were considered to be incapable of verification and hence meaningless, to the present stage in which the analytic approach to philosophy and language recognizes the distinctive functions of religious statements. In the initial stage, analytic philosophers sought to be so rigidly empirical that nothing except empirically verifiable statements could be acknowledged, and they therefore considered (nonempirical) religious language to be inappropriate language. Those who currently define their work as linguistic analysis, however, generally agree that we may indeed speak of the appropriateness of religious statements, and that the main question today is not "Is there religious language which is authentic?" but rather "How can religious assertions best be analyzed according to their function and context?"[26]

Contemporary theology's self-consciousness about language has been greatly informed by British and American linguistic analysis; for those theologians whose work is heavily influenced by Continental thought, however, the existentialist phenomenology of Martin Heidegger continues to be influential. Heidegger's more recent writings have been concerned with poetico-religious expression, and those who follow him have developed a more widely contoured hermeneutics than have the theologies based on linguistic analysis. In those theologians who emphasize the eventfulness of language-occurring (such as Ebeling and Fuchs), we are given a rich constellation of existentialist analysis *and* linguistic and aesthetic reflection.

This type of hermeneutical phenomenology has to do with what is being linguistically experienced—with what happens when language realizes itself. Language is understood as the revealing or expressing of existence, and so it is regarded primarily in terms of dis-closure, discovery. According to this view, language hovers about Being and brings Being to speech obliquely, in an allusive, indirect manner; hence language is thought of as being a limited occurrence, since it gestures toward, but is not itself what is. And this "that language is not quite," is the silence that surrounds language (in Heidegger's terminology, "primordial discourse," in Funk's, "the pre-reflective cogito"). The movement language traces is from event to logic, from liveliness to fossilization; "logical" assertions are those that dead-end in themselves, that have lost their original kinship with reality.

An analogy from the graphic arts may help explain this sense in which language (expression) is said to hover about being and to penetrate its silence. There is a way in which a striking painting may immediately persuade us of the validity of a point of view, of an opinion, or a feeling. The old cliché, one picture is worth a thousand words, is true not only because a picture conveys numerous items of information simultaneously but because often some emotions, concepts, or situations, are only "brought to speech" through the picture. The early Cubist paintings

---

[26] Paul M. van Buren, *The Secular Meaning of the Gospel Based on an Analysis of its Language* (New York: The Macmillan Company and London: Collier-Macmillan, Limited, 1966; orig. 1963), brings a linguistic approach to bear upon some of the themes of primitive Christianity. Ian T. Ramsey, *Religious Language: An Empirical Placing of Theological Phrases* (New York: The Macmillan Company, 1963; orig. 1957), and *Model and Mystery* (London and New York: Oxford, 1964), explores the possible applications of linguistic analysis to theological problems. John Macquarrie discusses the present situation in *God-Talk*, Chap. 5, "Theology and Logical Empiricism," where he identifies some five areas in which there is general agreement today among the analysts and theologians (pp. 111–118).

articulated the experience of twentieth-century anomie and disjunctive-
ness with an immediacy that was found in verbal forms only after several
generations of poets and writers. Similarly, after an artistic nuance has
become conventional, it loses its power to evoke directly the silent expres-
siveness that it originally had.

In art as in language, there are *levels* of expressive effectiveness, and
it is not always self-evident how these levels make their appearance.
Robert W. Funk, in *Language, Hermeneutic, and Word of God,* develops
a formal structure to analyze the levels of language in the NT; this structure is a creative adaptation of Heidegger's analysis of the stages in the
life of language. Funk's attempt is to be understood as part of a phenomenology of NT language, although we should be clear that "the
phenomenon" is not understood in a purely external or formal way, since
content is as much at issue as is shape (form). What Funk sees in parable,
for instance, is not just content or theology, not on the other hand just
formal structure, but rather for Funk, ". . . to grasp the parable in its
fullness means to see *what happens when parable occurs.* . . ." (p. 126,
my emphasis.) "What happens" is a phenomenology of parabolic language; "when parable occurs" is the language event—active and alive—
that takes place.

Funk's analysis of the linguistic levels of the NT may be schema-
tized as follows: first there is level I, *Primordial Discourse,* the silence
that surrounds language; the totality which exists in its wholeness.[27]
This primordial level cannot be grasped directly, since it is the creative
level that gives rise *to* linguistic expressions; it reflects the sense in which
". . . language participates in the creation, preservation, and modification of the appearances." (P. 226.) "Primordial discourse" is not something
that can be identified until it makes an impression and comes out in
someone's language—but then we are in the presence of language on
level II, *The Re-Flective Mode of Language.* Language at this second
level re-flects the "world" of primordial discourse directly; it is the primal
experience coming into linguistic form. Following Heidegger, now Funk
speaks of the "poetical" mode: re-flective language is language that
discloses the contours of existence and creates tradition; it is characterized by directness, immediacy, spontaneity, and non-discursiveness.

The type of language found at the second level is well represented
by parable. Parable provides an oblique view of the silence that surrounds language; it founds a parabolic world that opens out onto tradition (level III).

[27] See the brief critique of the monistic view of reality presupposed in such a
viewing in Roy A. Harrisville, review of Funk's *Language,* in *JournBibLit* 87(1968),
362–364.

At level III, *Language in the Mode of Primary Reflectivity*, is that language reflecting not upon primary language as such but upon the fate of reflective language (II) in the midst of competing worlds. As Funk puts it, it brings the "world" of level II "to stand," it holds up second-level language to what it intends—in terms of the ways in which it is heard. So this third-level language is language that has become tradition; it is language in the mode of recapitulation, of reseeing, of rehearing in terms of new and divergent contexts. (It is ". . . language which reflects upon its own intentionality in view of its auditory range," p. 287.)

Finally, level IV, *Secondary Reflectivity*, is attained. Here we have reflection upon tradition, attention to linguistic formulas established and past. This is common discursive language such as that late Christian language that attempts to expound belief. Although most NT language appears at levels III and IV, we might specify, though Funk does not in this context, a fifth level, *Logic*—language that has become completely "dead," representing ossification, solidification, and consensus—in short, dictionary language.

Some general examples of the way Funk's schema may be applied will be helpful: *poetry* would be considered language at level II, its interpretation at IV, its "world," level III. It is very difficult to bring the poem (II) or its "being" (I) into discursive language (description of its "meaning," IV), without reflecting upon the way it impacted its "world" (III).

Parable, as we have seen, appears at level II. The difficulty of forming a parabolic theology is apparent in the chasm between the parable itself (II) and its elaboration at second hand (IV); such a theology must take into account how the parable confronted its hearers (III) and how it was first transmitted. The parable itself ". . . stands on the frontier of language and mirrors without conceptualizing the kingdom of God" (p. 235); parable is ". . . the language event which brings the kingdom of God near" (p. 237).

The NT *epistle* is located by Funk at level III. If parabolic language (and I think this must be extended beyond parable to include other sayings-materials) founds a world, the epistle (considering now only the genuine, early Pauline epistles) reviews the destiny of that foundational language in other conceptual worlds—the worlds of the apostle and of his readers. A theology of the Pauline letters is not as difficult to develop as is a theology of the parables, and indeed this (IV) is just what the post- and pseudo-Pauline letters attempt to bring about. Understanding the epistles this way helps us grasp how it is that Paul's theology is not what we usually think of as "systematic" theology, but a contextual theology moving within specific contexts: it has to do with allowing ". . . what the proclamation intends, i.e., the Crucified, give [Paul] what is to be said in view of the hearer" (p. 247). Paul attends to the not-yet-spoken as well as the first-speaking, in order to speak. And so, "If the parable is a gesture pointing the way into the kingdom of God, the letter is only one step removed: it wonders why the gesture has been missed" (p. 248).

There are problems with Funk's schema, and perhaps he has worked it out more to generate further analysis than to suggest a final formulation. It is not always apparent, for instance, just how level II is to be distinguished (in actual analysis, rather than in theory) from levels III and IV, insofar as they all play upon the word reflectivity. (In earlier essays, Funk used the term "reflective" at level II.) And it is difficult to apply the analysis to particular passages. Where, for instance, would kerygmatic passages fit?

Funk states that "The letters presuppose the proclamation (kerygma) . . . and refer to it, in that Paul is reflecting upon the fate of that proclamation among his readers" (p. 238). This statement would seem to indicate that kerygma takes place at level II, whereas in reality it must be at level III (for example, the kerygmatic newness is always predicated *dia Christon*—through, by agency of—the Christ); and yet the earliest statement, the earliest linguistic falling-together of kerygma must be placed at level II.[28] How are we to distinguish the progression of development? Is a primitive kerygmatic statement closer to level I than a later kerygmatic statement? If kerygma comes to expression in specific contexts, then can we speak of "kerygma" as *the* kerygma? Suppose we determine that a parable absolutely cannot have originated with the historical Jesus: does that make it appear at a different level than an authentic parable?

Analyses such as this one are successful if they open up the fabric of critical analysis, and this Funk's proposal surely does. If the contemporary reader of the NT is made to appreciate that there are different *types* of language in the NT and that there are different *functionalities* and *levels,* then the first steps toward a fresh comprehension have been taken. Having worked through such a proposed system of analysis, the reader cannot help but pay more careful attention to the linguistic range of what was happening within the inner dynamics of the primitive Christian communities. In this sense such analysis must be considered a task of major importance for future study of the early Christian literature.

As we have seen, when analytical attention is focused on what happens in NT language, several levels of discourse can be identified. There is some language that betrays little primary creativity and seeks

[28] Also, Funk suggests that ". . . the kerygma is an abbreviated language-gesture of which the letter is an expansion . . . " (p. 238, n. 55), in which case kerygma functions at level III; hence we would have to differentiate between two levels of III. Or we might say that the historical Jesus (II ?) comes to expression only as the Christ of faith (III ?).

only to pass on information. Other language exposes reality, language that "acts," "performs," or "founds a world." We may briefly sketch some of the specific types of NT language, reserving discussion of the large units in which the traditions were formed, the genres,* for the next chapter.

Performative Language. It is especially owing to the British philosopher John Austin that linguistic analysts have come to differentiate a particular type of language that does not merely make a statement (a constative utterance, in Austin's terms), but also is an action. Performative language is that language that happens when one declares war, opens a highway, marries, apologizes, names, grants freedom, promises, elicits hope, or warns. Emphasis upon performative language has opened up a viewing of primal, effective language of major importance for the new hermeneutic. As Via notes, "It is because performative is one of the possible functions of language that language can become an event."[29] One contemporary interpreter claims, for instance, that Jesus' word can be understood as granting freedom, giving time, or releasing man into present responsibility for his fellows.[30]

No doubt many of the imperative statements of NT language are intended as performative: the clearest examples would be the word of healing that effects a cure, or Jesus' cursing of the fig tree (Matthew tells us, 21:19, that it "withered at once"). Paul's declarations of "grace . . . and peace to all of you" in the introductions to his letters, or in his concluding benedictions were no doubt understood as substantively giving grace and peace and blessing. And Paul, in Romans, reviewing and elaborating his own grasp of Christian theology, understood such words as "There is therefore now no condemnation for those who are in Christ Jesus" (8:1) as performative words—as words creating a grace-filled life possibility.

Aware that some NT language is truly primary and performative, critics and translators of the NT ought to be able to perceive more directly how primitive Christianity "worked," to sense more clearly its psychology and its inner dynamics. We are so caught up in a philosophical context that treats words as arbitrary ciphers that it may be especially

---

* See Glossary.

[29] *Parables,* pp. 52–53. A brief analysis by Austin is found in "Constatives and Performatives," in *Problems in the Philosophy of Language,* ed. T. M. Olshewsky (New York: Holt, Rinehart and Winston, Inc., 1969), pp. 242–250. See also Funk, *Language,* pp. 26–28, and A. C. Thiselton's discussion, relating Austin to Heidegger, Gadamer, Wittgenstein, and Fuchs, "The parables as language-event: some comments on Fuchs's hermeneutic in the light of linguistic philosophy," *ScotJournTheol* 23(1970),437–468.

[30] See Ernst Fuchs, "Jesus' Understanding of Time," in *Studies of the Historical Jesus,* pp. 104–166.

difficult to admit that there is religious language that performs, and that "works" quite in and of itself. But to ignore this dimension is to reduce language to the status of mathematical signs; it fails to recognize the complex wholeness of the language-act in which language *is* act, and vice versa.

Symbolic Language. It is almost impossible to speak clearly about symbolic language in the NT because the subject is overlaid with centuries of both popular and scholarly interpretation. We cannot enter the debate, for it would take an enormous amount of time and space just to review the history of symbolic theory (semiotics; in theology, symbolics), and equal time and space to develop a contemporary position. At the same time, no one can read John's Gospel, the Johannine letters, Hebrews, or the Apocalypse of John, without becoming conscious of their symbolic fertility. Perhaps it will suffice, then, merely to point to this fecundity as the essence of symbol, to suggest that symbol excites the imagination to a completion of what is "only" symbolized.

Symbols grow out of socially tense matrices. They represent an intensification of particular historical experiences which, though they resist specification, can become partially perceived in visualized forms. Symbols are not artificial in the sense of being arbitrarily chosen (the ancient swastika design of the Nazis was forcibly appropriated because of its explicit contrast to the Christian cross). They evoke rather than specify, in which sense symbols are like visual metaphors. We may call the symbol a metaphor that can be concretized without loss of evocative potential. At any rate, symbolic forms are located toward the immediate rather than the distant end of the spectrum of language forms; symbols evoke the presence of what they re-present in an eventful mode.[31]

Metaphor. It is as difficult to speak adequately about metaphoric language as it is to speak about symbolic language. Beda Allemann recently emphasized the tautological character of the phrase "metaphoric language" because language probably originated as metaphor.[32]

Metaphor attempts to say something that has never been said before, and for which there is consequently no available word. To use a metaphor means conjoining two disparate entities in such a way that a third entity comes into linguistic expression. Before metaphors cloy and decay, they, like symbols, evoke rather than specify—they enable us to give voice to what is yet inarticulate. True metaphor is richly evocative; it cannot be scientifically reduced. I can specify precisely the emotions evoked by

---

[31] See esp. Ray L. Hart, *Unfinished Man and the Imagination*, Chap. VI.

[32] "Metaphor and Antimetaphor," in *Interpretation: The Poetry of Meaning,* S. R. Hopper and D. L. Miller, eds. (New York: Harcourt Brace Jovanovich, Inc., 1967), pp. 103–123.

a simple metaphoric phrase such as Homer's "wine-dark sea"—I can elicit the sense of revelry and challenge of war ("wine") or the dismay and bloody tragedy of it ("dark")—but such elucidation never replaces the metaphor, which captures a spectrum of war's dreadfulness that cannot be otherwise expressed.

We can refuse "to metaphor," of course, either in our own life styles or in interpreting metaphors of the past. But ultimately our only real alternatives are to seek to apprehend reality more immediately (and hence to play scientific games) or to allow metaphor its own playfulness, its own ambiguous relationship to reality as it is usually perceived (and become poetic men):

> Poetry uses metaphor in a free, playful, and ironic manner. In poetry metaphor wins back its original color, spontaneity, and freedom. Poetry is a deliberate deception—but precisely through this deception poetry corresponds to the basically illusionary character of language.[33]

We may speak of two levels of metaphor in the NT: there is the obvious, traditionally defined figure of speech (James and John are sons of thunder) and there is the metaphoric construction that cannot be so traditionally defined. It is the latter that is being analyzed as a means of fresh attention to parable,[34] and that was an essential aspect of the inner creativity and freshness of the primitive Christian utterance. Such metaphor works by breaking up conventional viewings. It allows a speaking of that which is yet unspeakable,[35] and directs attention to what *happens* in the metaphoric situation.[36]

[33] Allemann, p. 106. I should emphasize that I do not limit metaphor to the traditional grammarian's "abbreviated simile." As Allemann points out, to do so with respect to contemporary literature would mean a necessary judgment that there is no use of metaphor in contemporary literature—a judgment that is immediately refuted by the works of Franz Kafka, Edward Albee, Kenneth Patchen, or John Hawkes. These and most contemporary writers (especially contemporary poets) reject traditional metaphors and indeed even the traditionally understood making of metaphors, but internally they are deeply rooted in the metaphoric tradition. Indeed they follow this road so far that they often seem in danger of dead-ending in what literary critics call absolute metaphor.

[34] Funk, *Language,* Chapter 5; "The Parable as Metaphor," Via, *The Parables.* References to contemporary non-theological criticism will be found in either book.

[35] See Allemann, p. 119: ". . . what stands between the lines and between the words, or, to be more precise, what is not patently there, but what appears between them as a kind of magnetic field, as tensions created by the interplay of relations." And Funk, p. 139: ". . . Metaphor shatters the conventions of predication in the interests of a new vision, one which grasps the 'thing' in relation to a new 'field,' and thus in relation to a fresh experience of reality."

[36] See Funk, p. 234: "Metaphor directs attention not to this or that, but to the whole background and foreground of an entity or event by means of imaginative shock or surprise. Metaphor seizes a focal actuality which it loosens from its mooring in everydayness (the 'received' world) in order to descry its penumbral field."

If, in the metaphoric situations of the NT, we can manage to get inside the primitive Christian perspectives, we will listen in as old worlds shatter—we will understand the Christians' sense of being present at the birthing of a new world. The new world comes unexpectedly (Jesus: like a midnight prowler). It is present only to those who participate in it (he who has ears to hear). And it cannot be ossified or codified; it permits of no gross simplification, nor does it provide easy copy for *The Reader's Digest.* "It" is a poem. The new world opens itself to participation not by coercion but by the virility of creative love. This metaphor is not the grammarian's figure of speech so much as it is the permission to take up one's bed and walk, or the announcement that this is the Age of Aquarius.

Myth. The study of myth is just as vast as the study of symbol or metaphor, and again we do not try to do it justice. Somewhat more space will be devoted to myth than to the other parts of this section, however, since the problem of myth is of pressing importance in contemporary NT interpretation. In fact in many ways "the problem of myth" is a peculiarly contemporary formulation. Today myth has a negative connotation not found in the original meaning of *mythos,*[37] and we hear of projects to interpret the myth or to do away with it. Especially in the debate centered around the writings of Rudolf Bultmann, the theme of demythologizing is continuously repeated. Some theologians[38] are afraid that we may throw out content of major importance if we seek to ignore mythic language or to substitute for it a logic of predication (such and such a myth "is really saying such and such"). The contemporary problem comes, to a large extent, from lack of clarity in the way the word is used and from the way mythic world stance is confused with mythic imagery. Several understandings come quickly into view:

Myth may be used neutrally: it is thought of as a story of the gods. In this more usual literary definition, myth designates a literary mode, "not a specific literary work, but a floating tale," which is the raw material for literary compositions, "a traditional tale common to members of a tribe, race, or nation, usually involving the supernatural and serving to explain some natural phenomenon."[39] The Persephone-type myth is a

[37] The meaning develops as follows: "thought," "word," "story," then "fiction," though the standards of antiquity are not as tensed as in our distinction between "real and unreal" myth. See G. Stählin, "MUTHOS," *Theological Dictionary of the New Testament* 4(1967),762–795.

[38] See Chapter 1. I think particularly of Amos N. Wilder, in *New Testament Language for Today* (London: SCM Press Ltd., 1956), and in *Early Christian Rhetoric.*

[39] L. H. Hornstein, ed., *The Reader's Companion to World Literature* (New York: Holt, Rinehart and Winston, Inc., 1956), p. 309. Also Mircea Eliade, *Myth and Reality,* trans. W. R. Trask (New York and Evanston: Harper & Row, Publishers,

common mythic explanation for the seasons found in many cultures. The Prometheus myth presents a pictured account of the taking of fire and wisdom from "the gods" to "man."

In another modern usage, myth is taken to refer to a means of objectifying, of historicizing and of seeking to regulate that over which man does not seem to have control. This is the negative sense in which Bultmann uses the word: "Mythology is the use of imagery to express the other worldly in terms of this world and the divine in terms of human life, the other side in terms of this side."[40] The story of the ascension of Jesus Christ from the earth into heaven is a myth insofar as it visualizes the differences between two of the three stories of the universe. Such an attempt to represent the world for primitive man, an attempt "to speak of a transcendent power which controls the world and man . . . ," is taken by Bultmann to represent the opposite of the scientific world view. Here myth functions as world stance; mythic world stance refers to man's place among the deep and mysterious powers that determine the course of human and cosmic affairs.

A third type of interpretation adjudges myth to be the necessary means of translating "the real into terms of the ideal, the punctual into terms of the durative and transcendental."[41] In such an interpretation, the mythic is a supreme form of enriching language by serving to conceptualize the trans-conceptual.[42]

I have drawn out only these three understandings of myth[43] because

---

1968, © 1963), pp. 5–6: "Myth narrates a sacred history; it relates an event that took place in primordial Time, the fabled time of the 'beginnings.' In other words, myth tells how, through the deeds of Supernatural Beings, a reality came into existence, be it the whole of reality, the Cosmos, or only a fragment of reality . . . ."

[40] Bultmann, "New Testament and Mythology," p. 10, n. 1; see also *Jesus Christ and Mythology*, p. 19.

[41] From *Thespis:* Ritual, Myth, and Drama in the Ancient Near East. Copyright © 1950, 1961 by Theodor H. Gaster. Reprinted by permission of Doubleday & Company, Inc. The quotation is from p. 24 of the 1961, 2nd rev. ed.

[42] See also Jean Danielou, *The Theology of Jewish Christianity,* trans. and ed. John A. Baker (London: Darton, Longman & Todd and Chicago: The Henry Regnery Company, 1964), p. 205: "The word 'myth,' as a technical term in the phenomenology of religion, no longer has the sense of 'fable.' It means 'an imaginative (not imaginary) representation used to convey symbols of value.'" Danielou is quoting H. Duméry.

[43] Many further definitional types could be cited, ranging from that of the social anthropologist to that of the iconographer analyzing medieval art. See esp. Macquarrie, *God-Talk,* Chap. 8, and Robert Luyster, "The Study of Myth: Two Approaches," *JournBibRel* 34(1966), 235–243. For a course on "Myth and Ritual," I had no trouble in identifying thirty-two contrasting definitions; they were organized into the following ten categories: (1) Aesthetic device; narrative; literary form. (2) Has to do with the gods, the "other" world. (3) Explain origins. (4) Enforce social order. (5) As mistaken or primitive science. (6) The words to a ritual. (7) Make universals concrete, intelligible. (8) Explicate beliefs or collective experience; convey values.

I think there is a vital difference between the application of the adjective "mythic" to language and literature (for example the myth of Persephone) and its function as world stance (for example as the opposite of science). The essential question is not Can we do away with myth? but Can we distinguish in each case between mythic language and a mythic orientation to the world? Before we become involved with demythologizing, we need to understand whether we are truly just bringing out the meaning of the myth or whether we are being asked to give up mythic language (resurrection, Prometheus, heaven and hell) or also mythic world stance (belief in someone who can overturn natural laws, acceptance of an external monitor upon the course of universal events). We may even be asked to choose between an ancient mythical system and a modern one, for there is little doubt that even modern scientific systems occasionally indulge in mythic self-justification.[44]

There is also the question of whether Jesus or the early church only expressed themselves in mythic language or also maintained a mythic world stance. What does seem to take place in primitive Christianity—especially in its foundation, Jesus' teaching—is the modification and revaluation of myth. Even when the traditional mythic language remains, we sense that it has been stripped of its mythic meaning by having been brought into conjunction with the primitive Christian understanding of God's historical participation in the world.

An example: the expectation of a Kingdom of God, ushered in by a messianic figure and featuring the final justification of a national Israel is found in mythic form in late-biblical Judaism. Especially in the apocalyptic writings of the OT apocrypha and pseudepigrapha, mythic imagery abounds; the final time will break into the present (or the very near future) as cosmic judgment. Mythically formulated miracles were expected, and there was speculation that a great mythic battle between the Sons

---

(9) "Spiritual" expression. (10) Inclusive definitions. Add to this list the master-definition by Henry Murray, "The Possible Nature of a 'Mythology' to Come," in Henry A. Murray, ed., *Myth and Mythmaking* New York: George Braziller, Inc., 1960; Boston: Beacon Press, 1969), pp. 300–353, and Joseph Campbell's four master functions analysis (Mystical/Metaphysical, Cosmological, Sociological, and Psychological), and one is well enough supplied with material! See Campbell, "Mythological Themes in Creative Literature and Art," in Joseph Campbell, ed., *Myths, Dreams, and Religion* (New York: E. P. Dutton & Co., Inc., 1970), pp. 138–144; and see, in Campbell's series, *The Masks of God*, the following: *Primitive Mythology* (New York: The Viking Press, 1959), pp. 461–472; *Occidental Mythology* (New York: The Viking Press, 1964), pp. 518–523; *Creative Mythology* (New York: The Viking Press, 1968), pp. 608–624.

[44] See Julius A. Roth, "Ritual and Magic in the Control of Contagion," *AmerSocRev* 22(1957), 310–314.

of Darkness and the Sons of Light would precede the dissolution of everyday reality before a final reestablishment of an Eden-like paradise.[45] In Jesus' teaching, however, the nationalistic element is in retreat; the Kingdom becomes less and less Israel's fulfillment as a political body.

Jesus picks up the interpretation of *basileia* (reigning, "kingdom") which plays not so much upon its nationalistic, political connotations as upon its focus upon God's way of life. *Basileia* refers to the style of Israel's adherence to its Lord; it may be said that what Jesus did was to speak this Reigning of God—to bring it very near—so that its mythical overtones are hushed before very concrete realities of life, such as the problem of dealing with the fall of an overly self-sufficient son and his jealous older brother (the good Samaritan story, Lk 10).

According to Jesus' interpretation, God's reigning was not something to appear only in a far-off future but was so near to the presently experienced world that one ought to be prepared for it at any time. Many of Jesus' parables, for instance, began to demythologize the traditional myths of the Kingdom, relating its contours to his listeners' contemporary experience. Jesus indulged in typical Hebraic hyperbole to make his point: the Reigning of God comes in a twinkling, so unexpected and quickly that one should be prepared all the time; its coming is so important that one will not even have time to settle his bank accounts or take up the social obligations of mourning.

God's reigning, Jesus went on, is so close, it comes so instantly and immediately, that one should really stop telling beautiful stories about "when God comes . . ." and live in the belief "that God already rules." Of course the Kingdom begins with John the Baptist—but who cares when it started? The point is that for Jesus, Kingdom meant the immediate now—Kingdom meant how one loved his neighbor.

The mythical view of the *basileia* was transmuted into the historicized mode in which God reigns; it became the moral possibility for renewing and reorienting everyday community. That which was the future ideal became contemporary possibility. Its turning point was no longer the great mythic battle, but willingness to let oneself go—to offer oneself as one who participated in God's new time. The Kingdom remained mythical in many respects—it was still entirely "God's" doing, and it was not consummated in present existence. The Reigning *is*, but *is yet to be*. "God" will consummate his reigning "in the future"; until then Christian

---

[45] Compare Helmut Koester, "The Role of Myth in the New Testament," *And NewtQuart* 8(1968), 186: "To be sure, some of its terminology derives from political language and thus, has positive historical connotations. But the Kingdom does not arise from the continuity and causality which characterize the history of world and men," and thus it is basically mythic.

man was to live in terms of the new reality of love and in sight of the ultimate promise.[46]

To be sure, Jesus' re-reading of the great mythic themes of Israel was itself not entirely successful: he is reported as telling conventional mythological stories (the synoptic apocalypse, Mk 13 and parallels); and in works like the Apocalypse to John, a fully mythological mind-set seems to have enabled him to ignore the newer, more radical approach.[47] There surely *is* mythological language throughout early Christian theology, and hence the problem of myth is not just a problem with respect to Jesus, but a problem with respect to how Christian theology as such should take on shape and form. One must not only attempt to identify the contours of myth in the NT, but must also evaluate the viability of myth in contemporary society; then the proper question becomes: Which myths (Christian or otherwise) can function to sustain the contemporary understanding of "world"?[48]

One of the briefest but certainly most telling attacks on Rudolf Bultmann's demythologizing program is to be found in Herbert Richardson's *Toward an American Theology*, Chapter 3, "The Myth is the Message." The chapter title is accurate, for Richardson develops the post subject-object dichotomy point that Marshall McLuhan has bowdlerized: an effective linguistic form *is* that which it says. Its content may not be neatly lifted out from its form, but *is* its form, the point made throughout this book.

Along with others, Richardson hopes to reinstate appreciation for myths as image-sets which act by evoking that which they express. The essence of myth, namely the story,[49] is a complex happening that must happen—not that must be rephrased into "scientific" logics. Bultmann's

---

[46] See Koester, "The Role of Myth . . . ," p. 189. Hence Bultmann interpreted Jesus rightly when he refused (against Buri and Ogden) to demyth or dekerygmatize the kerygma itself; the problem, however, is whether or not contemporary theology must demyth in a radical manner. On the possible ways of basing contemporary approaches on Jesus' teaching, see Jack T. Sanders, "The Question of the Relevance of Jesus for Ethics Today," *JournAmerAcadRel* 38(1970), 131–146.

[47] I know that the usual interpretation of the ApocJo is that its author speaks mythic language, but does not think mythically but "historically." I am not convinced that the distinction is helpful, nor do I believe that the author of the ApocJo was not essentially a mythologist in his beliefs.

[48] The question may be phrased in language other than the "world" concept of Heidegger and Gadamer: Herbert W. Richardson, *Toward an American Theology* (New York, Evanston, and London: Harper & Row, Publishers, 1967), p. 6 and elsewhere, coins the term "intellectus" to refer to a similar matrix of meaning/thought/feeling/perception. The question in his terms asks what sort of myths are necessary to undergird the intellectus of contemporary sociotechnical society.

[49] See Wilder, *Early Christian Rhetoric*, Chapter IV; Beardslee, *Literary Criticism*, Chapter II.

error (beyond category-confusion, for which he is scolded by several critics[50]) was twofold. First Bultmann is simply incorrect when he adopts the Romantic assumption that each era must become progressively more "scientific" (understanding this term in the narrow sense of meaning the opposite of subjective or humanistic). As Richardson notes (pp. 50–51), the contemporary world is not solely characterized by the growth of the empirical sciences but also by the high level abstract thinking in logic and mathematical theory and by the absolute imaginative knowledge of the artist. Hence an important rethinking of how we deal with myth as prescientific language (and hence outmoded) must occur. Richardson rejects the concept of evolution from mythical world view to scientific world view in favor of an analysis that stresses the movement from undifferentiated thinking (the primitive situation, where myths, empirical data, and theorized explanations are not distinguished) to modern differentiated thinking. Myths do continue to function for modern man—indeed modern man has become so aware of their existence and power that he now self-consciously creates and manipulates myths.

Bultmann, who introduced reflection upon the process of understanding to theological attention, secondly misconstrues the power of myth to be myth. That is to say he fails to recognize the intense linguistic power of myths in conveying ("translating") total perceptions. There may well be certain late Hellenistic myths that no longer function for us because they fail to coincide with or support our world views: certainly no one who has seen men walking on the moon can any longer affirm a three-storied universe, nor can we who know about DNA accept the explicit terms of the creation of man in Genesis.

The alternative to demythologizing, which seeks to extrapolate abstract formulas from such myths, may well be an outright rejection of those myths' viability for us. But instead of replacing the Hellenistic-Christian myths with rational or existentialist condensations of their meanings, we ought to learn *how* the myths were irreducible in their own contexts, how they voiced for their own world view those aspects of reality that could not otherwise be voiced. Then the task turns toward the place of mythic articulation of *our* experienced reality. The point is not to learn how to live without myths (Bultmann's scientific modern man), but how to evaluate myths, how to create and to sustain our own living mythologems—understood now not as prescientific but as aesthetic, sensuous explicaitons of reality (of "world") that persist coterminously

---

[50] Esp. by John Macquarrie and Schubert Ogden, and by Ronald W. Hepburn, in "Demythologizing and the Problem of Validity," in *New Essays in Philosophical Theology*, ed. A. Flew and A. Macintyre (New York: The Macmillan Company, 1955), pp. 227–242.

with science or abstract logic as articulators of reality which are self-validatingly real:

> The reality that the myth symbolizes is evoked by the myth itself and cannot be experienced apart from it. Hence, the truth of a mythical discourse consists solely in its power of illumination, or its ability to create feelings of wholeness, rightness, and well-being in a person. In producing these affections, a myth validates itself. . . .[51]

We need to recover the aesthetic and psychological importance of the story and of myths, to see how myths convey meanings by their sensuous and symbolic impact. And hence we need to comprehend the ways new myths are being forged today, to learn to judge myths (such as the Nazi or American white's myth of racial superiority, or the evolutionary-progress myth of Western consumerism) that have arisen in our own era.

Instead of replacing ancient myths with contemporary existentialist reductions, our need is for better comprehension of mythic functioning in our own society. The Ancient Near Eastern New Year's festivals, for instance, are less important to us for existentialist insights into our own personal experience than for reminding us of the ways the inauguration of an American president can be said to invoke ancient models of stability and world renewal.

We should also regain a sense of the importance of the close relation between ritual and myth: there is *some* truth in the classicists' judgment that the myth is the spoken aspect (*to legomenon*) of the co-ordinate ritual actions (*to dromenon*).[52] An age that scoffs at religious ritual and revises its religious patterns more and more in the direction of the formalism of the Quaker meeting needs to be shown how its need for ritual is satisfied by other equally ritualistic compensations (sports, education, sensitivity groups, dance and rock music). I seriously doubt that man is less needful of ritual today than in previous generations; what is needed is the sensitivity of the field anthropologist to descry rituals occurring in the present arenas of experience. The "strangeness" of myth and ritual may well be that the myths *we have identified* have to do with supernatural beings and forces. To be sure, our perceptions do not include such supernatural factors—or at least we generally do not think they do; we supposedly live in a "post-mythic" age.[53]

[51] Richardson, pp. 69–70.

[52] Jane E. Harrison, *Themis* (Cambridge, 1912); see also Northrop Frye, "New Directions from Old," in Murray, *Myth and Mythmaking*, p. 117; and on E. R. Leach, see G. S. Kirk, *Myth: Its Meaning and Functions in Ancient and Other Cultures* (Berkeley and Los Angeles: University of California Press, 1970), p. 23.

[53] Macquarrie, *God-Talk,* esp. pp. 181–182.

It must seem strange, then, for me to advocate recognition of myths' evocative powers—their availability to vocalize field-wide perceptions—and to urge that we seriously attempt to recognize and vitalize mythology. The strangeness arises however, from a narrow definition of religion. To call only that "religious" which refers to particular supernatural beings is a restriction demanded by very few theologians. Mythology is still necessary, still crucial, for mythology articulates felt-perceptions of power, especially of trans-personal power, and no society yet has found it unnecessary to describe linguistically the powers that transcend its ordinary experiences ("evolution," "democracy," "freedom," "purpose," "unity"—are these any less than "transcendent" or "religious"?).

Eschatological Language. To those accustomed to theological literary analysis, it might come as a bit of a surprise to find eschatological language included in a section that has dealt with myth, metaphor, and symbol, since "eschatological" is usually taken to be an adjective of content, not form. I argue however that the term is a legitimate and helpful one in such contexts, and that we may indeed speak of a form-and-content manner of expression that is eschatological. It is necessary to indicate briefly the place of eschatological thought in primitive Christianity before developing what I propose as characteristics of eschatological language,[54] although one of the most difficult problems in dealing with NT eschatology is the determination of its boundaries.

The extent of eschatological or apocalyptic influence upon primitive Christian theology has been a central issue in NT studies of the twentieth century since the work of Johannes Weiss and Albert Schweitzer, and even in the 1950s and 1960s, there were many articles and monographs devoted to this issue.[55] Scholars speak of the pervasiveness of eschatological thought: but how pervasive was it? Should we go so far as to agree with Ernst Käsemann, who speaks of *apocalyptic* as the "mother of the church"? Or should we accept Bultmann's modified acceptance of

---

[54] In "Identifying Eschatological Language," *Continuum* 7(1970), 546–561, I pursue the possibility of a phenomenological analysis of NT eschatological diction. This enterprise is carried forward in a paper on "Apocalyptic Style in the New Testament," being revised from the Symposium on Eschatological Language at the Society of Biblical Literature, October 1970.

[55] A series of important articles were published in the *Zeitschrift für Theologie und Kirche,* beginning with Käsemann's "An Apologia for Primitive Christian Eschatology" (ET now in *Essays on New Testament Themes,* pp. 169–195), and continuing with articles by Käsemann ("The Beginnings of Christian Theology" and "On the Theme of Primitive Christian Apocalyptic"), Ebeling ("The Ground of Christian Theology"), Fuchs ("Concerning the Task of a Christian Theology"), and Bultmann ("Is Apocalyptic the Mother of Christian Theology? A Disagreement with Ernst Käsemann"). Several of these articles are translated and brought together with American papers in the sixth volume of the *Journal for Theology and the Church* (New York: Herder and Herder, 1969).

this judgment, and call *eschatology* the mother of Christian theology?[56]

The massive impact of the new situation into which the primitive Christians understood themselves to have entered—the eschatological situation of the Last Days—can hardly be minimized. Whether or not we posit eschatology, or specifically apocalyptic eschatology, as the overriding influence upon the development of primitive Christian theology, we can never ignore the far-reaching affects of the new orientation. No little part of the enthusiasm of the primitive Christian movement is to be comprehended in its terms. Thus the usual orientation toward eschatology gets in the way of disclosing its far-reaching and encompassing features; textbook traditions take the word literally and assign it a place at the end (*eschatos:* end, goal) of the course of theological study. Hearing a "logos of the end," one finds many other topics of primary importance, and mentally places eschatology in his "work to do . . . someday" files. This is lamentable, for empathetic interpretation of the NT demands that we recognize the full extent to which eschatology influenced the NT writers.

Jesus cannot be fully comprehended unless we take into account his relation to the reigning or kingdom of God (*basileia tou theou*)—an eschatological concept. Paul's sense of urgency that drove him from country to country is the consequence of his belief in the nearness of the eschatological Day of the Lord (*hemera tou theou*). John the Baptist's preaching, the Apocalypse to John, the crucial immediacy of the kerygmatic outlines, the reasons for spreading the gospel, the purposes and motivation of Christian ethics: all these are overwhelmingly influenced by early Christian eschatology.

The question of eschatology is usually presented mainly in terms of When? rather than Why? and hence we are predisposed to think of anything eschatological as having to do only with matters of time, especially of the future. The time dimension is important, of course, but as significant are the dimensions of *purpose, direction,* and *goal,* which are central to eschatological thought. To be sure, eschatology is future oriented, and it proposes options as to how things will eventuate, but its central characteristic is its affirmation THAT GOD: that God rules rather than fate or some immutable law. In this sense, eschatological language is on a par with language about creation: both attempt to express God's purpose, will, and character.[57]

Primitive Christianity was "eschatological" in such a basic way that

---

[56] See glossary for the distinction between eschatology and apocalyptic eschatology. Also: Otto Plöger, *Theocracy and Eschatology,* trans. S. Rudman (Richmond: John Knox Press, 1968), Chap. 3.

[57] See B. W. Anderson, "Creation," *The Interpreter's Dictionary of the Bible* I (Nashville: Abingdon Press, 1962) 730: "Creation is fundamentally an eschatological doctrine. The opening words of Genesis: 'In the beginning God,' correspond to the prophetic expectation: 'In the end God.' " This correspondence was elaborated

its eschatological perspective is really its most characteristic feature. The primitive church seems to have conceived of itself as already participating in the benefits of the freedoms of the longed-for Last Days—a claim not exactly calculated to please its Jewish neighbors.

To a major extent, primitive Christian eschatology entered bodily into its language. What we are faced with in parable, for instance, is Kingdom *(basileia)* entering language: it may be said that Jesus did not just "illustrate" the eschatological reigning of God, but he brought his living it into speech. In the parables and in certain of his sayings, Jesus' eschatological conscience flooded his language. Kingdom became not description of some future socio-political order, but present event.[58]

The evangelists themselves found this sort of eventful immediacy too hot to handle, and so they presented the parables as typical Rabbinic parables, illustrating ideas and concepts. I am very skeptical about the present introductions and settings for Jesus' parables,[59] and even more skeptical that their conclusions were originally connected to the parables by Jesus; for instance, in the Unjust Steward (Lk 16:1–13) there are no fewer than six "concluding" sayings, each appended in an attempt to tell us what this difficult parable really means. Mark even allegorizes parables —in short, the second Christian generation had already relinquished the eschatological dynamism to which Jesus gave direct linguistic presence.

Modern parable interpretation has often been no less thick-headed than the evangelists, insisting upon the necessity to improve upon the parables and to spell out their metaphoric freshness into abstract theological systems. Such refusal to let the parables have their own head is especially seen in that manner of explicating Jesus' message which sees it as being within the mainline imagery of late-Jewish eschatology, but then qualifies by regarding Jesus' eschatological language as merely its "shell." So for example, E. F. Scott speaks of Jesus employing eschatological language as a "vehicle" for his real meaning; the language is only the external thing, symbolic, "little more than figurative."[60] Bultmann's own viewing of language leads him to a similar position: Jesus' eschatology is only mythology, the garments in which the real meaning comes clothed.[61]

If, however, we assume that what is being said *is* what is said, then

---

by Hermann Gunkel, *Schöpfung und Chaos im Urzeit und Endzeit*, 1895. To this topic, see David S. Russell, *The Method and Message of Jewish Apocalyptic* (Philadelphia: The Westminster Press, 1964), pp. 422 ff.

[58] This understanding of parable is similar to that developed by Eberhard Jüngel, *Paulus und Jesus*.

[59] A contrary view is argued by A. C. Thieselton, "The parables as language-event . . . ," *ScotJournTheol* 23(1970), 454–58, 468.

[60] *Kingdom of God*, pp. 82, 95, see p. 110, quoted by R. H. Hiers, "Eschatology and Methodology," *JournBibLit* 85(1966), 170, which gives other examples.

[61] *Jesus and the Word*, pp. 55 f., 131, and "Jesus and Paul," p. 186.

we may not so easily divorce the medium from the message. If language itself founds worlds, then we must not blithely rescue Jesus by modernizing him. We must not strip off his language by saying that he really meant something else. The risk, of course, is that Jesus remains back in antiquity. But such a risk must be taken lest we find ourselves having reverted to casting our own modern concepts of reality back into Jesus' thought.

Albert Schweitzer shattered the confidence of life-of-Jesus researchers by showing that most scholars' lives of Jesus were little more than projections of modern thoughts into Jesus' context;[62] but he failed to take his own medicine when he presented Jesus as an apocalypticist whose career ended in failure. We must learn from Schweitzer that it is not enough to remove the splinter from another generation's eyes, but that we must remove the log from our own, and this means that we must learn to evaluate more sensitively the role of the eschatology in NT language.

The problem involves the extent to which we consider eschatological language to be "real"; in this way it is similar to the problem of mythical language. And although the NT represents both a continuation of myth and its modification, as Bultmann consistently emphasizes,[63] we must ask to what extent the mythic language is supported by or differentiated from the mythical world view. The analysis of these two factors has much relevance to the attempt to grasp the dynamics of eschatological language.

Hans Conzelmann, for instance, distinguished two basic ways of treating the problem of eschatology in an analysis which reflects a distinction like that between mythic world stance and mythic imagery developed above.[64] In German scholarship, the problem of eschatology is almost always taken in its narrow aspect, that is to say, it is "the problem of the delay of the parousia"[65] that is the usual starting point, and hence Conzelmann proceeds to delineate two responses to this problem in NT literature, one that is time bound and one that is not.

From the standpoint of apocalyptic imagery, the Apocalypse to John

62 *The Quest of the Historical Jesus: A Critical Study of its Progress from Reimarus to Wrede.* (London: Adam & Charles Black, 1963, 3rd English ed.; orig. ed. 1906.)

63 Especially in *History and Eschatology*. Stählin, on the other hand, can only speak of myth being silenced by sacred history ("MYTHOS," cited above).

64 See pp. 195, 197–198. Hans Conzelmann, *Grundriss der Theologie des Neuen Testaments* (Munich: Kaiser, 1967) #40, pp. 338–348. In what follows, I am working out from Conzelmann's analysis; the examples are his. ET: *An Outline of the Theology of the New Testament*, trans. John Bowden (New York: Harper & Row, 1969).

65 *Parousia*: a Greek term for presence, coming. The term came to refer to the return of the Christ as End-Time Ruler. I suspect that the emphasis upon the delay of the *parousia* in German scholarship dates from the section in Schweitzer's *Quest* entitled "The Failure of the Parousia" (ET pp. 357ff.).

used apocalyptic materials to portray the final drama, and Luke worked out an interpretation of the period of the church which was to take place before the consummation or parousia. According to Conzelmann, both theologies are time-bound in that they operate with specific imagery and forms of conceiving the final time, and these conceptions tended to crystallize around their specific terms—hence it is not helpful to bring such varied eschatological presentations into consistency with one another. Instead of seeking consistency in eschatological imagery, we are alerted to the fact that several presentations simply lie side by side and cannot be reduced to common denominators.

In fact we can see several distinct concepts: (a) cosmological expectation was found, alongside (b) intensified hope for the individual, and there was both (c) a radical call to repent and be prepared for the final and conclusive appearance of God, at the same time that there developed (d) a "Christian way" (*vita Christiana*) with generalized rules of long-range conduct emphasizing endurance and witness in the face of heresy or persecution. The danger of the first, time bound, eschatology, is that it can too easily become fused with one particular type of eschatological formalism. A rigid set of categories and images replaces the original eschatological dynamic; translation becomes merely a matter of substitution and allegorizing, as when the impact of Graeco-Roman thought transformed the morally-conceived Kingdom of God into the trans-temporal heavenly reign of God.

In the second type of eschatology, the central concern is not to maintain the apocalyptic imagery intact, but to build upon its conception of faith. So in Colossians, Ephesians, Hebrews, and the Gospel of John, according to Conzelmann, the eschatological problem was dealt with by existentializing the apocalyptic imagery. Such a standpoint is no more satisfactory than the first, however, since the danger is now that the historical dimensions of Christianity are lost to view (as in Gnosticism).

As we spoke above about mythic language vs. mythic intentionality, we might speak here of apocalyptic or eschatological imagery vs. the understanding of existence in eschatology. In either case the question of interpretation and translation has to do with the limits that one sets. How much of the original language and how many of the original conceptions must be maintained? Once the eschatological language is relinquished, other primitive Christian language may be relinquished, so the question is an important one. To respond that nothing must be relinquished—that the primitive period of the church is the supremely inspired period of the church—is to invite an uncritical biblicism to determine how the churches shall look today. To respond that nothing is to be kept is to dissolve the historical dimensions of Christianity into gnostic speculation.

Whichever direction is taken, however, one should not allow his attention to be distracted from the fact that for the primitive Christians eschatology was not something peripheral. It was not, even in its apocalyptic extremes, the concern only of a select few who withdrew from daily affairs. We are often misled by the impressive image of the author of the Apocalypse silently and monastically composing in seclusion on Patmos, but eschatological language is not solo-language. The model of John in pious retreat furtively reveling in a great secretive ciphering tends to hide the fact that the language of eschatology is a corporate language intended to catch up the rich cultural associations of the past and weave them into a marvelously shining new tapestry of anticipation. There are social factors behind eschatological language which speak as loudly as theological factors, and we must be aware of assuming that eschatological terms are merely ciphers for the Transcendent (Karl Jaspers).[66]

Eschatology is a means for telling the story of the world, not in vague, mystical or decorative phrases, but in language that opens out of and into cultural realities. Symbols in eschatological language, for instance, are not chosen haphazardly. Rather:

> The symbol . . . is constituted of dramatic media, heavily charged with associations reflecting the plenitude of the moral and affective life of the group and its past. It thus has an evocative and as it were explosive force as a means of communication and shock.[67]

The symbols and the apocalyptic imagery as a whole sound strange to our ears, but they were not so strange to their first hearers. Eschatology was not a private language, but a language that gathered together expectations and hopes and gave them a framework of images. It was precisely not a privatizing but a publicizing of language that gave apocalyptic its relevance: apocalyptic eschatology brought an order to bear, a way of

---

[66] I do not have in mind an explicitly Marxist or anti-Marxist critique, but it should be stressed that such images as the Great Beast or the New Jerusalem carried very specific socio-political references. In a similar context, Wilder refers to a study of Negro slave songs which suggests that "crossing over Jordan" was not a vaguely spiritual reference, but referred to actual escapes into free territory or into Canada ("Scholars, Theologians . . . ," p. 1). Two other articles by Wilder are also relevant: "Social Factors in Early Christian Eschatology," in *Early Christian Origins*, ed. Allen Wikgren (Chicago: Quadrangle Books, Inc., 1961), pp. 67–76, and "Eschatological Imagery and Earthly Circumstances," *NTStud* 5(1959), 119–45 (New York: Cambridge University Press). I am not at all convinced of the correctness of the traditional evaluation of apocalyptic as a literature that turns away from the human level to a supernature and the spiritual beyond-history (see a typical such evaluation in Russell, *The Method and Message of Jewish Apocalyptic*, pp. 17–18).

[67] Wilder, "Eschatological Imagery . . . ," p. 243, see also pp. 232–3, 244–5. On the rich connotations of just one figure, see Mathias Rissi, "The Rider on the White Horse, A Study of Revelation 6:1–8," *Interp* 18(1964), 407–418.

conceiving reality. Eschatological language (like language about creation) is not concerned with a never-never land, but with politics and the social order, with blood and sweat and tears and success.

To be sure, eschatological language, especially apocalyptic, sounds weird to our ears; the fantastic eschatological imagery strikes us as only a sort of "divinatory brooding" (Austin Farrer), and having traced its background to Greek, Iranian, and Mesopotamian sources, we dismiss its relevance. Such dismissal misleads, however, for it is precisely a rebirth of the dynamics of its sources that marks truly creative eschatology.

What was happening was a rethinking of history—not a vague poeticizing (in the negative sense), but a re-tooling of concepts of time and mastery and power. This eschatology represented no gnostic flight into an arcane speculation about the titles of the rulers of the aeons, but rather the concrete recasting of categories of time and social intercourse:

> The eschatological mood represents a radical spiritual cultural effort of a group (or an individual) to overcome disorder and to define meaning, and to give body to possibilities and to the future, as well as to come to terms with dynamic and radical changes in the conditions of existence.[68]

Such massive recasting of convention is no easy task; it cannot be performed overnight, and it does not readily admit of terminological consistency. We should therefore not expect to witness uniformity, urbanity, or elegance in the primitive Christian eschatological literature.

Furthermore, we should look for a means of comprehending the full range of eschatological thematics rather than attempting to define the "essence" of eschatology. It is a longstanding conclusion that prophecy gives way before apocalypse in many circles of ancient Judaism; but it would be more adequate to speak of the tensions between apocalypse and prophecy as they coexist.

Perhaps there is a range of eschatological language that runs from that primary, creative, imaginative level of its first Israelite coalescences outward toward cliché and sterile repetition. Certainly there is tension between the liberation of images in some eschatological language—a radical reappropriation of ancient Israelite symbols and metaphors—and their historicization. Existentialist analyses have been quick to refer to myth rampant in apocalyptic: it would be more adequate to speak of mythic and nonmythic perspectives simply lying side by side (not so strange today, if one imagines the atomic physicist heaving spilt salt over his shoulder at the breakfast table).

[68] Wilder, "Social Factors . . . ," p. 76. Reprint by permission of Quadrangle Books from *Early Christian Origins* edited by Allen Wikgren, copyright © 1961 by Quadrangle Books, Inc.

There is much careful work that needs to be done on the literary features of eschatological language before its contours are fully understood. In the study of eschatology no less than in the study of other primitive Christian language, NT scholarship must hone its hermeneutical tools. The linguistic impact of eschatology's approach to reality is just beginning to attain adequate hearing. We who have heard from the poet (in this case a balladeer) that we are "on the eve of destruction," are perhaps more sympathetic toward primitive eschatology than were earlier generations. Perhaps the plurality of contemporary society will also be reflected in attempts to fully respect the diversities of eschatology, for eschatological expressions are often inconsistent with one another. They are often mytho-poeic. They sometimes verge on the dereliction of responsible theological discourse, something which occurs in later developments of Gnosticism as well as in Christian millenarianism.[69] But the primitive Christian eschatology is a world-founding language, and the subsequent progress of the church is a picture of the several language worlds of ancient society in rigorous competition.

There are no single linguistic characteristics that everyone can accept as delimiting what I have called a type of language on a par with symbol or metaphor. The usual approach is to treat eschatology as a matter of material content, and hence we have no historical treasury of noted linguistic traits. I am trying, however, to work out such criteria. Part of my working (and still tentative) typology for analyzing eschatological language is given here; I should first indicate in general terms that I take eschatological language to be that con-forming of language, content, and form, in which men evoke the dimensions of the future which, impinging upon their contemporary times, elicit comprehensions and expectations about the purposiveness of time and history. Such language understands itself as penultimately expressing a visionary wholeness uniting past experiences and anticipated futures. It is largely figurative language, richly textured with the language forms of symbols, images, and metaphors. And it is evaluative insofar as the present is brought before the critique of the possible.

It is my contention that we may trace a linear pattern of linguistic effectiveness: the pattern runs from primary creativity of expression, in which the fallability of present modes of conceiving and imagining is fully recognized and in which symbols and images are least specified, to a secondary, less effective level in which the openness and transitoriness

---

[69] An excellent study of the contrasts between the main lines of Christian development and the character of gnostic language is by Samuel Laeuchli, *The Language of Faith.* The arguments Professor Laeuchli expresses in his book and in personal conversations have impressed upon me the great difficulties with which patristic Christianity forged its linguistic tools.

of primary creativity gives way before desires to specify, to concretize, to delimit, and to make explicit. There may be a chronological progression from the one to the other level in a particular society, but I do not consider this to be a necessary development, and in a piece of eschatological writing like the Apocalypse to John, I find both levels at once.

The following typology represents my current exploration of the characteristics of eschatological language. I foresee, eventually, a rather formidable cross-referencing and classification system for comparing eschatological writings in which a particular writing or statement can be described in meta-language (positive valences in IA2, IB4, IIA2, IIB3 . . . , negative in IA3 . . . etc.), but that must wait a while. For any eschatological statement, I would explore the following matters:

I. Temporal Evaluation
   A. Evaluation of past
      1. Cosmic, universal perspective; parochial, nationistic, racial perspective
      2. Periodization in historiography (millenia, interim kingdoms, Two Ages)
      3. Importance of primordial or eventual period (creation imagery; primal time: end time correlation)
      4. Cosmological historical survey, ethically-religiously weighted
   B. Present in relation to future or eschaton
      1. When is eschaton? (purely future, partly realized or initiated, anticipatory, prolepsis, wholly realized already)
      2. Immediacy of the end ("existential" reality impinging upon everyday; merely a convention)
      3. Identification of beginnings, continuation, conclusion of end-period
      4. What follows "the End"?
   C. Day of the Lord
      1. Relationship to (prophetic) origins of the concept
      2. Stages of development of the concept
      3. Forms: Day . . . of the Lord, . . . of Jesus Christ, . . . of Wrath, . . . of God, . . . of Judgment; absolute: The Day
   D. Parousia concepts (immediate expectation, eventual culmination of historical processes)
II. Purposive Projection
   A. Argument for order, purpose, structure
      1. Relationship to classical paradigmatic events ("creation," exodus, exile, rebirth)
      2. Rationale for suffering of elect, for the witness (palliative, bolstering)

    3. Determinism vs. freedom of action (astrology, fatalism)
    4. Pessimistic or optimistic view of historical process
  B. Theodicy (justification of evil)
    1. Problem of evil; source of evil—how explained?
    2. Evil or suffering as just recompense, judgment (present vs. future; cosmic judgment)
    3. Victory of the righteous
    4. Righteous as enforcing justice (messianic militia)
  C. Reigning (Kingdom) of God
    1. Spatial or temporal conception
    2. Nationalistic overtones
    3. Rule of the Elevated/Resurrected/Enthroned One
    4. As ethical norm for behavior (exhortation, admonition)
  D. Utopian projection
    1. Moral perfectionism
    2. Societal reconstitution
    3. Righteous ones as demonstrating God's election
III. Conditions of End-period
  A. Political vs. Idealized Future
    1. Rebellion; conquering "the nations"
    2. As spiritual ideal; as rallying-point for action
  B. Position of Evil and Good
    1. Messianic woes
    2. Messianic militia; new covenant people; or new idealized Israel
    3. Overcoming of evil forces
    4. Individual's place in end and future
  C. New Revelation (mystery, secret plans, messianic torah, secret book, scrolls, seals)
  D. Cosmological changes
    1. Compartmentalizing (heaven, hell, etc.)
    2. Sun darkening, cosmic transmutations
  E. Life after death
    1. General resurrection of believers
    2. Hellish torments for the evil
    3. Rule of the elect
IV. Agencies Responsible for Eschatological Events
  A. Pluralities of agencies: angelology, demonology, astral powers, evil powers of the world; functions: persecution, messengers, avengers, rulers, misleaders
  B. Dualisms: light/darkness; gods/devils; false/true signs or messiahs
  C. Messianism
    1. Individual figure: messiah, son of man, others
    2. Group figure: new Israel, God's people

      3. Antichrist figures

  D. Preparatory eschatological groups (ascetic, libertinist)

V. Contexts

  A. Location within tradition history of eschatology (suggested progression: prophets; wisdom; Jewish apocalyptic, canonical, Essenes, apocryphal and pseudepigraphical; Christian eschatology: Jesus, Paul, early Catholic; Christian apocalyptic; rabbinical eschatological; gnostic apocalyptic; "establishment" eschatology)

  B. Sources (extent of extra-Israelite influences, such as Iranian)

  C. Modifications in transmission

  D. Acceptance: esoteric or popular

  E. How understood by writer? How much influence of tradition (lively? conventional? dead?)

  F. Relationships to actual socioeconomic matrices

  G. In cross-cultural view (Pacific cargo-cults, Amerindian Ghost Dance)

VI. Literary Description

    (The ways in which the above are expressed, but also the forms giving rise to new thoughts and expressions; the mutual interpenetration of concepts and forms; and then the "loading" due to use of already established [traditional] forms and images.)

  A. Imagic and imaginative language

    1. Mythopoeic expressiveness

    2. Symbolism (animate figures, non-animate figures)

    3. Sensual imagery (sounds, sights, smells, etc.)

    4. Traditional images (prophetic, later)

  B. Conventions: visions, pseudo-ecstasy, pseudonymity, historical surveys, symbols

  C. Numerology; Astrological material

  D. Mythological figures, stories, legends

  E. Specific forms (symbolic utterances, blessings, wisdom sayings, farewell discourses, prayers, paraenesis, poetry, liturgical fragments)

  F. Larger forms: the apocalypse (differences between "books," apocalypses, passages)

  G. Self-consciousness of being in particular "style," "content," or "form"; patterning, mixed forms

  H. Sociological nexus of form (liturgy, apology, etc.)

5

Primitive Christianity
and Interpretation Today

We are in a position now to look at the overall perspectives that produced early Christian literature. We have discussed the ways NT scholars probe the materials to disclose the various tendencies at work, and we have looked at the types of language; now we can begin to show the whole scope of the literary movement, dwelling once more on the kerygma, and including the impact of the larger literary types (genres). The second half of the chapter includes personal perspectives on how one moves from literary analysis—the primary focus of this book —into the complex discipline of NT theology.

EARLY CHRISTIAN LITERATURE

What happened in primitive Christianity was a new sense of orientation to reality. Primitive Christianity represents a new orientation to the world, and hence we must speak of a new language, since language and world are coextensive. The eschatological fervor of the early Christians may well represent the specific impetus that produced the new orientation: aware of living in a new aeon, the Christians forged a new literary form, the gospel, and adapted Hellenistic-Jewish epistolary conventions in a new way. That which belonged to the old aeon was not sufficiently tensed to serve the new. A people does not lightly break all bonds with the past, however, and Christianity found a way to have its cake and eat it too by claiming to have the *true* understanding of Scripture. All that was old was claimed as being at best an anticipation of what was new;

hence from then on Christians distinguished *Old* and New Testaments, although a neutral acronym from the tripartite division of the Jewish scriptures, Tanak, was available.

When we look carefully at the NT literature, we see quite a range of literary and theological impulses. To be sure, the eschatological understanding was the basic qualifier, but unless we are to subsume everything under the one unifying rubric of "eschatology,"[1] we must pay heed to many activities in which the many-faceted organism of primitive Christianity began to take shape and form. Such activities were carried out entirely within the sensitivities of the new eschatological outlook, but they are not necessarily comprehended by the specific themes, topics, and language of eschatology per se. The literary materials of the NT represent the reflection of the life of the early churches, molded and shaped by the needs and interests of those communities, as well as (in their present form) by groupings of traditions and individual authors.

We must take account of a wide range of activities, including preaching and instruction, formation of creeds and materials for worship, and propaganda and theological reflection. A literature is being formed, but for the most part it is formed almost as an afterthought, for of central prominence in the early church was the vivid immediate apprehension of the Spirit of God, once again conceived of as operative, creative. The early church regarded itself as having inherited the gift of the Spirit in the eschatological last days (claiming the fulfillment upon them of the promise in Joel 2: "I will pour my spirit on all flesh"), and this meant two things: first, the immediacy of the Spirit signified the presence of the Christ. The Christ about whom these documents speak was not a figure of historical significance in the past, but was rather the present, living Lord, Christ-with-us-today. Hence any sort of writing could only be an indirect reflection of this immediacy. Second, because of this vivid eschatological spirituality, there was a certain reserve about writing down anything at all.

---

[1] The recent book by Jürgen Moltmann, *The Theology of Hope. On the Ground and the Implications of a Christian Eschatology*, trans. J. W. Leitch (New York and Evanston: Harper & Row, Publishers, 1967), appears to me to represent just such an exaggerated position. Moltmann's criticism of recent movements within theology are incisively sharpened by his wide-reaching grasp of historical method, but I wonder if he has done much more than that for which he criticizes existentialist interpretation—advance *his* eschatological thematic (the theology of *hope*) as the way primitive Christian theology really ought to be read. The excitement of this book—an excitement more concisely borne out in his "Toward a Political Hermeneutic of the Gospel" (see Chap. 2, n. 48)—is the same excitement at engaging the contemporary situation as the fulfilled gesture of hermeneutics now familiar to us from existentialist interpretation. The corrective implicit in the book—that existentialist interpretation's romantic emphasis upon the individual must be re-formed into a more substantial concentration upon values of the societal matrices—begins to take on depth in the article.

It could be said of the Law (for example in late-biblical Judaism) that God *had spoken*—man's task was to explain and study this residue of his speaking. But in primitive Christianity it was felt that the Spirit *speaks* now and directly. What was written down participated in the Spirit's contemporaneity. In the NT, then, we encounter the power of language in a very primary sense, and this is reflected in the fact that the NT is only comprehensible by sensing the immediacy of the oral word that lies not only behind it but also alongside it.

Oral word continued to have pride of place in the later development of the early church, reflecting further the fact that the basic character of Christian communication was preaching (proclamation) and story telling (narrative; Wilder calls it "the basic mode of speech"). Even into the time of Augustine (fourth century c.e.), those who could recall Words of Jesus (*Logia Jesu*) or the sayings of the Apostles were highly honored as being able to vouch for and supplement the written accounts. Papias (Bishop of Hierapolis, end of the second century) collected every scrap of information from the earliest days of Christianity under the following rubric: "I did not think that what was to be gotten from books would profit me as much as what came to me from the living and abiding voice."[2]

All the modes of early Christian writing were closely related to oral discourse, although in later generations the literary form tended to become more conventionalized and its oral quality suppressed. This is especially true under the theological influence of those who, like Luke, were apprehensive about guaranteeing the tradition and were therefore more concerned with the authenticity of tradition than with its relationship to primal, oral situations.

But the direct, verbal communication also began to be less effective. Congregations arose in widely dispersed areas—beyond the control of Jerusalem-based leaders. Conflict arose between those who wanted to remain both Jews and Christians and those who wanted to utilize only some of the Christian beliefs along the lines of their own sects. Misuse of the traditions called for stabilization. A written word could be passed on when an oral word was impossible; indeed the size of the growing church, the need for controlling the use of the traditions, and the tendency to omit and forget some of the traditions pressed toward the written word as that which would shape the oral word. Hence we have the development of a literature.

---

2 As reported in Eusebius, Ecclesiastical History 3.39.4. Note the role within Judaism of the oral laws (toroth) supplementing the written Law (Torah); such oral materials, which were formalized and written down in the Babylonian Talmud and Palestinian Talmud, seem to have been generated primarily in the exilic and post-exilic periods—precisely the time when the written Torah was becoming established.

Jesus' words were collected at an early stage, along with resumés of the significance of Jesus. We have parts of the collections of Jesus' sayings in such gospel sources as Q, M, and L.† A coordinated presentation of Jesus' words and deeds, woven together according to particular patterns of belief, represents the next stage in dealing with the traditions. Now we have *gospels,* or booklets summarizing what was considered essential about the career and teachings of Jesus—especially in the interpretive theological framework of the kerygma. Since some argue that the kerygmatic outlines were of major importance as frameworks for the organization of the gospels, it will be helpful to explore a bit further the supposed nature of this kerygma.

In 1935 Charles Henry Dodd published *The Apostolic Preaching,*[3] a small book that was to have great influence upon NT research, for it argued that the most important aspect of primitive Christianity, so far as its eventual literary production was concerned, was not so much teaching (*didache*) as preaching (*kerygma*).

Dodd felt that Paul shaped his life work around the features of the kerygma, and that the gospels were also formally determined by the kerygma. He summarized those passages of the NT that present the central aspects of the messianic occurrence, displaying in a large chart the similarity between "the kerygma according to the Acts of the Apostles" (representing the Petrine preaching to Palestinian Jews: Acts 2:14–39, 3:13–26, 4:10–12, 5:30–32, 10:36–43), and "the kerygma according to Paul" (representing the extra-Palestinian preaching as found in Acts 13:17–41 and in Galatians, Thessalonians, I Corinthians, and Romans). Six or seven central items of this kerygma were common to both types of kerygma, differences being explained by differences in theological emphasis. Paul's kerygmatic teaching outline was as follows:

1. The prophecies are fulfilled and the New Age is inaugurated by the coming of Christ.
2. He was born of the seed of David.
3. He died according to the Scriptures to deliver us out of the present evil age.
4. He was buried.
5. He rose on the third day according to the Scriptures.
6. He is exalted at the right hand of God, as Son of God and Lord of quick and dead.
7. He will come again as Savior and Judge of men.

† M and L are symbols for the source materials used by Matthew and Luke, in each case independently of each other, of Mark, and of Q. (On Q, see pp. 9, 103, and Glossary.)

[3] The quotations and outline which follow are from *The Apostolic Preaching and Its Development,* by C H Dodd (London: Hodder & Stoughton 1936). Used by permission of the author and publishers.

The main burden of the kerygmatic formulae in Paul and in the Petrine teaching is "that the unprecedented has happened. God has visited and redeemed His people."[4]

According to Dodd the early gospels, and especially Mark, are to be understood as sympathetic renditions of the apostolic preaching and do not exist merely for the sake of reporting or passing along dry facts. They exist for the sake of kerygma, for the sake of continuing God's work in the Christ. Even though Matthew and Luke began to include secondary theological reflections about eschatology and morality, their gospels are still essentially kerygmatic in nature.[5] In John the kerygma is most loosely tied to the actual teaching of the historical Jesus, but in John the kerygma is enriched to its greatest extent, and "we have the most penetrating exposition of its central meaning." (P. 75.)

Dodd's lectures were influential because they so clearly laid out the centrality of the kerygma in the formation and shaping of the gospels at a time when scholarship was ready for such an emphasis.[6] Especially in English-speaking scholarship, Dodd's name became synonymous with the technical-exegetical side of "kerygmatic theology," and the small *Apostolic Preaching* was regarded as one of its best exegetical supports. While Dodd was not about to say that "everything is kerygma," his book certainly argued the centrality of this element:

> The *kerygma* is primary, and it acted as a preservative of the tradition which conveyed the facts. The nearer we are in the Gospels to the stuff of the *kerygma*, the nearer we are to the fountain-head of the tradition. There never existed a tradition formed by a dry historical interest in the

[4] Dodd, p. 33. Robert M. Montgomery and W. Richard Stegner have produced a programmed-learning booklet, *Kerygma* (Nashville and New York: Abingdon Press, 1970), which trains the student with no theological background to be able to recognize the stresses and uses of kerygmatic passages. According to these authors, the successive principles of the kerygma are:

1. The new things that are happening fulfill the scriptures.
2. The new age was started by the life and death of Jesus.
3. God raised Jesus from the dead.
4. Jesus has been exalted to the realm of God.
5. The Holy Spirit is now being given in the new age.
6. Men must repent.
7. Jesus is coming again.

[5] See Dodd, p. 53: "Matthew is, in fact, no longer in the pure sense a 'Gospel.' It combines *kerygma* with *didache,* and if we regard the book as a whole, the element of *didache* predominates."

[6] See esp. Dibelius' emphasis upon preaching. See also Bultmann, *Theology* (see index and both Vols., esp. I, 86ff., 96, 105 f., 307); N. A. Dahl, "Formgeschichtliche Beobachtungen zur Christusverkündigung in der Gemeindepredigt," in *Neutestamentliche Studien für R. Bultmann* (Berlin: Töpelmann, 1957, 2nd ed.), pp. 3–9, supplementing Bultmann, p. 106; C. F. Evans, "The Kerygma," *JournTheolStud* N.S. 7(1956), 25–41; and Conzelmann, *An Outline of the Theology of the New Testament.*

facts as facts. From the beginning the facts were preserved in memory and tradition as elements in the Gospel which the Church proclaimed. (Pp. 55–56.)

The emphasis upon the centrality of kerygma in the tradition history of the early church was a necessary theological emphasis and a corrective to liberal theology's assimilation of Jesus and the early church into its own vested interests in interpreting the life of Jesus. It was a helpful emphasis within the more literary and historical phases of NT research as well, insofar as it directed attention to the hidden agendas and the nuances behind the primitive Christian writings. It especially made scholars conscious of the redactional tendencies in early Christian writings and of the extent to which theological (and not biographical or historical) interests had shaped the materials. It is obvious, however, that not everything in the NT is exclusively kerygmatic. There are many passages that can be assimilated to "proclamation" only by the most forceful of interpretive sleights-of-hand. In the middle decades of our own century, and especially because of the attempt to bring to expression the fuller ranges of intentionalities lying in and behind the texts, exegetical attention has been focused on contexts such as liturgy and worship, missionary and propagandizing enterprises, catechetical instruction, and what may simply be called delight in narrative.

These contexts are especially represented in the materials in the NT outside the synoptic gospels, and to complete our tradition-historical sketch of the development of early Christian literature, we must summarize how the additional materials made their appearance. The Pauline epistles have chronological priority over the gospels and have not been discussed before now simply because of convenience of arrangement: that is, they are attempts to reflect and work out the significance of the new Christian world view that was rooted in the experiences surrounding Jesus. The letters contain theological reflections, practical instructions, liturgical formulations, missionary advice, and other materials Paul brought together in his own unique ways. Almost every passage in Paul's letters is to be understood as oriented toward a particular religious context; Paul attempted to hear the Christian message within the contexts he addressed. He both selected from the living traditions he knew and acted independently, creating new traditions. Paul's letters seem to have been collected and published by the end of the first century.

As we move into the second century, there are other developments: the Gospel of John interpreted the Jesus materials in a way that brought primary focus upon the meaning of the Christ-events and only secondary focus upon reproducing materials from the life of Jesus of Nazareth. Someone in John's name wrote short theological tracts about issues involved in forming the Christian style of life (I, II, III John). And someone else named John brought the interpretation of the Christ-events into another stream of religious writing, apocalyptic eschatology, writing the Apocalypse to John (usually termed the Revelation to John). This book shows very clearly that there were many attempts to portray Christianity within the religious matrices and expectations of the Hellenistic-Jewish world views.

To carry our survey further, Luke extended his Gospel further into a second volume, a chronicle of the primitive Church according to Luke's ideal of the new Time of the Church—namely the book of the Acts of the Apostles. The book really ought to be called something like The Sacred History of Primitive Christianity, for Luke did not use the literary genre familiar in Hellenism under the name of acts (*acta*); the title accrued to the book at a later date than its composition.

Other lines of interpretation were influential in other writings: Hebrews interpreted Jesus as the (Jewish) High Priest who had now finally performed a necessary sacrificial offering for mankind. Colossians interpreted the Christ in relation to cosmic powers. Then as we move well into the second century, further epistles were written. Because of the prominence of Paul, these were slavishly styled after his letters and may be called the Pseudo-Pauline writings (usually termed the Pastoral Letters; I and II Timothy, Titus). Already we have evidence that the period of primary creativity and adjustment is past, and these writers so missed the point of early Christian theologies that they contradict the earlier eschatology, faith, and ethics. We no longer have small groups fervently awaiting the End of time, with the Lord's return, but an ongoing religious structure that must be cultivated. In the so-called Catholic or Universal Letters (I and II James, Jude; usually also I, II, and III John), we have a lasting, structurally defined Institution. There are officials who "preside" and those who "teach" as career occupations; and there is "doctrine" to be believed.

Our survey, a sort of miniature tradition history of the whole early Christian canonical literature, must come to a halt, but not before mention of writings that did not make the canon. The NT Apocrypha are writings with varying claims to authority which were finally rejected by patristic Christianity in the fourth century; among them are writings of similar types to the NT literature. Some of the apocrypha, like the Gospel of Thomas, now have claim to serious attention, especially as we see that the central issue is how traditions are interpreted (rather than where they originated).

NT scholarship has explored many of the various types of materials in addition to kerygmatic materials of an explicit nature, and the synoptic traditions. Those given special attention in this century include: credal formulations,[7] catechetical and general instruction and teaching,[8] moral exhortation (paraenesis),[9] and cultic and worship materials.[10]

A full tradition history of the primitive Christian literature would need to encompass many more internal and external matters than can this brief sketch, but there are several "thrusts" or motives that deserve attention. There is, for instance, continued interest in apologetics.[11] We are not on certain ground until we encounter the full Hellenistic literary type, the formal apology, in the later Christian Fathers, but certainly much of Luke's writing fulfilled an apologetic purpose: he even has Paul present in mini-apology at Athens (Acts 17). The controversy dialogues in the gospels are to be understood in terms of their use in apologetic dialogue and encounter; and J. Louis Martin has recently argued that the gospel of John portrays the attempts of some early Christians to develop their Christian identity vis-à-vis contemporary Judaism.[12]

---

[7] Passages such as I Cor 8:6, I Tim 3:16. See R.P.C. Hanson, *Tradition in the Early Church* (London: SCM Press Ltd., 1962), esp. Chap. 2, "The Creed"; Oscar Cullmann, *The Earliest Christian Confessions* (London: 1949); J. N. D. Kelly, *Early Christian Creeds* (London: 1950); and Vernon H. Neufeld, *The Earliest Christian Confessions* (Leiden: E. J. Brill, 1963); also Zimmermann, *Neutestamentliche Methodenlehre*, pp. 192–202, on Ro 1:3–4.

[8] M. H. Bolkestein, "Die synoptischen Evangelien als Lehrstoff in der Katechese," *NovTest* 8(1966), 85–94; Gottfried Schille, "Bemerkungen zur Formgeschichte des Evangeliums," *NTStud* 4(1957–58), 1–24, 101–114, 5(1958), 1–11.

[9] In addition to generalized paraenetic materials (see Dibelius, *From Tradition to Gospel*, Chap. 9, entitled "Paränese" in the German ed.), three specific types are often specified: (1) *Haustafeln*, lists of household duties, as Col 3:18–4:1 and Eph. 5:21–6:9; (2) *Gemeindetafeln*, concerning duties in the church congregations, as I Tim 5:1–21 and I Peter 2:13–3:7; and (3) Catalogues of vices and virtues, as Col 3:5–14 and Gal 5:19–23. See Hartwig Thyen, *Der Stil der Jüdisch-Hellenistischen Homilie* (Göttingen: Vandenhoeck & Ruprecht, 1955), other studies by S. Wibbing, K. Weidinger, A. Vögtle; in English: O. J. F. Seitz, "Lists, Ethical," *Interpreter's Dictionary of the Bible*, III(1962),137–139.

[10] See esp. Oscar Cullmann, *Early Christian Worship*, trans. A. S. Todd and J. B. Torrance (London: SCM Press Ltd., 1953); C. F. D. Moule, *The Birth of the New Testament* (New York and Evanston: Harper & Row, Publishers, 1962); Moule, "The Intention of the Evangelists," Appendix II, in *The Phenomenon of the New Testament* (London: SCM Press Ltd., n.d.), 100–114; Joachim Jeremias, *The Eucharistic Words of Jesus*, trans. Norman Perrin (New York: Charles Scribner's Sons, rev. ed., 1966); and Edgar Krentz, "The Early Dark Ages of the Church—Some Reflections," *ConcTheolMon* 41(1970), esp. 73–85 (hymnic materials). Explicit materials may include: Lk 1, 2 (early Christian psalms), Hebr 13:20–21 (blessing), II Peter 5:11 (liturgical fragment?), Mt 28 (missionary commissioning), Jude 24–25 (ascription), I Cor 11:23 ff. (eucharistic), I Peter (baptismal sermon?), James (Christianized Jewish homily?), Eph 5:14 and I Tim 3:16 (hymn fragments).

[11] Apology, apologetic, come from the Greek *apologia*, meaning a defense (as Plato's justification of the death of Socrates, in his *Apology*). As a rhetorical device, an apology begins by stating the points on which the audience and the speaker find ready agreement, and moves on to justify a new position as being consistent with those points.

[12] *History and Theology in the Fourth Gospel* (New York and Evanston: Harper & Row, Publishers, 1968).

Theodore J. Weeden argues that there is an apologetic interest in the gospel of Mark: we should say an anti-heretical interest, for Weeden thinks Mark fabricated an opposition between Jesus and his disciples in order to excoriate heretical tendencies represented by members of his own congregation.[13]

The importance of history writing has also come into prominence recently: for a long time it looked as if NT scholarship was so entranced with the realization that it did not have to be ashamed of early Christian historiography—that the primitive Christian literature answered in terms of "witness," "confession," "proclamation," rather than being merely some sort of shoddy historical writing—that it would ignore or suppress that which seems rather obviously written for the simple purpose of recording what it was that had happened.

It was due to the impact of such studies as Hans Conzelmann's *The Theology of St. Luke* and to the conservatives' insistent rejection of the creativity of the Christian communities that more substantive attention is now given to materials written because of the desire "to write history." Of course such a desire looked rather different then than it would now,[14] but NT scholars are now more fully aware of the legitimacy of NT historiography and less inclined to continually refer to kerygma.

One influence upon the development of the primitive Christian literature that is just coming into view might be identified as that of "the genres themselves."[15] Certainly once a gospel had been written, the impulse to do it again was present; and doubtless the same situation applied with the letter, the apocalypse, and the history. A glance at the NT Apocrypha, however, discloses that some forms were not often copied: the *acta* of the apocrypha are not similar to the Acts of the NT, but to the Hellenistic *acta*, representing precisely the romantic, chatty type of spiritualizing and pious biography that is lacking in the NT materials. There are few apocryphal letters, although in the first centuries of Christian literary development, the letter form dominated the field.[16]

The gospels stand out in the progression of primitive Christian literature because of their length and because of their inclusiveness. The

[13] "The Heresy That Necessitated Mark's Gospel," *ZeitNTWiss* 59(1968), 145–158.

[14] Much of what the Hellenistic writer called history we should judge absolutely tendentious; see the selections in Arnold J. Toynbee, trans., *Greek Historical Thought from Homer to the Age of Heraclius* (New York: New American Library, 1964, orig. ed. 1952); see also William A. Beardslee, *Literary Criticism of the New Testament* (Philadelphia: Fortress Press, 1970), Chap. 4, "History as a Form."

[15] The focus on the self-conscious genre "gospel" is reflected in the fact that the Gospels Seminar of the Society of Biblical Literature, in its annual 1970 meeting, featured both a session on "Aretalogy [the story of a hero or miracle-worker] and the Gospel," and a Task Group on the Gospel as Genre. See also note 17.

[16] Doty, *The Epistle in Late Hellenism and Early Christianity* (Diss., Drew University, 1966), Chaps. 2 and 4.

canonical gospels all maintain the same general picture of the development of Jesus' career, as well as Jesus' message and impact. These are filtered through the theologies of the evangelists' communities to produce a literary genre that is not just a "life" of the religious hero, not just a collection of his sayings, and not just a contemporary volume of theological reflection.

It is a widely accepted axiom of NT studies that the literary form that served to dramatize, elaborate, and to specify the sequence of the christological events, together with the teachings of Jesus—in short, the gospel form—is a unique literary creation of some early Christian or of some early Christian community. To be sure, parallels to certain aspects of these writings are to be found within the Judaeo-Graeco-Roman religious milieu.[17] But the full-fledged gospel-form defined by the Christian gospels, such as Mark, is no direct descendent of any of these. Much as the first widespread use of the codex as a form of publishing can be traced to the needs of the early Christian communities, and as the ordinary slangy (*koine*) Greek was taken up in such a way that an ecclesiastical Greek (and later an ecclesiastical Latin) was elaborated, so the early Christian gospels took hold of a number of received traditional literary patterns and revamped them for their own purposes.

The specifically new qualities of the gospel were not really pursued until the development of NT literary criticism, with its emphasis upon comparisons of literary genres.[18] In the works of K. L. Schmidt and Martin Dibelius, especially, it was sensed that there is something about the gospel form that can be identified and laid out in such a way as to provide a basis of comparison with other similar literary creations. In Schmidt's and Dibelius' work, and in subsequent scholarship, what has begun to come to light is that the most striking of the larger literary types of primitive Christianity is more complex than had been supposed. We are beginning to have some sense of its dynamics, although conscious attention to the gospel form as such is a relatively new contribution; hopefully we will soon have more adequate analyses at our disposal. It would be quite an undertaking, for example, to follow through such richly programmatic suggestions as the following:

> Julius Schniewind: ". . . our synoptic gospels are—even in their final shape—still a form of primitive Christian kerygma."
> Amos N. Wilder: ". . . the gospel action is not a history so much as a ritual enactment or mimesis."

[17] See Moses Hadas and Morton Smith, *Heroes and Gods. Spiritual Biographies in Antiquity* (New York and Evanston: Harper & Row, 1965), and Dibelius, "The Structure . . . ."

[18] See for instance the brilliantly perceptive analysis of the need for attention to the gospel genre in Julius Schniewind, "Zur Synoptiker-Exegese," *TheolRund* N.F. 2(1930),129–189.

Helmut Koester: the gospel is "an extension of the kerygma of Jesus' passion and resurrection." (Compare Wrede's famous description of Mark as a passion narrative with an introduction.)

We can only hope that the gospel (seen as constituting a literary whole) will soon have its rightful chronicler and critic. A number of preliminary studies have paved the way, but several factors still need to be determined with care: the contours of the gospel, the matter of the sources used, the lasting problem of synoptic relationships, the function of the gospels in early Christian usage, the question as to what constitutes the "core" of the gospels, and finally, the way theological reflection has molded and shaped the gospel presentations.

We have some excellent analyses of the term "gospel,"[19] as well as summary presentations of the ways in which the gospels attained their present shapes; but what is needed is more precise characterization of how the actual contours of "gospel" took shape and what precisely characterizes the genre. If we are to continue to claim that the gospel is a unique literary creation, we need to have clearer ways of defining the nature of the gospel form.

There is also the unanswered question of why the primitive Christians were not satisfied with pre-Christian literary forms, and even the question of why the gospel form remained at the center of attention when other forms became popular. The relevance of Graeco-Roman and specifically Jewish sources for comparative analysis of the gospels has long been recognized. Obviously primitive Christian communities and authors had access to traditional materials coming from several cultural and religious backgrounds. The use of Jewish scriptural materials in forging the passion narrative or the birth stories of Jesus, for instance, has been exhaustively studied; more recent studies are pursuing the relationship of the synoptic gospels and John to other types of Jewish materials such as scripture exegesis and argumentation and wisdom traditions.

The synoptic gospels with John present a fascinating archive for the study of a particular religion in antiquity, since we have here the most unusual situation of several accounts of one basic phenomenon. How these accounts are interrelated, and whether or not they were based on a preliminary outline of some sort remains a question.[20] And we still need

---

[19] See Gerhard Friedrich, *Theological Dictionary of the New Testament* II(1964) 707; Martin Albertz, *Die Botschaft des Neuen Testaments* (Zollikon-Zürich: Evangelischer Verlag, I.1, 1947; I.2, 1952); W. Schniewind, *Evangelion. Ursprung und erste Gestalt des Begriffs Evangelium* (Gütersloh: 1927, 1931); and Marxsen, *Mark the Evangelist*, Chap. 3.

[20] See for instance Otto A. Piper, "The Origin of the Gospel Pattern," *Journ BibLit* 78(1959),115–124; Štefan Porúbčan, "Form Criticism and the Synoptic Problem," *NovTest* 7(1964),81–118; O. J. F. Seitz, "Gospel Prologues: A Common Pattern?" *JournBibLit* 83(1964),262–8. The questions are raised again in the context

clarity about the process of development of the gospel elaboration: was it simply a process "of the filling out of a given kerygmatic framework with the narrative material about Jesus and the traditional sayings of the Lord?"[21]

Attention to the actual use of the gospels by the early church has been confined by and large to the use of the gospels by the church fathers. We might more profitably explore the ways and frequency of use of gospel materials in the earlier period just following their "publication." The exploration of this tradition history is just beginning to be carried out, as is the exploration of redaction-critical nuances brought to bear by the evangelists and their communities.

The genre of epistolary literature has recently returned to the forefront of NT scholarship, as witnessed by the 1970 formation of a continuing working seminar on The Form and Function of the Pauline Letters in the professional Society of Biblical Literature. A number of recent studies has brought into prominence the formal dimensions of Paul's letter form. Robert W. Funk, for example, proposes that the following outline would have been in Paul's mind as he wrote (demonstrated in I Thessalonians and Philemon):[22]

Funk's Analysis	*Illustrated in I Thessalonians*	*Illustrated in Philemon*
1. *Salutation*	1:1	vv. 1–3
a. Sender	Paul, Silvanus and Timothy	
b. Addressee	to the church of the Thessalonians	
c. Greeting	Grace to you and peace . . .	
2. *Thanksgiving*	1:2–10 we give thanks to God always (+2:13 ff., 3:9 ff.)	4–6

---

of redaction-critical analyses and source analysis in several essays in David G. Buttrick, ed., *Jesus and Man's Hope,* Vol. I (Pittsburgh: Pittsburgh Theological Seminary, 1970).

[21] Conzelmann, *The Theology of St. Luke,* p. 12; see also Dodd, "The Framework of the Gospel Narratives," *ExposTimes* 43(1932), 396–400.

[22] See esp. *Language,* Chap. 10, "The Letter: Form and Style," and "Saying and Seeing: Phenomenology of Language and the New Testament," *JournBibRel* 34(1966),207–213. I have also consulted two unpublished papers: "Form Criticism, Literary Criticism, and the Phenomenology of Language," 1964, and "The Problem of the Integrity of I Corinthians," 1963. See also "The Form and Structure of II and III John," *JournBibLit* 86(1967),424–430; "The Apostolic *Parousia:* Form and Significance," in *Christian History and Interpretation: Studies Presented to John Knox,* ed. W. R. Farmer, C. F. D. Moule, and R. R. Niebuhr (New York: Cambridge University Press, 1967), 249–268.

Funk's Analysis	Illustrated in I Thessalonians	Illustrated in Philemon
3. (Theological) *Body*		
a. Formal opening	2:1–12 Background of relationships and purpose of ministry	7–19
b. Connective and Transitional Formulae	2:13–16 Eschatological era	
c. Eschatological Climax	breaking in	20–21
d. Travelogue (apostolic parousia)	2:17–3:8 Plans to visit	22
4. *Paraenesis (Ethical Exhortation)*	4:1–5:22 Moral requirements; sanctification; eschatological teachings	(lacking, but see 21)
5. *Closing*		23–25
a. Greetings	5:26 Greet all the brethren	
b. Doxology	23 May the God of peace . . .	
c. Benediction	28 The grace of our Lord . . .	

Congruence with this Form

I Thess	Perfect
Philemon	Perfect, except no paraenesis
Galatians	All elements except thanksgiving and greeting/benediction—modified order
Romans	All elements; modified order
I Cor, Phil	Paraenesis and closing missing

The importance of understanding what sort of form may have been natural to Paul is manifold: (a) We are provided with a more or less standard pattern according to which Paul intended to organize his writing (sequence analysis). (b) This is of great importance with regard to those letters such as I and II Corinthians, or Philippians, which have either been composed of several letters or have been rearranged in the process of being collected and copied. (c) Hence formal analysis is of importance for judging questions of authenticity: we may have a sense of what *should* have been included in a genuine Pauline letter as well as noting how the pseudo-Pauline letters do or do not imitate the Pauline form. (d) Such analysis provides important insights into the structure and theology of any particular letter, as when an expected element is lacking and we recognize that its function has appeared in another segment of the letter (for example Galatians, in which the Thanksgiving is omitted because impatient Paul was so upset with the Galatian church that he rushed directly into his treatment of the problem of freedom). (e) **The** relative weight of particular theological arguments in Paul's writings can be judged from the location within the formal structure of a particular letter (for example ethical or paraenetic discussions are dependent, in Paul's letters, upon the main theological developments in the Body of the letters). (f) Paul's own writing habits can be compared with those of his contemporaries, and we can begin to comprehend the ways primitive Christianity modified the literary traditions of its environment.

Additional features of the Pauline letters are being analyzed today as seldom before; the emphasis has shifted from the mainly theological analysis (as in Bultmann, *Theology of the New Testament*) to analysis of such factors as Paul's use of traditional materials and phraseology, his exegesis of scripture, his style (especially vis-à-vis Graeco-Roman epistolography), the influence of Paul's Judaic background, and the ways Pauline thought developed in dialogue and in tension with members of churches he addressed and his opponents.[23] Once the scholarly world has obtained some clarity on these issues, we may expect similar broad-scale inquiry into the post-Pauline letters in early Christianity.

NEW TESTAMENT THEOLOGY TODAY

A final aspect of NT interpretation to be discussed is the discipline and methodology of NT Theology—no simple task, because the way any "biblical theology" is to be conducted today presents a real question. A good many NT scholars would leave NT Theology to the theologians— they understand their own work to be fenced off from contact with contemporary developments in religious belief. While I share this view, by and large, my understanding of the hermeneutical circle is such that I do not think the NT scholar can avoid asking how his interpretations are "heard" by his contemporaries. This asking need not be done exclusively within perspectives of the Christian religion, because it is a matter of interpretation as such.

Furthermore, I conceive of NT Theology as being that aspect of NT scholarship that studies how the theologies within the primitive Christian writings are formulated and interrelated. The discipline will then be seen to deal primarily with the theologies of the NT in a phenomenological mode of questioning. In this section I reflect upon the tasks and func-

---

[23] The best popular summary of the status quo of contemporary scholarship is Günther Bornkamm, *Paul;* the range of technical problems was surveyed by Nils A. Dahl, "The Pauline Letters: Proposal for a Study Project . . . ," circulated at the October 1970 meeting of the Society of Biblical Literature. I engage some of these matters in *Letters in Primitive Christianity* (working title; forthcoming, 1972).

tions of such a discipline as it begins to gain some autonomy from normative or constructive Christian theologizing today.

Contemporary biblical theology portrays, no less than other forms of
contemporary theology, the attempt to reconcile the biblical mind with
the modern mind; "reconcile" however must not be taken to mean that
the process is simply one of matching situations or of "applying" a divine
word to "our situation." NT study in this century, in addition to its stress
on literary analysis, has stressed *theological* analysis: methodological procedures and types of historical approach have been discussed, but time
and time again the central activity has taken place in terms of the attempt to found a contemporary theology upon the theology "of the bible,"
or at least, to discover the appropriate categories for defining that biblical
theology.[24]

The names of those who are most highly respected in NT studies are
primarily names of those who have made specific methodological and exegetical contributions, to be sure, but who have also specialized in theological analysis (such as Bultmann, Conzelmann, Fuchs, Käsemann, and
Haenchen). Attention to the role of the theologies of the authors of the
biblical texts has been accompanied by attempts to develop contemporary
approaches to the biblical materials in such a manner that the original
contributions of these materials may be fully understood today.

In spite of significant advances and sophistications in theological
analysis, however, there are a number of questions as to the very nature
of the discipline at the present moment. Such questions include: How
does biblical theology make its appearance today? Is biblical theology
merely a process of reporting upon what the NT authors say? Is it sufficient to say that NT theology merely *reflects* what is present in the NT,
or does NT theology itself partake of the dynamic revisions of the hermeneutical circle? Does it somehow balance between Then (the theology
found in the bible) and Now (a theology based on the bible)? Is NT
theology influenced by the questions that face religions in the twentieth
century? Or does it stand clear of such contemporary problems?

My own initial response is to say that biblical theology cannot re-
strict itself to reportage: it cannot give us a photo album of how the
biblical authors performed theology in a manner that remains opaque to
our own concerns. We should be completely uninterested, I suspect, in
such a presentation: we would have little interest in such a picture other
than mere historical curiosity (unless our perspective be that of the biblicist who considers the periods of the bible to be the only inspired and
model-setting periods of history). NT theology cannot be considered to

---

[24] Brevard Childs, *Biblical Theology in Crisis;* Werner Georg Kümmel, *Die
Theologie des Neuen Testaments nach seinen Hauptzeugen* (Göttingen: Vandenhoeck
& Ruprecht, 1969), esp. pp. 11–16.

be a strictly "objective," reporting discipline,[25] but is rather a discipline that sympathetically reports on the NT theologizing. It need not be a religious or church discipline, working to secure religious institutions, but it must entail a certain amount of empathy with the NT church if it is to adequately comprehend that situation. I am especially in agreement with a statement by W. Paul Jones that: "Biblical interpretation requires that the biblical *meaning* be *experienced,* not necessarily as one's own, but experienced in a dramatic immediacy in which the subject-object distinction is transcended."[26]

Even if we agree that theology proper is found only at the furthest remove from primordial speaking, and if we accept the judgment that theologizing fails to elicit hope today because it is fossil language—trafficking in dead words—it cannot be said that NT theology is entirely composed of such trafficking. If it were, the whole enterprise would long ago have been foreclosed. We need not relinquish what has been done as Christian theologizing nor turn our backs abruptly upon the Christian or the Jewish history. We do not accept this history uncritically or un-creatively, but theology need not begin completely anew in each genera-tion—*cannot,* if it is to be a theology with historical relevance.

NT theology as interpretation has the massive and important task of revoicing the earliest Christian theology—the task of allowing that which was once lively to revive itself and be heard again. This revoicing need not be done for "religious" purposes, but it is a necessary task of the in-terpreter who wishes to listen accurately to his text. What happens is not, as Linnemann and Via have recently argued,[27] a repeating of the original language-events of the texts, although it may well be true that in the process of his analysis, the NT theologian will "hear" the "silence" of primordial discourse in such tonalities that he is able to re-speak it in his own day, and hence participate in more vital levels of language than are conventional.

Indeed there is no doubt but that interpretation itself may strike the hearer or reader with the impact of primary language, but in that case

---

[25] The contrary point of view is argued by Krister Stendahl, "Biblical Theology, Contemporary," *The Interpreter's Dictionary of the Bible* I(1962),418–432, and "Method in the Study of Biblical Theology," in *The Bible and Modern Scholarship,* ed. J. Philip Hyatt (Nashville and New York: Abingdon Press, 1965), pp. 198–209.

[26] "Aesthetics and Biblical Hermeneutics," *RelLife* 31(1962),404 (Abingdon Press).

[27] Eta Linnemann, *Jesus of the Parables,* trans. John Sturdy (New York and Evanston: Harper & Row, Publishers, 1967); Via, *The Parables.* See also Ernst Fuchs, "Must One Believe in Jesus if He Wants to Believe in God?," *Journal for Theology and the Church* I(1965), 165 (translation altered): "As theologians we should only be engaged in reflection [literally, after-thinking, *nach-denken*], without being able to determine before hand the boundaries of this reflection, since the truth of which we would like to speak remains entirely dependent upon its taking place."

what has happened is that the text's own primacy has come into its own or that the interpreter has himself been moved to speak in a primary mode. Insofar as interpretation carefully sets forth the primary text, it is secondary language, or even logical expression, which exists to expound the unfamiliar in terms of the familiar. When the hearer acknowledges himself grasped and challenged by the text, we may say that its language has regained its eventful potency in a secondary situation. But when the hearer experiences the text due to the interpreter's words and applications, we still have to speak of his ability to bring about *new* language events, not merely to repeat the original ones. Of course the whole situation is alive within the one movement from original text into our own situations. But we ought to distinguish between the original language event that is the text (assuming that "the text" has this character, though obviously many texts do not), and secondary language events that occur in subsequent situations, either as byproducts of competent exegesis or as the working out of the text's own life-stance and address in our own situations.

It is no longer as evident as it was to Bultmann and other kerygmatic theologians that the NT texts have for us the character of address (*Anrede*). To be sure, one must find some way to refer to the manner the material in certain texts "speaks" or addresses modern man, but there is impatience today with those who still speak of going to the bible to "get God's Word," which can then be proclaimed during the familiar Sunday hour originally set according to the schedule of the farmer's chores.[28]

Just before his death in a Nazi prison, Dietrich Bonhoeffer called for a "nonreligious" interpretation of scripture.[29] Perhaps such interpretation will strike us as appropriate when it is understood in the context of carefully delineating between the original situation, the accrued interpretations of successive Christian generations (the "religious" or "literal" interpretation, discussed below), and our own situation. Surely we are not called upon to reproduce the stance of antiquity. We have every right to be perfectly bored with Jordanian and Israeli advertising appeals to "walk where Jesus walked." And neither are we bound to the explicit

[28] The problem has to do with the credibility of the bible itself; see Herbert Braun, *The Problem of a New Testament Theology*, p. 176: "We are also able to grasp the oracular character of the Torah only as a phenomenon of the history of religion; for the concept of God which lies behind it (that there are holy texts full of profound divine meaning), is unattainable to us."

[29] See esp. *Letters and Papers from Prison* (London: SCM Press Ltd., 1953). The extent of the debate aroused by Bonhoeffer's use of this phrase may be seen in the fact that a 400-page collection of essays dealing with this subject is to be edited by Peter H. A. Neumann (Darmstadt: Wissenschaftliche Buchgesellschaft).

patterns of faith set by our honored mothers and fathers, for these are their patterns, not ours.

Difficulty has been caused by the very distance of ancient culture from our own—difficulty compounded by the fact that biblical language is richer, less logical, and possesses greater linguistic dynamics than our own daily language. We need little tutoring to attend to logical expression: the theological finesse of Hebrews or James does not strike us as difficult to understand. But we are ill at ease when we are rammed up against that which is not so literal—against that which is multi-valent in its imagery, or that which, like the early eschatology, represents an immediacy we do not share.

Our uneasiness may lead us to resort to allegory or some other method of interpretation in which we can specify "what it means" in no uncertain terms. Patristic exegesis knew this trick, especially when it linked the two sets of scripture: Justin tells us that the story of Noah is actually a prefiguring of the Christ and his wooden cross—after all, "Noah also was saved by wood, riding on the waters with his family."[30] In our own day, interpretation has become less arbitrary; in main-line Christianity and Judaism, at any rate, such fanciful exegesis would be laughed at today. But there are no fewer arbitrarily assigned interpretations, even if less fanciful, and they frequently go under the guise of being called (usually with arched eyebrows of the interpreters) the "literal truth." The literal interpretation or meaning is, however, the meaning that has become customary in a particular setting—it is establishment criticism, or in the popular usage, the "religious" interpretation.

The "literal" represents the fusion in our own world of description and convention: it is the one particular viewing specified by our milieu. When the literal meaning (or the conventional "religious" meaning) is sought, one usually seeks—albeit unconsciously and uncritically—a mixture of the real (what is really there, what matters) with what we have come to expect in terms of logic or convention. The literal is not that which really describes what is there so much as it represents the ways in which Mr. Everyman has traditionally, conventionally come to refer to it: in short, the literal is just as much a matter of cultural conditioning as is the allegorical.[31]

---

[30] *Dial.* 138.2, quoted by R. P. C. Hanson, *Allegory and Event* . . . (Richmond: John Knox Press, 1958), p. 104. See also similar examples in the same work, pp. 104–5, 107, 179, 214–15.

[31] Critic Northrop Frye notes that it is this uncritical acceptance of the conventional as the literal or as "realism" that frustrates the artist, since ". . . when the public demands likeness to an object, it generally wants the exact opposite, likeness to the pictorial convention it is familiar with." *Anatomy of Criticism,* by Northrop Frye (Copyright © 1957 by Princeton University Press; Princeton Paperback, 1971), p. 132, quoted by Funk, in his discussion of the "literal," "Myth and the Literal

Interpretation therefore not only involves recognition and appreciation of what is actually present in the text but also the necessity to rehear the text, which will often then be received as an anti-literal, unconventional, or even nonreligious interpretation. The biblical critic, especially, must expend a great deal of energy just convincing people of the necessity to position oneself critically toward one's own history. (The problem is particularly clear with reference to academic generations: Gerhard Ebeling remarked in class that the professor's students are always his pallbearers also.)

Interpretation today also involves restoring plurality and richness of signification to biblical language that has been unnaturally narrowed and arbitrarily specified. The interpreter finds it necessary to remind readers that the biblical language is better comprehended as metaphor than as theology. If theology specifies, defines, and stipulates, metaphor hints, beckons, and opens out onto a broad and loosely textured theatre. Metaphor (and I mean metaphoric language in the sense discussed above, not merely "shortened simile") has the unique ability to speak that which cannot fully enter discursive language; it gestures in the direction of its meaning, but does not permit a "literal" description of that to which it points. What is metaphorically expressed must be taken *as metaphor* lest what metaphor brings to expression vanish.

Since so much of the early Christian language is not easily reduced to an arbitrary set of theological points, and since such reduction only reflects our desires to have mastery over the texts, we must school ourselves to listen for the faint hint and the clue as much as to the discursive language. We must learn to catch the rich implications of figured language in its own dynamism; we must learn to recognize that some symbols, for instance, are used in a questioning mode—setting the listener on his ear and asking for his self-evaluation rather than "explaining."[32] In what we usually refer to as "nonliteral" language, we need to try to hear the echoes of a reality that is not less real for being said in ways that

---

Non-Literal," in Stoneburner, ed., *Parable, Myth, and Language*, p. 59. See also the careful article by Owen Barfield, "The Meaning of the Word 'Literal,'" in L. C. Knights and Basil Cottle, eds., *Metaphor and Symbol* (London: Butterworth's Scientific Publications, 1960). Barfield concludes (p. 57): "In this factual sense there is indeed no such thing as literalness. The most we can safely say, therefore, is that the literal and discursive use of language is the way in which it is used by a speaker, who is either unaware of, or is deliberately ignoring, that real and figurative relation between man and his environment, out of which the words he is using were born, and without which they could never have been born."

[32] The concept of "Israel" is surely such a symbol in the questioning mode—referring to that ultimate hope for human peace for which Jews, Christians, and others have sought throughout recorded history. And the "messianic banquet" of apocalyptic Judaism and primitive Christianity is similarly charged: by its implied perfection, it exposes the imperfection of relationships that we now experience.

are not usual to us. We need to feel that tension between what the author was trying to say and what now comes through to us because of the ways we have been told to interpret his language.

Of course we still have to attempt to interpret. We are not granted the luxury of a hermeneutical moratorium during which we may simply emote and enjoy. But we may begin to listen more carefully. We may begin to be present when an author finally chokes out words that only partly express the full reality that grips him. And we may begin to read, to teach, and to preach as if we were really listening; to resist ideational reduction ("literal" readings) in such a way as to interpret parable by parable, story by story. Our attention can be focused upon the NT's non-propositional event-inverbalizing language rather than upon the relative sophistication according to our standards. Regaining a sense of awe before the imaginative discourse of creative primitive Christianity, we are remanded to linguistic happening rather than to semantic quarrels, asked to participate in the NT's own rich polyphony rather than being given a theological outline.

It is essential to give the text its own voice, and this means first of all listening to it in its pristine originality. The interpreter's work as literary critic is not done away with: he has still to perform his task of analyzing the state of the text and its history. But where he goes with such analysis now takes the forefront. If he rushes to apply the usual categories (the supposedly literal meanings), he endangers the freedom of the text and may well only hear what he already knows. What must be done is to allow the richly endowed metaphors and images their unique excitement. By not forcing texts into his categories or his system, the interpreter must listen to their wholeness, giving texts such as those of the NT the same sensitive attention that would be directed to a poem:

> . . . If the poem is a real creation, it is a kind of knowledge that we did not possess before. It is not knowledge "about" scmething else; the poem is the fullness of that knowledge. We know the particular poem, not what it says that we can restate.[33]

The touchstone of adequate interpretation is not so much whether it is comprehensible in terms of the history of interpretation as whether it strikes us as real, as genuine. Genuineness is as much a problem in interpretation as in contemporary religious life in general: I suspect that the primary reason religions cease to be influential is that they lose the ability to convince their adherents that they refer not to a super-world but to reality—to everyday experienced life together.

[33] Allen Tate, "Narcissus as Narcissus," repr. in *The Critical Performance*, ed. S. E. Hyman (New York: Vintage Books, 1956), p. 177.

In the middle of his essay on Bonhoeffer's nonreligious interpretation, Gerhard Ebeling makes two statements that sum up the demands placed upon the contemporary interpreter and theologian:

> *The demand for intellectual honesty is the obligation to keep my thinking in agreement with my reality.*

> Anyone who in his thinking (from cowardice or laziness or whatever the reason) culpably bypasses a part of the reality that concerns him, or who does not exhaust the possibilities ascribable to him of recognizing what concerns him, transgresses the precept of intellectual honesty.[34]

Ebeling has grasped the essential insight behind Bonhoeffer's call for nonreligious (nonchurchly, nonpseudo, *real*) use of language in Christian speaking, and it refers to an extremely important aspect of the theological process. It is the sort of insight appropriate to the frequent complaint that language used in religious discussions does not ring true, that often words such as "god" are used in the same way words like "coffee" are used—that hence only confusion results, and theologians seem to be engaging in talk that is too specialized, too abstract, too remote from everyday affairs.[35]

The theme is not introduced merely for the sake of urging people to be "intellectuals" or even to stop doing shoddy research, be it a student's term paper or an instructor's lecture. Rather the call to intellectual honesty has to do with taking seriously the modern world—our world, our language—in such a way that one is cognizant of deadness, decay, fossilization in language, whether social language or theological language. Such cognizance may then be paid out as one seeks out the terms that are newly alive in one's own day. "The demands of intellectual honesty are," Ebeling reminds us, "subject to historical change."[36] This in turn then means that truth and freedom and genuineness are historical concepts and that in each generation we must win anew an understanding of what they mean.[37]

The language of the NT has informed Jewish and Christian thinking and theology, but affirming its historicity leads us to state that it is limited to its own world. NT theology will therefore be exercised to rehearse its own tradition to see what NT theology has been historically (and hence will deal with traditional topics such as "atonement," the nature of the

---

[34] *Word and Faith*, pp. 112–113, my emphasis.

[35] See *Post Bultmann Locutum. Diskussion der Professoren Gollwitzer und Braun zu Mainz* (Hamburg: Herbert Reich Verlag, 1965), esp. the Foreword by Horst Symanowski.

[36] *Word and Faith*, p. 112.

[37] See further *Word and Faith*, pp. 28–29, 56–57.

church, justification, et al.), but it will seek to do its speaking in the historical language of its current setting. Theology must be done critically, historically—what Ebeling calls the "obligation to keep my thinking in agreement with my reality." Such thinking understands that religiosity tends to replace faith as the antithesis of faith. The Pharisee is exposed as he who is essentially anti-historical, since it is he who desires to insulate himself within religious verbiage of the past, and so escape the rigors of confronting his own historical situation.

The process of theological interpretation begins to appear as a never-ending struggle—and so it is. It also begins to have aggressively contextual aspects as we see that truth and freedom are historically bounded factors of relationship. The process of theologizing finds its essential basis not in a special sort of magical language or history, but in attending to the same basis as any other discipline, namely the reality of man's experience. This means that interpretation (as well as preaching) will not revolve around the already religious, but around man who decides to be religious or nonreligious, partly on the basis of the call of the biblical text. It means that Christianity is ultimately concerned not with *homo religiosus* but with what makes man man.

SOME CONCLUDING NOTES ON LIVING WITH FIRE

We are almost always at fault, when we interpret early Christianity, for selling its language short. Of course ideally we should be able to listen to language and to what happens behind and around the spoken words—to hear all of the subtleties that attend the multiform linguistic interstices. That we cannot is the tragedy of the poetic soul in every generation—what is new now is simply the recognition that it is not just the poet's *poesis* to which we should so carefully listen. If we operate out of the cultural context in which we assert that there is something of value for us that happens in texts of the past—which only the acultural boor can deny—then we must work very hard indeed at really listening. This learning to hear begins to look like a perpetually self-sharpening operation. We never fully hear, and yet the effort is worth it.

We have to listen especially to the self-consciously directed language of our text: we do this out of fairness to the text's integrity. Otherwise we do not really wish to hear, but only to illustrate our own ideas out of the panoply of others' images. We have also to listen to the spaces between the paragraphs and the sentences and the words. This takes great skill and it sends us again and again to the language schools of interpretation. It sends us to theology and philosophy and also to literary criticism, to psychology and depth analysis, and to the great cross-cultural comparisons of past and present. And we must be anthropological historians in the best sense if the political, social, and ecological milieus of our texts are to be properly voiced.

We must learn to live with the half-gesture as intimately as with the boldly shouted kerygma; with the importance of why something is not stated, as well as the reasons why something is stated. We must learn to appreciate the fascinations of the complex as well as the solo beauty of one clear note. Nor should we miss the magical beckoning that comes from time to time, asking us to pay out not more than the rational, clear-sounding exposition. Especially in this twenty-first century of transistorized instant nonhearing machines, we need to be caught up in the multiphasic and the splendid and the paisley.

Of course Hesse is right: "Words do not express thoughts very well; everything becomes a little different, a little distorted, a little foolish." But words are our lot, and with care, they are not just our fate (*fatum:* that which is spoken) for confusion and disappointment, but our fate for a new and exuberant present and future.

One thing is certain: no one can live with too much "primary expression." That would be like living with raw electricity coursing through one's system (this image describes well the psychology of primitive Christian eschatology), and that is more than any of us can take. Just this common sense factor should retard us when we are tempted to accuse the primitive Christians of encapsulating the brilliance of primary Christianity so that it became a dim shadow of its origins.

Of course it is true that the church did "reduce the current"; the church utilized a good deal of mortar because of fear of losing its great originative potentiality, as in Lk 16:1–13, in which a parable is walled in by appending some seven different sayings, each specifying what the parable was "literally" supposed to mean. But we have a little warrant for taking such examples as a banner under which to found some "back to the bible" Christianity, for the real point should be that modern men are (by their schools, publications, teaching, and preaching) engaged in precisely the same securing enterprise that led to the incredibly stupid heaping of concluding sayings in Luke. We stand alongside the early church, not against it, seeking to appropriate without being seared, just as they were seeking to pass on the lively new words of freedom without having their fingers burned.

The problem is not one that affects the theologian alone. Rather it is a problem of the development, progress, and regression of any culture. It is essentially the problem of how we are able to coexist amid the fertile tensions of creativity and newness. It is the problem as to how we are able to appropriate religious or artistic creativity without extinguishing it in the very process of passing it on. And because there is always resistance to that which seems new, it is a problem of the survival of that which makes us uncomfortable.[38]

It is no wonder that religion as "the dead hand of the past" is often the last holding action against ideas that have become accepted everywhere else (J. K. Galbraith: "The familiar is always defended with much more moral fervor just before it becomes foolish"). And it is not surprising that times of radical change and consequent confusion produce syncretistic or simplistic movements. The popularity of Zen or flower children illustrates the sort of fusion of ethical-cultural-religious sentiments, as do the growth of Christian Pentecostal groups, the political right-wing resurgence, or the reductionist sentiments in our own time. We have, indeed, to be on our guard, for it was this sort of intolerance of cultural ambiguity that provided fertile ground for Nazi reductionism with its simple choice between good Aryans and bad Jews.[39]

Then insofar as we share the perspective of the primitive church—each of us standing in relation to the primal traditions—we have not the luxury of shaming their attempts. It is true that modern men might have written the NT differently, with greater respect for modern criteria of historical and theological literature. But it is also true that to each generation there remains the task of bringing about its own new utterances. We are not to stop with criticism of how the early Christians did it wrong; if the real dynamics of the gospel (giving the term its widest theological sense—good news) are to be pulsed through contemporary religious life, then we should be about our task of writing gospels (now understood in the sense of expressing insights into the meaning of reality).

How one becomes an effective gospeler is, of course, the question. Nothing characterized the years in which my theological training took place as much as the attempt to "find the right medium." Was it to be the cinema form or religious dance? Television or rock-and-roll folk masses? Was it to be a secularized religiosity little distinguished from Rotary or Kiwanis? Did it mean slick magazines and noise, or "religious art," or the recovery of solitude and meditation in a bustline-oriented universe? I suspect that these questions will no longer be so freely

[38] This is similar to the problem of the playwright, as expressed in the complaint by Arthur Miller, *Collected Plays* (New York: Viking Press, 1957), p. 10: "An idea, if it is really new, is a genuine humiliation for the majority of the people; it is an affront not only to their sensitivities but to their deepest convictions. It offends against the things they worship, whether God or science or money."

[39] Richard Rubenstein's articles in *After Auschwitz: Radical Theology and Contemporary Judaism* (Indianapolis, New York, and Kansas City: The Bobbs-Merrill Company, Inc., 1966) provide a very lucid and telling exposition of this phenomenon.

bandied about in this period when the message itself is no less in question than the media.

From contemporary analyses of the roles of communications media theologians seem to have learned only that more up-to-date means of verbal and non-verbal expression are required. More important than worrying about the appropriate modes of expression, however, are the attempts to give religious awareness a cutting edge that is fully interpretive, integrative, and creative. By this I mean that the future of theology may well lie in giving transitive stress to "metaphoring," to "worlding"—the hermeneutical enterprise has at last gained a sense of how texts of antiquity were evocative of new worlds, and now our task is to train our own metaphoring capabilities. Interpretation is the actual flowing give and take of human existence; we now recognize this flux in texts of the past, but our culture still focuses more on the past than upon the future.

But primitive Christianity has only a little to tell us about dealing with the past. It has a great deal to tell us about how new worlds are anticipated, formed, and brought to linguistic expression. There is a certain irony in suggesting that we look to the ways one *past* culture edged its way into a new world in order that *contemporary* men may best meet their own challenging future. But ironical or not, there are many similarities between the formation of the Christian religion in Graeco-Roman Hellenism and the formation of patterns of life now which will serve us in the twenty-first century. We will have only ourselves to blame if our refusal to learn from the past leads us to a dead end of international annihilation instead of peaceful and productive encounters with the amazingly new and different modes of human existence which lie ahead.

Appendices

1. CHART OF THE FORMAL ANALYSIS OF FORM CRITICISM

A comprehensive presentation of the form-critical method is out of question within the scope of this book. The following chart of the main features in the classifications of Bultmann and Dibelius, with selected examples, will, however, show how the formal analysis of synoptic materials can be structured.[1] The basic division of the synoptic materials is twofold. First the "sayings materials" are treated, then the "narrative materials." The arrangement of the chart is that of Bultmann's *History,* chosen because it is more tightly arranged and more comprehensive.[2] Dibelius' classifications (primarily from his *From Tradition to Gospel*) are **given in a second column;** their original order is indicated by **—A, —B,** etc.

In each case one or more rather clear examples are given, and a copy of the Huck-Lietzmann *Synopsis of the First Three Gospels* (New York:

[1] My article "The Literature and Discipline . . ." gives additional charts demonstrating how Dibelius and Bultmann classify some of the same materials in different categories.

[2] See also Bultmann's articles, "A New Approach to the Synoptic Problem" and "The Study of the Synoptic Gospels," which have been consulted in addition to the original German editions of the main books in drawing up the following classifications. The English edition of the *History* can never be used for serious purposes without checking the translation; the same situation applies for the translation of Koch, *Was ist Formgeschichte?*

American Bible Society) or the English version based on the Revised Standard Version, *Gospel Parallels* (Burton H. Throckmorton, ed.; New York: Nelson), should be consulted. Numbers in parentheses refer to the consecutively numbered paragraphs in the *Synopsis* and *Parallels*.

The major differences between the classifications of Bultmann and Dibelius are that for Dibelius, "Paradigm" is the more inclusive term, and Dibelius' "myths" are usually Bultmann's "legends," while Dibelius' "legends" are classified under several of Bultmann's categories.

I. Sayings Materials
   A. *Apophthegms:*
      Terse sayings set into a framework giving the situation and occasion. (The term comes from analysis of Greek literature, is often translated simply "apothegm." Dibelius calls them "paradigms," Beare, "controversy stories," Taylor, "pronouncement stories.") Sparse detail; emphasis upon typical characters and situations
      1. *Controversy and School Dialogues*
         Starting point: some action or attitude used by opponent in an attack by accusation or question; reply made by counter-question or metaphor. "Ideal" scenes serve to visualize an idea. Sitz im Leben; the apologetic and polemic of the Palestinian church (typically the opponents are the Scribes and Pharisees)
         a) Occasioned by Jesus' healings
            Mk 3:1–6 (#70, Sabbath healing)
         b) Occasioned by Jesus' or disciples' conduct
            Mk 2:23–28 (#69, Sabbath corn plucking)
         c) Question by disciples or others
            Mk 10:17–31 (#189, Rich young man)
         d) Question by opponents
            Mk 10:2–12 (#187, On divorce)
      2. *Biographical Apophthegms*
         Personal sayings about Jesus. By and large provide edifying patterns for sermons; created in Palestinian church.
         Mk 1:16–20, 2:14 (#11, #53, Calling of disciples)

          —A.   **Paradigms: Supplied as examples for early Christian preaching; edifying and religious, not "worldly" in character.**

   B. *Dominical Sayings:*
      Similar to apophthegms, but with different purposes; usually only one or two sentences.

1. *Logia*

   Jesus presented as the Teacher of Wisdom, hence this form fits Jewish wisdom milieu; least guaranteed to be authentic, since many probably taken over from Jewish sources.

   a) Principles
      Mk 9:49 (#132, Salt); Lk 10:7b (#139, Wages of laborer)
   b) Admonitions
      Mt 8:22b (#49, Dead heal the dead)
   c) Questions
      Mk 2:19 (#54, Bridal party)
   d) Longer passages
      Mk 7:7–11 (#38, Ask and . . .)

2. *Prophetic and Apocalyptic Words*

   Jesus proclaims arrival of Reign of God and preaches call to repentance in preparation; brief and vigorous, these have parallels in ancient prophecy. Sitz im Leben: edification of primitive Christian communities.

   a) Preaching of Salvation
      Lk 6:20–23 (#73, Beatitudes)
   b) Minatory Sayings
      Lk 6:24–26 (#74, Woes)
   c) Admonitions
      Mk 1:15 (#9, Repent and believe)
      Lk 21:34–36 (#223, Watch . . .)

3. *Legal Sayings and Church Rules*

   Catechetical and legal interests have governed collection of these materials from Jewish sources, added solutions to practical problems the Christian community then attributed to Jesus. Some are (as I.A.1. above) for polemic or debate, others rules for the pious life
      Mt 5:17–19 (#21, On law)
      Mk 2:27–28 (#69, On Sabbath)

4. *"I"-Sayings*

   Specifically "non-Christian" (pre-Easter) materials expected from Jesus of Nazareth; their development began in Palestinian churches, but they are primarily, with respect to form, the work of Hellenistic churches.

   a) Jesus speaks of his coming
      Lk 19:19 (#194, Son of man)
      Lk 10:16 (#139, Those who reject me . . .)

b) Jesus speaks of his person
Mt 8:10 (#46, I have not found such faith . . .)

c) Risen Lord speaks of his person
Lk 24:49 (p. 190, I send the promise . . .)

d) Exalted Lord speaks of himself
(Gospel of John; Odes of Solomon)

5. Similitudes and Similar Forms

Reflect Judaism's love of imagery and stories, hence we can seldom be sure they originate with Jesus; "We can only count on possessing a genuine similitude of Jesus where, on the one hand, expression is given to the contrast between Jewish morality and piety and the distinctive eschatological temper which characterized the preaching of Jesus; and where on the other hand we find no specifically Christian features" (*History*, p. 205). Most of Palestinian origins; editorial work of evangelists especially visible in contexting and introduction they have provided.

a) Figures of speech

b) Metaphors

c) Comparisons

d) Pure similitudes
Lk 15:4–10 (#172, Lost sheep and coin)

e) Parable proper
Lk 13:6–9 (#162, Fig tree)
Lk 16:1–8 (#174, Unjust steward)

f) Exemplary stories
Lk 10:30–37 (#144, Good Samaritan)

—E. **Paraenesis (exhortation, edifying utterance)
Not a formal genre, but a subject classification; edificatory passages grew out of Jesus' sayings; originally collected because of paraenetic value (practical guidance and community discipline). ". . . Here tradition was so sensitive to the current need of the community that all the paraenetic material goes back to Jesus himself."**

1. Wisdom Sayings

2. Comparison

3. Parable

4. Prophetic Cry

5. Short Command

6. Expanded Command

II. Narrative Materials

(There are characteristics of narrative technique which apply to all the following: law of scenic duality—no more than two persons on the scene at once; conciseness of duration and theme; group often treated as unity—Pharisees, disciples; motives and emotional feelings seldom represented; use of direct speech; repetition.)

A. *Miracle Stories:*

Told not just as remarkable occurrences, but as deeds demonstrating Jesus' messianic authority or divine power—which functions as something apart from his own will (see healing of woman with an issue of blood—Jesus senses some "power" has left him), for this reason evangelists see no problem in reconciling these miracles with Jesus' consistent refusal to give authenticating "sign."

Characteristically lack interest in personalities of healer or healed; nothing but the point matters (see Johannine tradition, where this tendency more explicit). Some Palestinian origins probable, most of Hellenistic origin

1. *Miracles of Healing (including Demon-Healings)*

Typically have four distinct moments: description of patient's illness and inability of physicians to heal; healing, in which demon recognizes exorcist; departure of demon, often in some spiteful and destructive act; impression of cure upon spectators (though no one present at time of healing itself)—this is "witness" to the cure.

Mk 5:1–21 (#106, Gerasene Demoniac)

(—A. Paradigms)

2. *Nature Miracles*

Typically, menace of the elements and impression created by miracle related.

Mk 4:37–41 (#105, Stilling of storm)

—E. Novellen

Jesus as Healer; delight in details; "secular" events; present concealed epiphany of god's messenger. Motivated by need for propaganda and as model for Christian miracles. Often represents a "degeneration of the tradition," in response to "worldy curiosity"

B. *Historical Stories and Legends:*

Legends: "Those parts of the tradition which are not miracle stories in the proper sense, but instead of being historical in character are religious and edifying. For the most part they include something miraculous but not necessarily so. . . . They are distinguishable from miracle stories chiefly by not being, as they are, unities, but gain their point only when set into their context . . . the life of some religious hero: that yields a biographical legend. Or the context may be the faith and the cult of the community: that yields a faith—or cult—legend." "I do not think it is possible to separate historical stories from legends . . ." (*History*, pp. 244–45).

"It is characteristic of all these stories that they arise out of the spirit of messianic hopes and institutions and that in them the Christ-myth of Hellenistic Christianity of the Pauline sort has no influence at all, that Christ does not have the place of a cultic deity" (*History*, p. 302).

1. From Baptism to Triumphal Entry
   Mk 1:1–8, 9–11, 12–13; 8:27–30; 9:2–8, etc.

2. Passion Narrative
   Mk 14:1f., 12–16, 17–21, 22–25, 26–31, 32–42, etc.

   Expansions on a primitive narrative—of historical date close to first kerygma (proclamation); motifs: proof from prophecy, apologetic, pure novelistic detail, paraenetic (exhortatory, ethical), dogmatic, cultic

3. Easter Narratives
   a) Stories of the empty tomb
      Mk 16:1–8, etc. "Completely secondary"; neither Paul nor speeches in Acts mention them; Ascension story necessitated by Easter legends
   b) Stories of appearance of risen lord
      (1) Motif of proving the resurrection by the appearance of the risen lord
      Lk 24:13–35
      (2) Motif of the missionary charge of the risen lord. Late Hellenistic; universalistic
      Mt 28:16–20

4. Infancy Narratives
   Mt 1:18–25, etc.

—C. **Legends**

Form: portrayal of secondary things or persons, lack concentration, manifold interests; not form but telling is what characterizes; casts religious hero into stereotyped mold of man of piety

Aetiological and biographical interests motivate transmission. ". . . Not portions of the
gospel important from either the material or
the literary point of view."

Twelve-year-old Jesus in Temple.

—D. The Passion Story

—E. Myth

Intends to relate the cosmic significance of
cult hero; restrained use in synoptics; interest not in history but in theological idea it
clothes—supernatural breaking directly into
human scene.

Baptism, Temptation, Transfiguration;
mythological traits elsewhere.

2. Bibliography of Works by Rudolf Bultmann Cited in the Text

Existence and Faith: Shorter Writings of Rudolf Bultmann, sel., trans., and intro. by Schubert M. Ogden. New York: The World Publishing Company, 1960. (Abbreviated here as *ExF.*)

Glauben und Verstehen. Tübingen: Mohr, I. 1933 (1961, 4th ed.), II. 1952 (1961, 3rd ed.), III. 1960 (1962, 2nd ed.), IV. 1965. (Abbreviated as *GuV.*) An ET of Vol. I has been edited by Robert W. Funk, *Faith and Understanding.* New York and Evanston: Harper & Row, Publishers, 1969. (Abbreviated *FU.*I.)

"Allgemeine Wahrheiten und christliche Verkündigung," *GvV* III, 166–177. ET in *JournTheolChurch* 4(1967)153–162.

"Antwort an Ernst Käsemann," *GuV* IV, 190–198.

"Ist die Apokalyptik die Mutter der Christlichen Theologie? Eine Auseinandersetzung mit Ernst Käsemann," in *Apophoreta* (Festschr. E. Haenchen). Berlin: Verlag Alfred Töpelmann, 1964, 64–69.

"Die Bedeutung der 'dialektischen Theologie' für die neutestamentliche Wissenschaft," *GuV* I, 114–133; ET in *FU* I, 145–164.

"The Case for Demythologizing," in *Kerygma and Myth,* ed. H. W. Bartsch. London: S.P.C.K., 1962, Vol. II, 181–194.

"A Chapter in the Problem of Demythologizing," in *New Testament Sidelights* (Festschr. A. C. Purdy). Hartford: Hartford Seminary Foundation Press, 1960, ed. Harvey K. McArthur, 1–9.

"Die christliche Hoffnung und das Problem der Entmythologisierung," *GuV* III, 81–90.

"The Concept of Revelation in the New Testament," *ExF* 58–91.

"Is Exegesis without Presuppositions Possible?", *ExF* 289–296.

"Die Frage der natürlichen Offenbarung," *GuV* II, 79–104.

Die Geschichte der synoptischen Tradition. Göttingen: Vandenhoeck & Ruprecht, 1958, 4th ed. ET: *The History of the Synoptic Tradition,* New York: Harper & Row, Publishers, 1963, trans. John Marsh. (The latter, cited here as *History*, should be used for critical work only with the German original at hand.)

"The Historicity of Man and Faith," *ExF* 92–110.

History and Eschatology: The Presence of Eternity. New York: Harper & Brothers, 1957.

"History of Salvation and History," *ExF* 226–240.

"How Does God Speak to Us Through the Bible?" *ExF* 166–170.

"Jesus and Paul," *ExF* 183–201.

Jesus and the Word. New York: Charles Scribner's Sons, 1958.

Jesus Christ and Mythology. New York: Charles Scribner's Sons, 1958.

"Karl Barth, 'Die Auferstehung der Toten,'" *GuV* I, 38–64; ET in *FU* I, 66–94.

"Die liberale Theologie und die jüngste theologische Bewegung," *GuV* I, 1–25; ET in *FU* I, 28–52.

"The New Approach to the Synoptic Problem," *ExF* 35–54.

"New Testament and Mythology. The Mythological Element in the Message of the New Testament and the Problem of its Re-interpretation," in *Kerygma and Myth,* ed. H. W. Bartsch. London: S.P.C.K., 1957, Vol. I, 1–44.

"Preaching: Genuine and Secularized," in *Religion and Culture* (Festschr. P. Tillich). New York: Harper & Brothers, Publishers, 1959, ed. Walter Leibrecht, 236–242.

Primitive Christianity in its Contemporary Setting. New York: Meridian Books, 1956.

"Zum Problem der Entmythologisierung," *GuV* IV, 128–137.

"Das Problem der Hermeneutik," *GuV* II, 211–235.

"Das Problem einer theologischen Exegese des Neuen Testaments," *Zwischen den Zeiten* 3(1925)334–357; repr. in *Theologische Bücherei* 17/2, 47–71; ET in *The Beginnings of Dialectical Theology.* Richmond: John Knox Press, 1968, ed. James M. Robinson, Vol. I, 236–256.

Der Stil der paulinischen Predigt und die kynisch-stoische Diatribe. Göttingen: Vandenhoeck & Ruprecht, 1910 (FRLANT 13).

"The Study of the Synoptic Gospels," in *Form Criticism*. New York: Harper Torchbooks, 1962, trans. and ed. F. C. Grant, 11–76.

Theology of the New Testament. New York: Charles Scribner's Sons, I. 1951, II. 1955, trans. Kendrick Grobel. (Abbreviated as *Theology*.)

3. GLOSSARY

Words given in italics within a definition refer to other entries in this Glossary. See also the Index to locate discussions of terms in the text.

Anthropology (Grk. anthropos, "man"): In theological use, the term refers to theoretical evaluation of man's place in the universe, especially in relation to deities.

Apocalypse (Grk): 1. An unveiling, a revelation, especially of future events; 2. As a literary form, characterized by being esoteric, secretive, rich in symbolic imagery, frequently presenting an ethical dualism; 3. The Apocalypse of John: the last book of the Christian *canon*, referred to by custom as "The Revelation of John."

Apocalyptic: 1. A form of *eschatological* thinking characterized by fascination with the end of time breaking into the near future; 2. A literary type, see *apocalypse*.

Apocrypha: Christian writings which were excluded from the *canon* in the first centuries; there are apocryphal gospels (especially infancy and childhood legends, and the Gospel of Thomas), epistles, and acts associated with important apostolic leaders.

Apophthegm (or apothegm) (Grk.): brief saying or maxim.

Apostolic Fathers: Christian writings from the first three centuries widely read in early Christianity; mostly formal epistles; contain valuable insights into development of the early Christian religion and institutional order; include: I Clement, "II Clement," Ignatius, Polycarp, Papias, Barnabas, Shepherd of Hermas.

Apostolic Parousia: see *travelogue*.

Aretalogy: A literary account of a hero or miracle-worker in Hellenism; possible influence on aspects of the gospel genre; examples: Porphyry —Life of Pythagoras; Philo—Life of Moses; Philostratus—Life of Apollonius of Tyana.

Canon (Grk. "reed," then "measure," then "list"): Primarily the list of books to be considered sacred Christian scripture, set in the fourth century.

Catechesis, catechetical (Grk.): moral and religious instruction, especially in fundamental or elementary beliefs.

Catholic (Grk., crasis of kata + holos—"according to the whole"): 1. Universal; 2. designation for the whole Christian church; 3. designation for certain NT letters (The Catholic or Universal Epistles: James, Jude, Peter, sometimes I–III John and Hebrews) understood to be universally addressed and conceived.

The Christ of Faith: Used in contrast to *the historical Jesus* to designate the worshipped Christ, the preached (*"kerygmatic"*) Lord, rather than the human Jesus of Nazareth.

Christology (Grk. christos + logos): Theory of the meaning of the christic events, e.g., how God's acts in the history of Jesus had significance for man's well-being.

Demythologizing: Rudolf Bultmann's program for interpreting the existential meanings of religious language that appear in mythic form.

Diatribe (Grk.): 1. A literary form of rhetoric used by the Hellenistic (especially Cynic and Stoic) popular philosophers; some conventions of the diatribe are reflected in Paul's letters 2. (the term has acquired a secondary meaning in English: abusive criticism, denunciatory preachment.)

Early Catholicism (Ger. Frühkatholizismus): Technical term used to describe early Christianity as it took on formal, institutional dimensions, as opposed to a supposed earlier noninstitutional form.

Eschatology (Grk. a logos of the eschaton, a doctrine of the end): The religious orientation that assumes purpose and meaning in the movement of history toward its conclusion or perfection, with emphasis upon the end-time itself. The primitive Christians thought they were already living in the final times because of God's intervention in history in Jesus Christ; such messianic intervention was expected during the period of early Christian development. A related term is *apocalyptic*, which refers to the type of eschatology that stressed not so much the perfection of history, but God's decisive and climactic incursion into history that would be completely discontinuous and new.

Exegesis (Grk. "to show the way"): Critical analysis of a text, especially a biblical text, which seeks to disclose its true meanings; often opposed to "eisegesis," or reading meanings into a text.

Form Criticism: See *Formgeschichte.*

Formgeschichte (Ger., form "history" or "criticism"): The type of literary and historical criticism developed in Germany in the beginning of the twentieth century by Schmidt, Dibelius, Bultmann and others. The method (at first applied only to the *synoptic* gospels) attempts to identify the *genres*—the types and the forms of literary materials —and to determine, by comparison with other occurrences of the type, their original form, their growth and modification. See *Sitz im Leben.*

Frühkatholizismus: See *early Catholicism.*

Gattung (Ger.): Generally *"genre"; *sometimes used in studies of Israelite literature to refer to pre-literary units, usually called "forms" in NT studies (Ger. Formen).

Genre (Fr., from Lat. genus): Literary type, mainly with respect to large units such as the *gospel* or epistle. See *Gattung.*

Geschichte (Ger.): 1. Story; 2. "history," especially meaningful history in modern contrast to *Historie* (history as chronicle, facts)—the distinction is sometimes between inner and outer histories; 3. in combination may take on either the English sense "history" (*Heilsgeschichte,* Zeitgeschichte) or "criticism" (*Formgeschichte*). The adjectival forms are geschichtlich- and historisch-.

Gnostic (Grk. "to know"): A religio-philosophical direction within Hellenism that emphasized salvific "knowledge" (gnosis) of the secret nature of the spheres. Its *anthropology* stressed the meaninglessness of the flesh, hence led either to a libertinistic or an ascetic morality. Gnosticism proper was developed out of oriental, Jewish, and Christian sources, but a proto-gnosticism or a gnosticizing tendency is found within the NT, primarily in the epistles.

Gospel (English term from Anglo-Saxon god-spel, a tale of the deity): Used to translate euangellion, although often used to replace the active form euangellizesthai. Euangellion (Grk.): 1. good news (as the pre-Christian Priene calendar reference to the euangellion of the birth of a god), usually found in the active verbal form, to speak good news; 2. the message that God acted on behalf of man in the event of Jesus Christ (theologically considered, this was always God's act, part of the event itself); 3. about the middle of the third century, if not before, designation for the books in the NT *canon* which contain this story.

Heilsgeschichte (Ger. salvific, saving, redemptive, or salvation history): 1. Used to characterize the biblical conception of God acting in history—which therefore becomes salvific itself (Luke, for example, presents such a view of the sacredness of history); 2. more generally used to describe modern versions of this theology, as by O. Cullmann.

Hermeneutic, -ics (Grk. "to interpret"): the principles and theory of exegesis and interpretation; studies of how understanding, especially of events of the past, takes place; (hermeneutics requires singular verb, like mathematics).

Hermeneutical Circle (or arc or spiral): The process by which the interpreter's initial questions to a text are modified by the exegesis of the text, resulting in new interpretive questions.

Historical Criticism: Method of interpretation that seeks self-criticism and fully historical appraisal of its own *hermeneutics* as well as of the original conditions in which a text arises.

The Historical Jesus: Modern convention describing the human career and teachings of Jesus of Nazareth (as opposed to his position for Christian faith, as *"the Christ of faith"*).

Historie: See *Geschichte.*

Kerygma: Theologians' shorthand for "the central message of the NT," or "the gospel message"; refers to the central sketch of what was proclaimed by primitive Christians about Jesus Christ: that in him God acted decisively to benefit mankind.

koine (Grk. "common"): Designation of the type of popular Greek found in NT literature; spoken as the street language of the Hellenistic world.

Literary Criticism: 1. Classical technical meaning: careful analysis of the process by which a complex text came about, including *source analysis;* 2. approach that studies the NT as literature, especially as comprised of literary *genres* and features found in other literature.

Logion, logia (Grk. "word(s)", "saying(s)"): Generally a discrete unit of statement-material; specifically (as Logia Jesu) sayings reported as being spoken by Jesus.

Paraenesis, paraenetic (Grk. "advice"): Ethical, edifying, hortatory material; also spelled parenesis.

Parousia (Grk. "presence"): Meaning acquired in primitive Christianity: the eventual (second) coming of the Christ as Lord, especially his return as Judge at the end of time.

Phenomenology: As used here, the approach to happenings of the past that seeks to elicit an understanding of what happened in terms of the original situation(s); especially with respect to ways in which language may be said to bring an event (phenomenon) "to expression."

Pre-understanding (Ger. Vorverstãndnis): Prior conception about the nature, value, or viability of something to be studied; concerns the cultural mind-set of the interpreter and especially, therefore, the questions he is inclined to ask of a text; more implicit and less formative than prejudgment (Vorurteil).

Provenance: (Fr. "origin," "source"); used to refer to the original place where a NT writing was completed.

Q (Quelle): (Ger. "source"); arbitrary designation for *synoptic* materials common to Mt and Lk, but lacking in Mk.

Redaction: Process of selecting, ordering, and polishing material for publication; used specifically to contrast composition out of common traditions (oral or written) with independent authorship.

Redaction Criticism (Ger. Redaktionsgeschichte): method of analyzing complex literary documents in terms of identifying use of shared materials, and especially how they have been composed into a particular framework or coherent whole; for NT materials, may differentiate one person's perspective from another (as gospel writers).

Redactor: Agent who redacts—edits materials into a unified whole. See *redaction.*

Religionsgeschichte (Ger., lit. "history of religion," but best American equivalent is "comparative religion"): A type of comparative analysis of (especially) Hellenistic religions begun toward the end of the nineteenth century; now used to identify analyses of comparative religious traditions in general or especially study of non-Western religions.

Salvation History: See *Heilsgeschichte.*

Sitz im Leben (Ger. "setting in life"): The sociological setting from which a particular form is thought to have come.

Source Criticism (or source analysis): Method of identifying the specific strata of earlier materials in a complex literary work.

Synopsis (Grk. "viewing together"): Mt, Mk, and Lk, the synoptic *gospels* which contain a large amount of parallel materials, especially compared to John; a synopsis may be a summary, but usually (technically) refers to a printout of the three (or four) gospels in parallel columns, displaying agreements and divergences visually.

Tradition History (Ger. Traditionsgeschichte): Best given full translation as "the history of the transmission of the traditions"; 1. method of analyzing the ways historical traditions attained highly valued positions in a community's religious structure; 2. the historical traditions that have become highly valued.

Travelogue: The element in Pauline letters in which Paul indicates his plans to visit, identifies his emissaries; a part of Paul's indication of his power and authority when present (apostolic parousia) with the addressees.

Index

A

Achtemeier, P. J., 30n, 37n, 40n
Albertz, M., 142n
Allemann, B., 112–13
Allport, G., 73n
Anderson, B. W., 122n
Anthropology, 23–25, 45, 49, 165
Apocalyptic, 8, 44n, 46, 66, 83, 101, 103, 116, 121–31, 138, 165–66
Apology, 139, 139n, 140
Augustine, 106, 134
Austin, J., 111, 111n

B

Barfield, O., 3n, 150n
Barth, H., 33n
Barth, K., 15–17, 21n, 31, 45, 91
Bauer, W., 93–94, 93n, 96
Baur, F. C., 12, 54
Beardslee, W. A., 56, 56n, 140n
Beare, F. W., 74n, 158
Beatitude, 82–83
Bolkestein, M. H., 139n
Bonhoeffer, D., 148, 148n, 152

Bornkamm, G., 72n, 104n, 145n
Bourke, M., 105n
Braaten, C., 23n, 44n, 76n
Braun, H., 24n, 148n, 152n
Brown, R. E., 10n
Bultmann, R., 5–6, 7n, 17–31, 32n, 33, 37n, 42, 42n, 45, 47, 55, 61–66, 61n, 68–69, 71, 72n, 73, 73n, 82n, 89, 92, 105, 114–15, 115n, 118–19, 121, 121n, 123–24, 136n, 145–46, 148, 157–66
Buri, F., 24n, 118n

C

Campbell, J., 116n
Canon, 9, 10, 102–105, 102n, 103n, 138, 165
Chapman, G. C., 93n, 94
Childs, B. C., 49n, 51n, 146n
Christ of faith, the, 7, 23, 23n, 29, 69, 94, 110n, 133, 166
Christology, 23, 24n, 40, 41n, 44, 59n, 74, 77, 99, 101–2, 141, 166
Cobb, J. B., 5, 44n
Conzelmann, H., 72n, 73, 124–25, 124n, 136n, 140, 143n, 146